10546

The
Travail of
Religious Liberty

Books by Roland H. Bainton

Published by The Westminster Press
The Travail of Religious Liberty
The Martin Luther Christmas Book

By other publishers
Here I Stand, a Life of Martin Luther
George Lincoln Burr, His Life
The Church of Our Fathers
Bernardino Ochino
David Joris
Sebastian Castellio, Concerning Heretics

The
Travail of
Religious Liberty

Nine Biographical Studies

by ROLAND H. BAINTON

10546

The Westminster Press · Philadelphia

PRINTED IN THE UNITED STATES OF AMERICA

To
HILDA AND GLEN KING

" *Him that overcometh will I make a pillar*
in the temple of my God."

Foreword

Mr. James Sprunt, of Wilmington, North Carolina, in 1911 established a perpetual lectureship at Union Theological Seminary in Virginia, which would enable this institution to secure from time to time the services of distinguished ministers and authoritative scholars as special lecturers on subjects connected with various departments of Christian thought and Christian work. The lecturers are chosen by the faculty of the seminary and a committee of the Board of Trustees, and the lectures are published after their delivery in accordance with a contract between the lecturer and these representatives of the institution.

The series of lectures on this foundation for the year 1950 is presented in this volume.

B. R. LACY, JR.,
President

Union Theological Seminary,
Richmond, Virginia.

Preface

The material in this book represents in large part lectures delivered at the invitation of the faculty and trustees of the Union Theological Seminary, Richmond, Virginia, on the James Sprunt foundation. Portions of these lectures were delivered also at the Danforth Conference at Camp Miniwanca, Shelly, Michigan; at the Eden Theological Seminary, Webster Groves, Missouri; and at the Vermont Congregational Ministers Conference, Montpelier, Vermont. For publication, these lectures were revised and in some cases amplified.

ROLAND H. BAINTON.

The Divinity School,
Yale University,
New Haven, Connecticut.

Contents

The
Travail of
Religious Liberty

INTRODUCTION

The historian who set out twenty-five years ago to write the history of the struggle for religious liberty believed the subject peculiarly suited to his pen because the evidence was all in. The victory had been won, and to recount the tale was a task of filial piety in order to extol the exploits of those who had put to flight armies of aliens. Today the armies of aliens hold the field in many quarters, and the history of religious liberty is a chapter in the intelligent man's guide to the reading of the newspapers. We approach the story now not simply to laud but to learn.

The contrast, however, between the now and the then is not wholly due to the resurgence of persecution but in part to an earlier provincialism which took into account only the Western world. Even twenty-five years ago the picture would not have been so rosy had the survey included the Near East and the Far East and the Russian steppes. Russia has never been a land of liberty. Under the old regime there was a graded system of toleration determined by considerations of political security. The religions of the annexed territories were granted that degree of recognition requisite for tranquillity. The scale ran through the Catholics, Lutherans, Mohammedans, and Armenians, to the Jews and the Russian sects which enjoyed the least consideration of all. Moreover, in the predominantly Catholic countries of Europe, Protestantism could never be said to have enjoyed a genuine parity, and certainly not in South America. Yet unquestionably the last quarter of a century has seen retrogression. Fascism, first in Italy and then in Germany, was the earliest setback, and then the emergence of Communism has exhibited the major characteristics of a militant religion the like of which has not been seen since the rise of Mohammedanism. Liberty has receded even in Russia, and notably in those countries that have been sucked into the Soviet orbit. We tremble for ourselves lest we too be engulfed, and even more lest in the effort to extricate ourselves we succumb to the very methods that we abhor.

We turn now to the record of the earlier gains for religious liberty in order to be instructed, both as to why men persecuted and as to how persecution can be overcome. A very facile answer is that the Communists persecute because they are atheists and if they were but Christians they would be gentlemen. This answer is shattered on the concrete base of history. With shame we must confess that the present appalling methods employed to cow resistance by disintegrating the very integrity of opponents is only a refinement along technological lines of the devices elaborated under the auspices of the Church. The story of persecution related in this book was practiced entirely by Christians.

Then comes the equally facile answer that really religions and religious ideas have nothing to do with the case. The causes of persecution are sociological, and if the existence of a people or a party be menaced, even though it profess the religion of brotherly love, it will find some casuistry whereby to bend even brotherhood to the service of suppression. The difficulty with this explanation is that it fails to account for crusading religions whose adherents are not content to insure the cohesion of their communities by purges from within, but with no provocation set out with a fanatical sense of mission to benefit the world by constraint. As a matter of fact, both the ideological and the sociological, both beliefs and situations, exercise a continual interplay.

The like is true also with regard to religious liberty. In part tolerance has displaced persecution because the presuppositions of persecution have been undercut, but in part also because the entire religious question has been relegated to a position of lesser importance in comparison with secular concerns. Political security, economic prosperity, and aesthetic enjoyment have come to appear more significant than religious rectitude. At this point liberty has come to depend upon a diversion of interest.

The present study is distinctly limited — first, as to scope, because it deals only with the struggle in Christian lands in the West and there chiefly with Protestantism. The selection may well appear invidious, because there is a chapter on Catholic persecution but none on Catholic liberalism, and to recognize the possibility of a liberal Catholicism is particularly important at the present juncture when such fears are entertained of the possibility of Catholic dominance in the United States. Yet the omission can be justified, partly because Catholicism is capable of tolerance on far fewer counts than Protestantism, and partly because these lectures were delivered at a Presbyterian seminary where a centering upon our own tradition was not inappropriate.

There is a limitation also in time, in that the period selected runs from the late fifteenth century to the late seventeenth, a span of only two hundred years, and of course persecution had been rife long before the fifteenth century and liberty was far from wholly won in the seventeenth. Nevertheless, the essential struggle is bracketed within these years.

Finally, the biographical approach entails very serious limitations. The impression may be created that the whole problem was simply one of personal clashes, whereas entire peoples and cultures were in convulsion. The nine persons selected were all passionate Christians and their lives therefore afford no illustrations of the secular motives for liberty. They were likewise private persons and not subject to the pressures of political responsibility, which induced even a bigot like Charles V to moderate his severity and engendered indifference to religion in Queen Elizabeth and Henry IV as they observed the disruptive force of confessional controversy for the body politic. The economic arguments for liberty might have been illustrated through Jakob Fugger or William the Silent, who were not disposed to see the transport of goods wrecked on transubstantiation. If these limitations be adduced as objections, the answer is simply that this is but a little book and leaves abundant room for another manner of treatment, and this way has also its merits. To deal with specific persons keeps continually to the fore what is so readily forgotten, that persecution thwarts, warps, and crushes individuals. The drowning of a thousand Anabaptists or the exile of ten thousand Huguenots may leave us cold, whereas a picture of one man burned, one man broken, one man exiled, may invest with meaning all the thousands and the tens of thousands.

The nine selected fall into three groups. The first trio have been chosen to illustrate persecution, Catholic and Protestant. They consist of two persecutors, the first Catholic, the second Protestant, namely, Torquemada and Calvin, and one victim of persecution from both parties, namely, Michael Servetus. The second three epitomize the struggle for liberty on the Continent in the sixteenth century. They are Sébastien Castellio the Frenchman, David Joris the Hollander, and Bernardino Ochino the Italian. The third three exemplify the struggle in England and the colonies in the seventeenth century, namely, John Milton for the Puritan revolution in the Old Country and Roger Williams in the New, and John Locke for the age of the Glorious Revolution and the Act of Toleration.

Before turning to these men, a word is in order with regard to the theory of persecution and in justification of the remark that Protestantism can be more readily tolerant than Catholicism. The prerequisites for persecution are three: (1) The persecutor must believe that he is right; (2) that the point in question is important; (3) that coercion will be effective.

On all three counts Catholicism and Protestantism, in so far as they were persecuting, were agreed. Both believed that outside the Church there is no salvation and that heresy damns souls. Lord Acton was quite mistaken in portraying the Protestant theory of persecution as diametrically opposed to the Catholic on the ground that Protestants had nothing left for which to persecute save error, whereas Catholics withstood the disruption of society through dissent. This picture is utterly misleading. Neither Catholic nor Protestant ever persecuted mere error but only obstinate error. Both persecuted heresy as heresy, and both believed that heresy, if unchecked, would disintegrate society. Both were driven by the exigencies of the situation to suppress dissent.

A few differences there are between the Catholic and Protestant theories, but they are not important. Luther sought to limit persecution by restricting it to blasphemy instead of heresy, but the gain was slight because he well-nigh identified heresy and blasphemy. Calvin declined to avail himself of this subterfuge and burned Servetus outright as a heretic. At several points Calvin intensified the Catholic theory of persecution. First, he accentuated the feudal conception of sin, according to which the enormity of an offense depends on the rank of the person against whom it is committed. When Calvin exalted God to dizzy transcendental eminence, heresy as an insult to his majesty became a crime of infinite depravity. In consequence the Catholic proviso that only a relapsed heretic should be put to death was abandoned. On no pretext could Servetus be regarded as relapsed. The other great difference was that the doctrine of predestination necessarily altered the purpose of persecution, which could not be to save souls, since they were saved or damned already, but could only be for the glory of God.

The greatest difference lay in the legal basis for persecution. For Catholics this was the canon law which was jettisoned by the Protestants. For it were substituted the Bible and the Roman law. In the long run this shift made for liberty, because the Bible provides but an insecure basis for the persecution of heresy, and the Roman law, while explicit enough, was to enjoy only a temporary vogue. The difficulty in the case of the Bible is that, although the Old Testament is severe in its penalties, they are directed, not against heresy, but only against idolatry and apostasy, whereas the New Testament, though mentioning heresy, is mild in its treatment of the offender. The Protestant persecutors had to combine the offense of the New with the penalty of the Old Covenant, a combination that the liberals were not slow in prying apart.

The Roman law was more explicit with regard to both the offense and the penalty. The two heresies penalized by death in the *Codex Justinianus* were a denial of the Trinity and a repetition of baptism. This ancient legislation directed against Arians and Donatists was revived in the sixteenth century and applied to Anti-Trinitarians and Anabaptists. Luther, Melanchthon, and Calvin all appealed to the imperial law. Joris, Gentile, and Servetus, and the Anabaptists as a whole, suffered under its terms. In fact the very name " Anabaptist," meaning " Rebaptizer," was invented in order to subject to the imperial laws those who preferred to call themselves simply Baptists. They would never admit that they baptized over again, for infant baptism was to them no baptism, but rather a " dipping in the Romish bath." The prevalence of the imperial code goes far to explain why Anti-Trinitarianism and Anabaptism were the two heresies visited with the severest penalties in the sixteenth century. Significantly, the last infliction of the death penalty for heresy in England under James I was for just these offenses. Roman law, however, was destined to succumb in favor of national codes, and a policy of persecution resting on no deeper legal basis than the old imperial laws could not indefinitely survive.

Differences, then, there are between the Catholic and Protestant theories of persecution but they are comparatively trivial. When one turns to the theory of liberty, the case is different, for Protestantism can be tolerant on more grounds than Catholicism, which cannot relinquish so many of the requisites for persecution.

With regard to the first prerequisite for constraint in religion, that the persecutor must believe he is right, the Catholic can never admit any uncertainty as to the cardinal affirmations of the Church. Neither can he concede that a willful denial of an article in the ecumenical creeds is a venial offense, since it will certainly entail damnation. The only ground for tolerance is expediency; but this is a larger ground than the word at first connotes, for expediency may be ecclesiastical, political, or religious. The Church can argue from the ecclesiastical point of view that persecution will recoil upon Catholics and do the Church more harm than good. This has been the situation in the United States. If any Church had been established, it would not have been the Catholic, and if any Churches were persecuted, the Catholic would not have been exempt. Leading American Catholics have clearly recognized this situation and in the past have wholeheartedly endorsed the American system of toleration.

Again expediency may be conceived in political terms. Persecution is then regarded as indiscreet because it wrecks the State. Here is the program of the French Politiques. As a Catholic, Henry IV promulgated the Edict of Nantes, and as a Catholic, Joseph II established the Decree of 1781. He was actuated by distress over the impoverishment and depopulation of the land through the expulsion of wealthy Protestants. As a corrective, toleration was granted openly to Lutherans and Calvinists and tacitly to Husites, though not to Deists who presumably mattered less.

Finally, expediency may be religious. From this point of view persecution is ineffective because incapable of engendering that heartfelt adherence which alone the Church can regard as adequate. Such a feeling presumably lies behind the repeal in the latest edition of the canon law of every penalty for heresy save excommunication.

In saying, however, that Catholics can be tolerant only on grounds of expediency one must not forget that Catholicism has nurtured three movements that made for tolerance, especially when transferred to Protestant soil, namely, mysticism, humanism, and sectarianism. Mysticism contributes by diverting attention from dogma to experience and by equating the way to God with the way of suffering, which comports more readily with martyrdom than with persecution. Humanism demands freedom for investigation in a limited area, and sectarianism, as in the case of the Spiritual Franciscans, places obedience to God or to the founder of the order, or to the Holy Spirit, above obedience to the pope. Such movements, to be sure, were restricted or suppressed by Catholicism, but nonetheless served in a measure to check dogmatic intolerance within Catholicism and proved a powerful solvent when transmitted to the Reformation.

Protestantism has made for liberty in much more varied ways, because it has been able to attenuate all three reasons for persecution. Certitude with regard even to the most cardinal doctrines and with regard to the authority of the

Church and the Bible has wavered in the face of attack on Protestant soil. A vein of rationalism runs from Erasmus through Castellio to Locke.

The second prerequisite for persecution, that the point in question be regarded as important, was demolished in part by a shift of interest within the realm of religion itself and in part by a secularism which diverted attention from religion as a whole, though this of course is extraneous to Protestantism.

Within the sphere of religion the importance of the dogmas supported by the sword of the magistrate was minimized in favor of the mystical and ethical elements. The one elevated inner experience, the other right conduct, as more significant than correct opinions. In Protestantism the ethical attack was the more prevalent. The argument was that in the eyes of God deeds count for more than creeds and creeds themselves must be subject to ethical tests. Just as the medical theories are judged by the cures which they effect, so too must theological affirmations be evaluated in terms of the correction of sins. Creeds are even ethically conditioned, for correctness of opinion is valueless apart from sincerity of conviction. From this position the step was easy to the assertion that sincerity is to be esteemed even though the opinions held be incorrect. Thus even error has rights as a stage in the quest for truth. Error is not the goal, but honest error is nearer to the truth of religion than dishonest correctness.

On this basis alone does conscience acquire any rights. The dominant Reformers of the sixteenth century scoffed at any conscience save a right conscience. *Conscientia,* they claimed, means nothing apart from *scientia; Gewissen* must be based on *Wissen.* Heretics have only a fictitious conscience. One recalls how Knox scoffed at Queen Mary's appeal to her conscience. The plea for conscience becomes relevant only when moral integrity is prized above dogmatic impeccability.

Another way of minimizing the importance of the points over which persecution raged was to make a distinction between one dogma and another. In this way fundamentalism arose. It was an attempt to segregate the fundamentals from the nonessentials in the interests of liberty. This type of thought has a long history. The *Devotio Moderna* had deprecated theological speculation to the point that Wessel Gansfort declared no ampler theology necessary for salvation than that of the penitent thief who was admitted to Paradise on very minimal terms. In the same vein Erasmus upbraided those who dissipated their energies on arid trivialities. The mediators between the Lutherans and Zwinglians relegated the sacramentarian controversy to the periphery. Other examples will appear in the course of this study.

The third premise for persecution is the belief that persecution is of some good. Here the Protestant was compelled to inquire, "Good for what?" The Catholic would have had an immediate answer, for the obvious purpose of persecution for him would be to save souls. But the Protestant, if he were a Lutheran or more particularly a Calvinist, could never say this, because according to the doctrine of predestination the salvation of souls is predetermined by God. The purpose of persecution is not to alter his decrees but to vindicate his honor. To this, the liberals replied that also here persecution is ineffective, since God is quite able to look out for himself. Neither can his honor be vindicated by burning men, for he takes no delight in holocausts.

The champions of liberty, while hammering at the notion that persecution either should or can glorify God, at the same time drew from the predestinarian arsenal in order to batter the Catholic position that persecution can be of any avail in saving souls. The doctrine of predestination at this point became a weapon of liberty, on the ground that if man's salvation depends wholly on God, then constraint is futile. On the Godward side it means indifference to the fate of the damned, but on the manward side it means impotence to alter matters by coercion. The particular determinist slogan on which the liberals fastened was a phrase from the apostle Paul that faith is a gift of God (Eph.2:8).

Because, however, the liberals in general were not themselves predestinarian in their thought, they preferred to give the determinist argument a different slant and shifted it from the soul to the mind. There is a determinism of the intellect. No more can the mind assent to that to which it does not assent than can the eye see as red that which it sees as blue. Constraint will not mend matters. In some cases this determinism is absolute. A moron never can grasp an argument; but in other cases the point is simply that apperception is slow and impeded by many obstacles. To effect conversion we must then master the art of persuasion. The greatest hindrances to clear sight are passion, pride, and prejudice, and these are only accentuated by vainglory and arrogance on the part of the one who is seeking to persuade. Humility and obvious devotion above everything else to the truth are the prime requisites for winning converts. Beneath the argument, of course, lies a confidence in the ability of truth to shift for itself and in the long run to command assent.

In the realm of theory certain considerations had an indirect bearing on the problem of persecution, and among them none was more important than the theory of the Church. Christian history exhibits two main views, and they are sometimes distinguished by calling the one the church type and the other the sect type. In England the terminology has been more frequent of the " parish " versus the " gathered " Church. They differ markedly in their attitude to religious liberty. The church type is based on a sacramental theory of salvation in which force is more appropriate because the sacrament can be regarded as a "medicine of immortality" which will benefit the recipient whether he likes it or not. The sacrament of Baptism is administered to babies. In a Christian land the Church is then considered to include all those born and baptized into the community. Alliance with the State becomes more natural because both Church and State comprise the same persons. Salvation outside the Church is impossible because the Church, even the visible Church, is like the ark of Noah, outside of which no souls were saved. To be in the ark one must receive the sacraments, subscribe to the doctrines, and obey the officers. Achievement of the moral demands is not so imperative because the unclean beasts were allowed in the ark. They are the tares to be left until the harvest. The heretics are not the tares. To them applies the text, "*Compelle intrare*," for they are comparable to Noah's wife in the mystery plays, who, incredulous of the flood, refused to board the ship until picked up bodily and shoved up the gangplank by her sturdy sons, whose place in the Christian commonwealth is taken by the secular arm. This theory of the Church is entirely compatible with a latitudinarianism which makes the gangplank broad, that as many as possible may enter the ark.

The sectarian theory of the Church looks upon the institution less as an ark of salvation than as a city set upon a hill to save itself and the world by an example of righteousness. The emphasis is ethical rather than sacramental. The tares are the heretics, who must be left outside and not compelled to come in lest they sully the purity of the community. The moral offenders are not the tares, and they must be excluded by excommunication. Babies are not to be baptized and church membership depends on mature conversion. This the State cannot effect by the sword of the magistrate. All constraint in religion is renounced, and commonly any alliance with the State is repudiated, since the State is instituted by

God because of sinners and is to be administered only by sinners. This view of the Church makes it exclusive. The ideal of comprehension is rejected and liberty is demanded to form small purist groups. The slogan of this party is:

> We are the choice elected few:
> Let all the rest be damned:
> There's room enough in hell for you.
> We won't have heaven crammed.

These two types can be combined, provided the community itself be select, granting residence, or at any rate the franchise, only to the saints.

Another question of significance for liberty is that of the form of political organization. The assumption is common that democracy is the form most conducive to tolerance, but democracy of itself is no guarantee of liberty. In Cromwell's days toleration could be achieved only by dictatorship. Cromwell could accord liberty to the Anglican Church, as he was disposed to do, only by flouting Parliament, which he was not disposed to do. On the other hand, religious restrictions were progressively removed under enlightened despots like Frederick the Great. The democratic form of the State means most for religious liberty in those cases where the Church seeks to influence political issues. Such activity will be tolerated only by a State that grants a similar liberty to various groups within its structure, like trade-unions. The totalitarian State will concede freedom to those Churches alone that confine themselves strictly to divine worship. Hence we may say that although the democratic State need not be tolerantly disposed, nevertheless in no other State is there so wide a scope for the activity and influence of the Churches.

As an administrative problem, the policy to be adopted by the State to dissident groups is conditioned only in part by its own constitution. Much more depends on the number and the temper of the groups themselves. Only if they are willing to live and to let live can the State drop the matter. If they are not so disposed, some measure of control becomes inevitable. Three solutions have been tried: territorialism, comprehension, and complete religious liberty. The first two methods were tried when the sects were intolerant of each other. The third became possible only as their temper changed.

Territorialism was rooted in the view which went back to antiquity that the State must be supported by a religion and that a single established religion is the best guarantee of the security and unity of the people. Such a motive led to the adoption of Christianity as the most favored religion of the Roman Empire. The division of Christendom occasioned by the Reformation was far from shattering the ideal. Since it could no longer be realized on a universal scale, the attempt was made to conserve it in many miniatures. The welfare of the State was still the determinative factor, and the prince was permitted to decide which religion should prevail in his domains. No other religion should be tolerated. Dissenters could be banished. The system of the union of Church and State, of the fusion of religion and the community, was thus conserved by an exchange of populations, and that was the point at which the system of territorialism enshrined liberty of a sort. Extermination was displaced by emigration.

This solution was adopted in Europe at the Peace of Augsburg of 1555, which recognized, however, only the Catholic and Lutheran Churches. The Peace of Westphalia of 1648 was conceived after the same pattern, but added the Reformed. And the American Constitution of 1787 was still cast in the same mold. Though no religion was to be established by the Federal Government, the states were free to retain or introduce any or none. The colonies had naturally grown up on the principle of territorialism. The Congrega-

tionalists gravitated to Massachusetts and Connecticut, the
Baptists to Rhode Island, the Presbyterians to New York and
New Jersey. The Catholics went to Maryland, the Quakers
and Pietist sects colonized Pennsylvania, and the Anglicans
predominated in the South. Established Churches prevailed
everywhere save in Rhode Island and Pennsylvania, which
latter presented the anomaly of religious disabilities without
an establishment. The Federal Constitution interfered with
none of this. Certain prerogatives of the Episcopalians in
Virginia lasted until 1802. The establishment of Congregationalism continued in Connecticut until 1818 and in Massachusetts until 1833. As a matter of fact, territorialism was
nowhere so compatible with liberty as in the American colonies because the right of emigration was not too difficult of
realization so long as the frontier remained open.

But to pull up with goods and kin was never easy, and for
that reason governments had recourse to another expedient
for solving the problem through a system of comprehension,
which sought to satisfy as many as possible in the community by latitude as to their most cherished tenets. These being
conceded, they were then asked to subscribe in other matters
to a scheme of uniformity. The recusants on the fringes to
the right and the left were subject to one penalty or another.
The Augsburg Interim which Charles V endeavored to impose on Germany enshrined this plan, and only after it
failed did he have recourse to the territorialism of the Peace
of Augsburg.

The English settlement was built on the same theory and
succeeded. The reasons for the failure of comprehension in
Germany and the success in England are a matter of speculation, but some differences are obvious. Charles V tried to
reconcile the Catholics and Protestants. Elizabeth attempted
comprehension only within the Protestant frame. Charles
was half Spanish. Elizabeth was English and Tudor. And the

date was later. England was already wearied by change and persecution from Henry through Edward and Mary. The disastrous effects of the religious wars on the Continent had given dramatic reinforcement to the theories of the Politiques. Besides, Erastianism from the outset had been deeply rooted in England. This, by the way, was not the doctrine that the State might introduce any religion it chose, but that in a Christian community the king held the two keys rather than the pope. Here we have the culmination of medieval imperialistic thought transferred to the head of one of the new national states. Perhaps deeper than any other reason is the closer continuity of the Reformation with the Renaissance in England than in other lands. The comprehensive philosophy of the Florentine Academy, with its candles for Plato as well as for Christ, suggested chapels for diverse cults beneath the one dome of the universal temple. The incursion of the Arminians further reinforced universalist tendencies. The system of comprehension, however, succeeded only relatively in England, since the champions of the narrow way refused to be comprehended and at length won for themselves an unmolested place outside of the Establishment.

The same thing happened in the American colonies, for if our Federal Constitution is an instance of territorialism, the individual colonies, whatever the religion established, displayed the same basic pattern as that of England. The rigidity of the first settlements soon moved in the direction of comprehension. At the same time the dissenters on the fringe gained an increasing footing: Baptists, Quakers, and Presbyterians in Virginia; Episcopalians, Baptists, and Quakers in Connecticut; and these, plus Unitarians, in Massachusetts. The process was arrested at this stage in England, but in America passed on to the third solution of the problem, that of a complete religious liberty in which the dissidents agree to differ.

The *pax dissidentium* had its first exemplification in Poland, in 1573, when those who frankly differed in religion
covenanted to preserve the peace among themselves, to shed
no blood, to impose no penalties, and to confiscate no goods
because of diversity in faith and practice. This peace, however, was made only between Protestant groups, and was
soon upset by the Counter Reformation. The next great attempt at this type of settlement was made by Oliver Cromwell, and will be discussed in connection with Milton.

An idea of great moment for the entire problem is that of
a united Christendom. The advance in liberty has actually
been associated with the disintegration of this ideal. The
Protestants of the sixteenth century had lamented the rending of the seamless robe of Christ and did their best to mend
the rents among themselves. But the sectaries of the seventeenth century definitely abandoned the ideal of unity and
regarded diversity and competition as wholesome and stimu-
lating, sometimes adducing the analogy of *laissez faire* in
trade.

The previous discussion refers several times to liberals over
against persecutors, as if there were two parties within Protestantism. That is correct. The one strain stemming from
Luther, Zwingli, and Calvin was dominant and continuous.
The other, stemming from Erasmus, asserted itself at recur-
rent intervals in all the rationalist movements and notably in
the Age of the Enlightenment. Coupled with the rationalist
approach were sometimes mystical and sectarian motifs. The
implication appears, then, to be that if Protestantism became
tolerant, it was only because of the triumph of the one party
over the other. The case, however, is by no means so simple.
Persecuting Protestantism also made its contribution to liberty — not, of course, by its persecution, but rather by its utter
intransigence. The liberals were in danger of securing tolerance by the evaporation of faith and the dissolution of the

Church. The intransigents were in danger of springing from resolute defiance to an imposition of their own creed, but their very defiance required that they be either exterminated or tolerated, and if they were numerous, toleration commended itself as the wiser expedient. They thus wrung toleration for themselves from the Catholic powers. To extend the same liberty to others was, however, possible only after some modification of their own position. They might, of course, wring their hands if unable to suppress their rivals, but if they became genuinely tolerant, as indeed they did, it could be only because they had come to esteem honest error as a stage toward truth, and even to conceive of themselves as possibly mistaken. But to concede this was to go over to the other camp. Very largely in Protestantism this is what has happened.

These themes will not be pursued systematically in the following study because it is set up around particular men. Rather, an attempt will be made to show the continual interplay of forces both in the realm of idea and in the realm of external circumstance, the tensions between the struggle to uphold truth and the effort to achieve tolerance. The story is carried through the most significant milestone, namely, the Act of Toleration in England in 1689.

PERSECUTION:
CATHOLIC AND PROTESTANT

Chapter One

THE PEAK OF CATHOLIC PERSECUTION:

Thomas of Torquemada

A bald enumeration of the presuppositions of Christian persecution gives no sense of the devastating intensity of conviction that could impel men to banish, imprison, torture, strangle, behead, drown, and burn. The supreme example and symbol is Thomas of Torquemada who, more than any other, fomented persecution in Spain, was instrumental in establishing and heading the Inquisition, and was the prime mover in the expulsion of the Jews. Torquemada was a bigot; he was also a Spaniard, and in him religious fanaticism and nationalist zeal were combined.

Thomas of Torquemada

The passion of his life was to unify Spain under the banner of Christian orthodoxy. Spain occupied a unique position. Prior to the Crusades this land had been the meeting point of three religions — Islam, Judaism, and Christianity. Under the tolerant regime of the caliphs the three dwelt in peace. Cultural interchange was fostered. Spain was the bridge between the Arabian and the European worlds, the crossroad of Islam and Christendom, where the Jews also had free passage. The ability of these religions to lie down together was due to no inherent tolerance, because each of them on occasion had been highly intolerant. Each makes exclusive claims. In this instance they manifested mutual respect, perhaps because the Saracens, like the Romans and the British, discovered that tolerance of religions is a convenient instrument for a tranquil administration. Wars, to be sure, there were, but not along confessional lines. Spain stood at the meeting of East and West.

This situation was not to last. The great disturbing factor was the Crusades. The root idea was religious, to protect the holy places from profanation and the holy pilgrims from molestation by dislodging the Turks and the Saracens from the Holy Land. An incidental effect was to forge a sense of European unity, to give reality to the ideal of Christendom. But this could scarcely be realized so long as the infidel retained a foothold in Europe itself. The Moor must be dislodged from the Iberian peninsula. The Mediterranean must become a Christian sea.

In this strife for unity the Jews were caught. The Crusaders on their way to the Holy Land, wearying of the long trek, vented their fanaticism in pogroms. In Spain the plan of reconquest demanded, not merely that the political power of the Moor be broken, but that the Christian faith be everywhere recognized, in which case the devotees of Jehovah were as alien as the worshipers of Allah.

As military pressure was applied to the Moor, popular antipathy was inflamed against the Jew. Friars preached hate. Archbishops, kings, and even popes might remonstrate, but those who had dedicated themselves to the most rigorous forms of the Christian life would not suffer themselves to be intimidated from attacks upon those alien to the Christian faith. Late in the fourteenth century a wave of anti-Jewish riots swept Spain.

They are better described as anti-Jewish than as anti-

Semitic, because race played no part and the Jew by renouncing his religion could relieve himself of all persecution. The temptation was acute, especially because no safe asylum was anywhere open. The Jews had been expelled from England in 1290, and from France in 1306, and in Germany were subject to periodic outbursts. For the first time in history a mass movement occurred in the Jewish community of wholesale conversion to Christianity. Thousands accepted baptism. The laver of redemption then washed away all disabilities, and the *conversos,* as they were called, became not only immune from molestation but eligible to the highest offices of the State and likewise of the Church. Converted Jews became treasurers, chancellors, bishops, and even archbishops. The more flourishing married with the Spanish nobility, so that scarcely any prominent family could claim purity of blood. Conceivably this process might have continued until assimilation was complete.

But it was not to continue, and one of the chief figures in arresting the process was Thomas of Torquemada, a Dominican friar who is said himself to have had a Jewish grandmother. He fell into one of the two classes of the *conversos.* The majority accepted Christianity only superficially, and in their homes continued to practice the rites of Judaism, to keep the kosher regulations, and to observe the feasts and the Sabbath. Some in clandestine circles may even have made mock of Christianity, but others by way of compensation became fanatically orthodox and sought to secure themselves in the Christian community by excessive zeal against any who lapsed into Judaism. Of such was Torquemada, or at any rate so he is explained, though the extant evidence is too scanty to warrant a confident judgment.

Apart from his personal motives this is clear, that Spain had reached a point of turning. The intolerance fanned by the Crusades had rendered impossible its former position as

the link between the crescent and the cross. Now it must belong either to Islam or to Christendom, oriented toward the
East or toward the West. And in the latter case there could
be but one religion, the orthodox faith of the Catholic
Church. Torquemada may or may not have sensed the full
import of the situation. From his behavior one can only
judge that he was fanatically committed to a Christian Spain,
purged of all alien elements, a veritable Gibraltar of Christendom.

In all this one observes that religious persecution was
closely tied to social concomitants. The kernel was the concept of a Christian society, the Church itself built on a pure
faith. But this ideal could readily fuse with some earthly
entity, whether the Holy Roman Empire or one of the rising
national states. This time it was Spain.

The instrument on which Torquemada seized for the
achievement of his purpose was the Inquisition. In his day it
was already fully two hundred years old, and back of the
Inquisition itself lay a still longer history of persecution. To
understand what it was all about a little review is necessary.
For this purpose one need not go back quite to Adam.
Moses will do as a point of departure, because he is the
founder of Judaism and Judaism is the parent of Christianity, notably with reference to the presuppositions of persecution. On the three counts of certainty, importance, and expediency, Judaism entertained no doubt. There could be no
question that the faith of Judaism was true, because delivered
by God upon the Mount to Moses. Neither could one deny
the supreme importance of maintaining the faith, since Jehovah is a jealous God who will visit his displeasure upon the
disobedient unto the third and fourth generations. And coercion certainly could preserve the purity of the elect people
by eliminating any apostates. The book of Deuteronomy
therefore decreed in the thirteenth chapter, the classic passage

on persecution alike for Jews and Christians, that if any Isra-
elite should entice his fellows to follow after other gods, he
should be taken beyond the camp and stoned. And in this
purge no son of the covenant should spare his brother, his
child, or even the wife of his bosom. Elsewhere in the Old
Testament, to be sure, one will find more liberal sentiments,
but here is the manifesto of persecution.

Christianity was the heir to Jewish exclusiveness and even
increased its claims. To the one and only God was added the
one and only Lord. The conflict in the Roman Empire was
not, as in Judaism, between Jehovah and Baal but between
Christ and Caesar. In place of the one chosen race arose the
one chosen religious community, the new Israel of God, the
Christian Church. Very soon emerged the view that outside
of this Church salvation was impossible. The Church was a
spiritual ark of Noah beyond which all were drowned. Obviously, then, adherence to the Church was of supreme importance. Adherence entailed submission to the Church officers, acceptance of the Church's rites, and subscription to
the Church's faith, the acceptance of a creed. This was a new
element. In the Old Testament the offense was apostasy, defection from the community. In the New Testament the
offense was heresy, a wrong belief, the rejection of an article
of the faith. The penalty in the Old Testament was death,
in the New Testament only avoidance. " Him that is a heretic
avoid " (Titus 3:10). The day was yet distant when the New
Testament offense and the Old Testament penalty were combined, but it was to come.

During the period when the Church was itself subject to
persecution there was of course no possibility of utilizing the
arm of the State for the punishment of heresy. But the presuppositions of persecution were further intensified by the
growth of a spirit of fierce antipathy toward those of a different persuasion. The Early Church swarmed with sects,

and hostility was bitter. When the orthodox and the Montanists were condemned to die in the same arena for the same Lord, they separated themselves to opposite corners rather than be eaten by the same lions. Such an attitude could manifest itself in active persecution. After the acceptance of Christianity by the Roman Empire, Constantine inflicted banishment upon the dissenting bishops at the Council of Nicaea. By the end of the fourth century the death penalty was actually exacted by the Emperor Theodosius, a Spaniard, of the heretic Priscillian also from Spain. Churchmen were aghast at this shedding of blood over a matter of the faith.

But churchmen were willing to condone and justify less extreme measures, particularly when heresy coalesced with social disorder in northern Africa, a region which by the end of the fourth century had come to be dominated by the party of the Donatists, who, after the persecution of Diocletian, had seceded from the Catholic Church rather than commune with those who had been lenient in receiving back collaborationist bishops. Once the schism was consummated, the Donatists attracted to themselves all the elements of discontent in northern Africa, where the old Punic population, after the demolition of Carthage, had long survived in the condition of peonage. To the Donatists flocked the oppressed and the dispossessed. Violence ensued. Saint Augustine, the bishop of Hippo in this region, still would countenance no retaliation. But when the government despite his remonstrance, stepped in and compelled the Donatists by fine and imprisonment to attend Catholic services, and when many of the Donatists then averred that formerly they had been intimidated by their own party from learning the truth and that now, through the forcible unstopping of their ears, their minds had been voluntarily opened, Saint Augustine declared himself no longer able to withstand the testimony of events.

He had questioned hitherto, not of course the truth of the faith or its importance, but only the effectiveness and propriety of constraint. With this example before him, he succumbed and proceeded to elaborate a theory of Christian persecution based on the premise of Christian love and concern for the welfare of the person coerced. If there is salvation only in the Catholic Church and if constraint can remove obstacles to genuine conversion, then to employ it is an act of kindness. Surely a father may properly hold back a child from playing with a snake and a son may restrain a crazed father from throwing himself over a cliff. A horticulturist prunes a rotten branch to save a tree and a doctor amputates a diseased limb to conserve a life. Even so may the erring be constrained. Augustine was here using fateful analogies which for him were comparatively innocuous because he did not personify society and did not admit of the death penalty. But if and when the body to be saved should be identified with the Church or the State, then the rotten member would become an individual to be destroyed. That step in the chain of logic was, however, not taken for centuries.

In between came the barbarian invasions in the West. The intruders were tolerant. Some were themselves heretical Arians; some were at first pagans. None of them were concerned about or so much as understood the intricacies of Eastern theology. Persecution slumbered. It was not to be invoked again for some six centuries. The reason is that heresy and sectarianism also slumbered. Why that should have been the case is distinctly puzzling. The Early Church was rent by sects, and likewise the Church of the late Middle Ages. Conceivably during the intervening period the collapse of culture and the decline of intellectual interest removed one of the causes of conflict. Again the winning of the West for Christianity consumed all energies, and monasticism provided a sufficient outlet for the urge to diversity.

Persecution was revived when sectarianism and heresy recurred. The beginnings are found in the eleventh century and culminated in the thirteenth, when, paradoxically, the Church reached the zenith of its prestige and power as a controlling and integrating factor in European civilization and coincidentally was menaced with disruption by a proliferation of sects. Both developments stem from a great reformatory movement which essayed to purge the monasteries, purify the Church, and Christianize the world. The effort produced new monastic orders, holy wars, and the papal theocracy. But even such glittering successes were a disappointment to ardent reformers, who deplored the resurgent wealth of the monasteries, the bestiality of the Crusades, and the secularization of the papacy through the acquisition of temporal power. The inference was that society cannot be Christianized and the Church as a whole cannot be reformed. Consequently small convinced groups must undertake the reformation, even at the price of secession. Conjoined with this moral urge was defection at one point or another from the faith. Such a dissipation of forces the Church could not abide at the very moment when a united effort appeared capable of erecting a new Jerusalem on earth. The arm of the State was therefore invoked to allay dissent. The result was the Inquisition, an institution founded by the popes in the thirteenth century and directly subject to their control. The Inquisitor was commissioned to ferret out heresy, undeterred by fear, favor, or affection. The convicted should be committed to the secular arm to be burned, rather than beheaded, because the Church abhors the shedding of blood.

Such was the instrument that lay at hand for Torquemada's purpose. Yet it was not entirely suitable for all that he envisaged. To begin with, its jurisdiction was too restricted, because the Inquisition could take cognizance of offenses only when committed by Christians. The test of a

Christian was exceedingly perfunctory, since it consisted in infant baptism. The unbaptized were free. This meant that the Inquisition might deal only with the *conversos,* and not with the loyal Jews and Moors. Increasingly Torquemada was of the persuasion that they too, notably the Jews, must come within the net, because the *conversos* could never be held to the Christian faith so long as the Jews were at hand to seduce them. Either, then, the scope of the Inquisition must be enlarged or some other device must be discovered.

Still another question was whether in any case the Inquisition could be bent to deal adequately even with the *conversos,* because the Inquisition was directly subject to the popes and the popes in this era were not fanatical. The late fifteenth century was the period of the Renaissance, when the popes had become Italian despots, elegant, loose, sometimes flippant, and often indifferent as to the faith. Crusading zeal, now at its peak in Spain, had cooled at the very seat of its origin, and Pope Alexander VI, himself a Spaniard by the way, actually made a treaty with the Turk against the most Christian king of France. It looked almost as if the former role of Spain as the bridge between religions and cultures might be taken over by Rome. Although such fraternization was but of short duration, Torquemada was rightly dubious as to whether the popes would abet his implacability.

The only recourse was to extricate the Inquisition from papal hands, and no other power was strong enough to accomplish this save the crown. Already in France, Philip IV had turned the Inquisition into an instrument of State to suppress the Templars. Torquemada undertook to do the like in Spain in order to extinguish the Judaizers. The sovereigns of Spain at this time were Isabella and Ferdinand. Isabella deserves to be named first, for she was the abler and more enterprising of the two. The contemporary verdict on their relative endowments was registered on their tombs. The head of Isabella sinks deeply into the stone cushion, whereas the brains of Ferdinand make but a slight impression. Isabella was a visionary, hospitable to the schemes of madmen. She suffered herself to be persuaded by two such in her lifetime. The one induced her to sponsor his wild plan to reach the Indies by sailing westward; and the other enlisted her for the expulsion of the Jews from Spain. To contemporaries, Columbus probably appeared the madder of the two. Torquemada became the confessor of Isabella in 1467, when she was sixteen and he was forty-six.

Ferdinand was of a different breed. His primary concern was to complete the process, already advanced in France, of the establishment of order through the reduction of baronial power and the concentration of authority in the crown. This was one aspect of rising nationalism. The great nobles and the great churchmen, who were also nobles, stood in the way, and sometimes the pope interfered. An institution that would not only preserve the unity of the faith but might at the same time break the nobility, both lay and clerical, was greatly to be prized, and just this the Inquisition might achieve. The goods of the convicted were subject to confiscation. If they could then be awarded, not to the Church, but to the State, the victim would be impoverished and the crown enriched. Furthermore, any who harbored heretics were themselves subject to prosecution. If, then, any of the feudal lords and great churchmen offered an asylum to the *conversos,* to whom they were frequently bound by ties of blood, they would at once come under the jurisdiction of the dread tribunal. Ferdinand perceived that the Inquisition could be highly serviceable, provided he and not the pope controlled it. Torquemada was not averse to playing upon the bigotry of Isabella and the cupidity of Ferdinand. The Inquisition was thus to become the great weapon for the purity of the faith and the honor of Spain. Orthodoxy and nationalism were combined.

Torquemada well knew that he would not have easy going even in Spain. The masses were not in a continuous state of eruption against the *conversos,* and the process of assimilation had actually gone so far that only by a din of propaganda could it be arrested. And propaganda in those days could not employ the radio, nor to any large extent even the printing press. The great instrument was the spoken word, and the speakers were the friars. Long had they been the preachers of intolerance. They were practiced in the art of inflammatory harangues. For rougher work there were the *familiares,* young nobles who were given certain clerical immunities in return for running down and rounding up suspects. Children even were encouraged to inform against their parents. Ordinarily a boy must be fourteen and a girl twelve to make their testimony admissible. But a case is reported of a girl of but ten who was forced to depose against her mother.

One of the chief weapons in the hands of Torquemada was any act of indiscretion or retaliation on the part of the *conversos.* Every incident was magnified in proportions and generalized in extent. The first episode occurred when a young Spanish noble, visiting his mistress among the Jewish converts, overheard her father and his friends reviling the Christian faith. The young man's orthodoxy was above his morals, and he promptly reported the case to the Church. The penalty imposed was lenient. The noble then remonstrated to the queen, and at this point Torquemada stepped in to plead that the local clergy could not be trusted. Therefore an independent tribunal must be introduced, namely, the Inquisition. The queen consented. Then the white-and-black-robed Dominicans marched in solemn procession into Seville and set up the Holy Office. One of their number would post himself every Saturday on the roof of the convent to scan the chimneys of the city. If any were without smoke, the house was investigated to learn whether the Jewish Sabbath was being observed within. One wonders why the Jews could not have been suffered to retain certain of the externals of Judaism just as the early Christians were not required to abandon the observance of the law. But unhappily in times of stress the trivial externals commonly become the symbols of diversity and the objects of attack.

Torquemada pushed for the extension of the Inquisition from Seville to the whole of Castile and Aragon and demanded further from the pope that the officials be appointed, not by the pontiff, but by the king. The pope refused and demoted Torquemada. Ferdinand promptly backed the friar and threatened financial retaliations against the papacy. The pope, seeing his income jeopardized, at once capitulated, and in October, 1482, Torquemada became the Grand Inquisitor for Aragon and Castile.

The campaign began by exhorting all in the community to confess or to inform. Those who confessed and did penance could thereby forestall the confiscation of their goods. Three days of grace were allowed. Then arrests were made of suspects. If they proved tough, various methods of softening were employed. The prisoner would be brought into a darkened chamber. Before him sat the Inquisitors robed in white. Behind him stood the guards. A notary was ready to take down every word. The Inquisitor in silence fumbled papers, casting a dubious eye at the accused. After he had been made sufficiently apprehensive, his examination began. If the suspect proved obdurate, the Inquisitor might announce that he had to go on a journey and would leave the accused in chains until his return. Or the hearings might be accelerated. Again the prisoner might be transferred to pleasant surroundings and allowed visits from his friends, who would insinuate the suggestion that he confess. A spy might come, pretending to be himself a prisoner, and would seek confidences. A complete pardon might be proffered in return for confession and the implication of others, though after the information was elicited, the pardon would be interpreted as that of God and not of the Inquisition, or the reward might be merely strangling prior to burning. The witnesses for the prosecution might be heretics or criminals, but for the defense only good Catholics.

All other attempts having failed, torture might be used. The rack and the burning of the feet became popular later. In Spain the commonest modes were the hoist and the water torture. The hoist consisted in tying the hands behind the back. One end of a rope was then secured around the hands and the other end of the rope passed through a pulley on the ceiling. The victim was raised and then dropped by sudden jerks. Each time the elevation was increased and weights

A Burning at the Stake in the Spanish Inquisition

might be placed on the feet. In the water cure the suspect was bound to a ladder, so placed that the feet were above the head. The mouth was held open by an iron clasp and the nostrils plugged. A rag was placed down the throat. The mouth was then filled with water. Swallowing took the rag down the gullet and cut off breathing. When the victim was on the point of suffocation, the rag was pulled up and the soft voice of the Inquisitor appealed for a confession.

If the accused were adjudged guilty, he suffered the confiscation of his goods. If penitent, he might be imprisoned for life or at least placed under close surveillance. If impenitent, he was burned at the stake, often after previous mutilation. Penitents were required to wear the sanbenito, a single shapeless, sulphur-colored garment, on Sundays and on all religious festivals. The only possible extenuation that can be urged for these practices is that civil penalties were at that time no less severe.

In the year 1488 the Inquisitors in Toledo handled 3,300 cases. Torquemada had to request the king to construct special dwellings for the throngs of the accused since the dungeons were full.

Further incidents played into his hands. The *conversos* divined that he meditated their extinction and resolved on retaliation. The most expedient method appeared to be to assassinate the Inquisitors. A band of six formed a conspiracy. One of their number was himself the son of a condemned *converso*. Two Inquisitors were to be dispatched. The task would not be easy because they were known to wear coats of mail beneath their Dominican cowls. The plotters concealed themselves in the church where the friars came at midnight for Mass. On the night in question only one of the Inquisitors appeared. The assassins debated whether to postpone their coup until both could be caught. When the lone Inquisitor went to a side chapel but a few yards distant, the opportunity was not to be missed. The son of the *converso* drove his sword through the coat of mail. And the other Inquisitor died shortly thereafter under suspicion of poison. The populace was inflamed. The *familiares* unearthed several of the conspirators. Some fled to France; one took his life. Those who were caught had their hands cut off on the steps of the cathedral. They were half hanged, castrated, and quartered. The attempt of the *conversos* to protect themselves by rebellion had failed.

Next a handful of *conversos* and Jews sought to protect themselves, not by the arm of man, but by the assistance of the powers of darkness. In place of assassination came magic. The whole story is to be reconstructed from the single dossier of one of the accused, preserved in the files of the Inquisition. The records begin in June of the year 1490 with the examination of a converted Jew, Benito Garcia by name, fifty years of age. He had been returning from a pilgrimage to Compostela, and stayed at an inn where, for lack of space, he had to share a room with some drunkards, who rummaged in his bag and found a wafer which they took to be a sacred host. The case was referred to the vicar. Under torture Benito confessed that he had relapsed into Judaism and that at the house of two Jews, Mosé and Yucé Franco by name, he had eaten meat on a Friday. He had declared the Corpus Christi to be humbug and spat during the procession, but he confessed nothing about the wafer.

He had incriminated two Jews. Strictly speaking, they were not subject to the Inquisition, but they were investigated. Mosé Franco turned out to be dead. Yucé was a lad of twenty. He was arrested. For good measure his father, eighty years of age, was also taken into custody, unbeknownst to the son. In prison Yucé fell sick and, believing himself to be on the point of death, asked for a rabbi. Such a request compromised him in no way because he was a Jew and had never been a Christian at all. The Inquisitors saw here a providential opportunity and introduced in the robes of a rabbi a *converso* fully conversant with the dialect of the local Jews. He inquired of Yucé for what reason he had been arrested. The boy replied that he did not know, unless perchance because of what had happened some eleven years previously, namely, the *mita* of a *nahar* after the manner of the *Otohays*. These three words were not Spanish but Hebrew. *Mita* means " killing." *Nahar* means " a boy," and *Otohays* is a combination of two words meaning " that man," the expression used among the Jews to signify Christ. In other words, eleven years before there had been a killing of a boy after the manner of Christ, that is to say, by crucifixion. The feigned rabbi reported the conversation and Yucé was confronted with what he had said. He then incriminated a family of converted Jews of the town of La Guardia. Like himself, they were named Franco, though not related to him. These Franco brothers, he claimed, had crucified a boy on Good Friday.

The Inquisitors then pieced together the separate items and constructed the charge that Benito had stolen a sacred wafer and Yucé had participated in a crucifixion in order to obtain the heart of a Christian boy. Heart and wafer were to be used together for purposes of magic. Yucé denied any complicity.

Then Benito and Yucé were placed in adjoining rooms with a crack between. An Inquisitor was listening in. Yucé began to strum on his guitar. Benito told him to stop lest he disturb his father. This was the first intimation he had had of his father's arrest. Yucé then asked Benito for what reason he had been apprehended, and Benito related the story of the discovery of the wafer at the inn. He had been subjected to water torture. The Inquisitors he considered were worse than Antichrist. If he ever got out, he would go to Judea. Better die than be tortured. Let Yucé, when he recited the prayer, "*Helohay nesamá*," remember him. Yucé then began plying him with questions about the wafer until Benito grew reticent.

The Inquisitors who had tapped the conversation were confident that Yucé was privy to the theft of the wafer. They laid before him the report of all that he had said to Benito, and extracted thereby the confession that he did know that Benito and the Franco brothers of La Guardia, who like Benito were *conversos,* had stolen the wafer to employ it in magic to protect them against the Christians. But the magic had not been successful. Nothing more would Yucé confess. After two months he made a reference to a human heart. After another month he was promised immunity for his father if he would confess more. And then he admitted that the human heart had been taken from a boy who had been crucified. Then the father was shown his son's confession. He corroborated the crucifixion and laid the responsibility upon the Francos of La Guardia. He and his sons, who were Jews and not *conversos,* had merely been present. The heart had been extracted to make a spell and the body had been disposed of.

The next procedure was to bring prisoners together in pairs. The Franco brothers of La Guardia were of course by this time under arrest on the orders of " Frey tomás de Torquemada." What one suspect had told about another was related to him in the hope that he would be angered and would retaliate by telling something against the informer. In this way Yucé came to be charged with having conducted the Francos of La Guardia and Benito to a cave for a crucifixion. He had himself opened the veins of the child and had declared Christianity to be humbug.

The defense — and the prisoner was allowed defense — pointed to discrepancies in the testimony and called in question the participation of Yucé in view of his youth. The objections were overruled.

Then came the torture. According to the record, on the second of November in the year of our Saviour 1491, the Inquisitors entered the dungeon and besought Yucé lovingly and with all humanity to tell the truth. He should relate whose child this was, how he was obtained, and who was the first to start this business. If he would tell the truth, they would deal with him mercifully. Then Yucé confessed that fifteen days after the crucifixion they had made fetishes, but the Inquisitors were sure that he was not telling the truth and committed him to torture. He was roped to a ladder and his arms pinned. He was assured that if they proceeded to the torture it would be his fault, and not theirs, because he had not confessed, that in any case they would treat him mercifully without effusion of blood or mutilation of members. Then Yucé confessed that Juan Franco had obtained the child at Toledo, having enticed him with candy, but whose child he was he did not know. The purpose of the fetishes was to obtain protection against the Inquisition, and the child was crucified after the manner of Christ because if he who represented Christ were destroyed, the power of Christ would be destroyed. In other words, this was representative magic.

The confessions were forwarded to Torquemada. He had followed the progress of the case but had not hurried, since he wanted the evidence to be unimpeachable. Nine months had elapsed in eliciting this much. Torquemada submitted the documents to seven of the most learned professors of the University of Salamanca. They rendered the verdict that Yucé and the others were all guilty. And now came the crucial point. Could the Inquisition exercise any jurisdiction over Yucé and his father, since they were Jews and not *conversos* like Benito and the Francos of La Guardia? The reply was that in such a case the authority of the Inquisition extended also to the Jews.

Invoking then the name of Christ, the judges pronounced the sentence of death. The auto-da-fé took place on the sixteenth of November, 1491. Certain of the *conversos* returned to the faith and were rewarded by strangling before burning. Young Yucé and his aged father adhered resolutely to their Judaism. Their flesh was torn by red-hot pincers before the fires were lighted.

What shall we make of this story? Some modern historians have assumed that the charges were a pure fabrication, concocted by the Inquisitors and corroborated by torture. Against this may be said that, unless the entire deposition is false, the first testimony as to the crucifixion came from the statement of Yucé to the feigned rabbi, and the first admissions as to the wafer were derived from his confidential conversation with Benito. The Jewish historian Sabatini was so far impressed by these facts as to concede the reality of the crucifixion. He insisted only that it was not a case of ritual murder by the Jewish community, but an instance of representative magic practiced by a few Jews and *conversos*. We need not be surprised if some Jews were no more enlightened and no more humane than many of their Christian neighbors. And we may even be able to understand how among a people threatened with extermination a few unbalanced spirits might summon the aid of the powers of darkness.

But they merely succeeded in supplying Torquemada with the means of their complete undoing. He pressed upon Isabella that the *conversos* could never be held to the faith so long as the Jews remained to seduce them. The unbelievers must be banished from the land. Isabella hesitated. Ferdinand hesitated. Well they might, because the Jews were the tax collectors and the crown needed taxes. But Ferdinand became more amenable when the immediate object of taxation was removed. The great drain was the constant war to expel the Moors from Spain. On January 2, 1492, Granada fell.

The war was over and Ferdinand could afford to dispense with the Jews. Their banishment was decreed after three months. They could take with them only what they could carry away. The leaders of the Jewish community appeared before the king and queen to protest their former services and to proffer their future contributions. As a token they presented 30,000 ducats. The sovereigns hesitated. Torquemada advanced to the table. " Judas," he cried, " sold his Master for thirty pieces of silver. You would sell him for thirty thousand." Holding aloft a crucifix, he flung it on the table, saying, " Take him and sell him, but do not let it be said that I have had any share in this transaction."

The edict of expulsion stood. The Jews disposed of their goods, a house for a donkey or a vineyard for a piece of cloth. The galleons of Columbus setting out for the New World passed the ships taking the Jews into a new dispersion.

This is of course but a single instance from the whole story of the Inquisition. After the fall of Granada the process that had been applied to the Jews was extended to the Moors. Later the Inquisition was to be employed against the Protestants. But quite enough is here to illustrate the principles and the procedures. The point to be emphasized is that this was primarily religious persecution. The fact that orthodoxy could be fused with nationalism must not obscure the fact that friars preaching in the name of religion had created a situation out of which the fusion could arise. Nor is persecuting religion to be regarded as insincere. Dostoevsky misrepresented the Spanish Inquisitor when he portrayed him as cynically ready to burn even Christ should he return. The Torquemadas were not cynics, but passionately sincere fanatics. All of which should make abundantly plain that virtues are not without their vices. A concern for truth can end in inhumanity and love itself can be perverted into cruelty. This, too, is obvious: that Christianity as such cannot be regarded as the panacea for all the ills of the world. It all depends on what kind of Christianity. And whatever else may be added, this certainly is an appalling reflection: that the barbarities practiced in modern times to ensure conformity to the program of a party are but refinements of the methods employed by those who invoked the name of Christ.

Chapter Two

THE PEAK OF PROTESTANT INTOLERANCE:

John Calvin

On the monument of the Reformation at Geneva stand in stone four massive figures. The tallest and most imposing is John Calvin, in life a frail and emaciated Frenchman, whose colossal proportions are here justified only because his spirit fashioned Geneva, divided Holland, convulsed France, molded Scotland, and guided New England. Beside him

Monument of the Reformation at Geneva

stands his henchman, Theodore Beza, who, after Calvin, held the citadel of Geneva begirt by foes. On one side stands William Farel, of the red beard, of whom contemporaries said that "no one bellowed more vociferously," and on the other side John Knox, who intimidated a queen and turned the Scottish nation from raiding cattle to raiding hell and rearing a nation of saints. One could scarcely find in the sixteenth century, apart from Luther, four more intrepid and influential figures, and they were all persecutors. John Calvin was responsible for the execution of Michael Servetus at the stake. Farel attended the execution. Beza justified the holocaust, and John Knox applauded.

At the far end of this monument of the Reformation stands a figure who, if he had been in Geneva in the sixteenth century, would have been drowned if not burned. He is the Baptist and Seeker, Roger Williams by name, a champion of religious liberty and of the separation of Church and State. What is he doing flanking this phalanx of persecutors? The paradox of the monument is that it includes men who would have destroyed each other had they met in life, but who nevertheless are placed in a line of succession. And the line is valid, as the sequel will reveal.

Another anomaly is that at the moment of its beginning Protestantism was more intolerant than contemporary Catholicism. The Catholic Church is not monolithic, and in the days of Torquemada the popes were more tolerant than were the Inquisitors. When Luther emerged, he was, in temper at least, vastly more intolerant than Pope Leo X. Luther was aflame for the Word of God. Pope Leo X was titillated by elegant tapestries. Catholicism again became deadly in earnest only in the Counter Reformation. The basic reasons for the comparative tolerance of the opening decades of the sixteenth century lay, however, not in the flippant indifference of individual popes, but partly in a sense of security, inasmuch as the menace of the Moors and the Jews had passed and the menace of Protestantism had not yet emerged. In such an interlude the philosophy of tolerance was able to flourish.

This was the age of the Renaissance. One of the strains in that movement is called humanism. It was in part an attitude to life, aspiring to fulfillment rather than renunciation. The ideal was to encompass all departments and master all disciplines. Nothing was alien; all learning, all systems, and even all religions should be studied and sympathetically understood. The pious pagans were esteemed as almost Christian saints and were not excluded from paradise. And Christianity was at times on the verge of losing its absolutely unique place among religions. Coincidentally, the essence of Christianity was attenuated, and defined as comprising little more than those universal beliefs and moral maxims common to all peoples. Christianity tended to be expressed in terms of the Fatherhood of God, the leadership of Christ, and the brotherhood of man. These were of course later the slogans of the Enlightenment and of liberal Protestantism. They were first formulated in the age of the Renaissance.

Another aspect of humanism was free inquiry, particularly with regard to historical documents, including those on which rested the claims of the Church and of the Christian religion itself. The textual and literary critics demonstrated the spuriousness of many bulwarks of orthodoxy and theocracy. The Apostles' Creed was shown not to have been actually by the apostles. The Donation of Constantine was exposed as false. And many of the decretals buttressing papal claims were demonstrated to have been fabricated. Even the text of the Bible was shown to be incapable of restoration with perfect assurance, and certain texts such as the one on the three witnesses, the great proof text for the Trinity, was proved to be an interpolation. The humanists demanded for themselves freedom to conduct such investigations and stoutly resisted interference. Humanism, whether within Catholicism or Protestantism, was one of the great strands in the fabric of liberty. Another was mysticism, which likewise flourished in this period, especially in the Rhine Valley and the Low Countries. Mysticism views the end of religion as the union of man with God. The devotee loses himself in the abyss of the Godhead as the drop of water is merged with the ocean. But this process is not easy, because there are alien elements impeding the union which must first be eliminated by a purgative process. The subduing of the flesh is at this point a wholesome discipline and any suffering imposed from without is to be welcomed. In this whole approach to religion there are three points making for religious liberty. The first is that the object of the quest is not the understanding of God by some intellectual process but absorption into his Being. Hence interest in speculative theology is diminished and rigid orthodoxy becomes less a ground for persecution. Secondly, if suffering is an essential stage upon the way, persecution is never to be inflicted, but rather to be endured with patience, if not indeed with joy and gratitude. The inference is not far removed that a persecuting Church cannot be a true Church, and the afflicted are by that very token to be regarded as true Christians. Finally, in the third place, the entire process of mystical absorption cannot be hastened or helped by any external constraint. Force may elicit a confession to a creed. It can scarcely unite the believer with God.

The man in whom all these tendencies converged was Erasmus of Rotterdam, and he deserves mention here because he was the father of so many of the liberal tendencies within Catholicism and Protestantism alike. In the early decades of the sixteenth century his spirit prevailed. Even in Spain he enjoyed an enormous vogue in the 1520's. The reason was of course in part that the Inquisition had done its work all too well, and the rigors could safely be relinquished. Throughout

Europe before the emergence of Luther the pressures were relaxed. Reformers might criticize and scholars might probe without throwing the Holy Office into hysteria.

The tolerance of Erasmus was based partly on rationalism. He deplored even discussion, let alone constraint over matters that cannot be known on this side of the Judgment Day. Many problems, he thought, were commonly deferred until the meeting of a general council, and it would be better to defer them still further, " until no longer we see in a glass darkly but behold God face to face." Among such questions he would include the problem of the relation of the three persons in the Trinity and the distinction between the nativity of the Son and the procession of the Holy Ghost. Speculation in any case appeared to him inimical to piety. " The sum of our religion is peace and unanimity and these can scarcely stand unless we define as little as possible and in many things leave each one free to follow his own judgment."

The ethical note also was prominent. Erasmus always sensed a perversion of values in leniency toward clerical concubinage and severity toward queries with regard to the consubstantiality of the second member of the Trinity. " What does it matter if there be no blasphemy of the tongue if the whole life breathes blasphemy against God? . . . If the Beatitudes which bless the meek and the persecuted are called a lie? What blasphemy could be more detestable than this? "

Again Erasmus, in keeping with the mystical tradition, sharply differentiated the spiritual from the physical and situated religion in the realm of the spirit. For this reason most of the controversies of his day appeared to him irrelevant, because centering on things outward, which in the eyes of God are of small significance. The chief heresy and the supreme blasphemy in his judgment was to turn the spiritual into the carnal. To burn men simply for observing kosher laws would be in his eyes a monstrous perversion of true religion and utterly ineffective in producing the right spirit, which alone matters.

But if Erasmus deprecated theological hairsplitting, it was not because he was not an intellectual. In the domain of literary studies he demanded the freedom of the scholar to carry on his investigations without dogmatic presuppositions or ecclesiastical interference.

Humanism and mysticism thus converged in him, and from him they flow out into much of liberal Catholicism and liberal Protestantism. On the other hand, one must not regard him altogether as the enlightened liberal. He had a very deep feeling for the authority and integrity of the Church, and when he saw the structure buttressing the European unities menaced by sectarianism, he was aghast and not unwilling to take some restrictive measures. Against blasphemous heresy that looked in the direction of sedition he would use the sword.

Protestantism arose during the Erasmian interlude, when the fires of the Inquisition smoldered and men might think and men might speak. Those who spoke were affected by the mood. Luther in his youth had been as intolerant as an Inquisitor, and declared that he would have been willing to bring a fagot for the pyre of John Hus. But when he found himself suspected of heresy, he endorsed the Erasmian principle that to burn heretics is against the will of the Holy Spirit. And this statement was one of Luther's propositions condemned by the Roman bull. He did not relinquish this position even after the pressures became intense. His view altered, however, when he passed from the status of a fugitive to that of a builder of a Church.

After a year in exile at the Wartburg, he returned unauthorized to Wittenberg and commenced the construction of what came to be known as the Lutheran Church. The first problem was what to do with the Catholics and their serv-

ices. Luther's followers resorted to violence, intimidating and
mauling priests and the religious. All this Luther roundly de-
cried. " Of course there are abuses," said he. " So also the sun
has been abused by being worshiped, but shall we therefore
pluck the sun from the sky? And men have gone wrong with
wine and women, but shall we on that account prohibit wine
and abolish women? " His counsel was to correct the abuses
by patience and a process of education. Faith is too inward
and spiritual to be judged or forced by outward means. Constraint leads the weak to deny their convictions. Better to let
them err than force them to lie. The Mass actually continued
for three years after Luther's return to Wittenberg. Much
more disconcerting was the rise of sectarianism within his
own ranks. He was cut to the quick when he discovered that
the predictions of his Catholic opponents were being all too
abundantly fulfilled — that one secession would lead to another and the seamless robe of Christ would be reduced to
shreds. Yet Luther was extremely loath to countenance any
constraint. " Let the spirits fight it out," was his advice.

It was not he who started Protestant persecution, but rather
Zwingli, and that may be all the more surprising because he
was a son of the Renaissance, a disciple of Erasmus, and very
cordial to the pious heathen. But the form of dissent that
arose in Zurich was not so much directed against dogmas,
with regard to which Zwingli might have been tolerant, as
against the very nature of the Church and its relation to civil
society. Here is another case where the eternal mingled with
the temporal. The Anabaptists (they preferred to call themselves Baptists) had a theory of the Church that necessitated
its separation from the State, because they claimed that the
Church should be composed only of heartfelt believers of
upright life, whereas the State should include the total body
of the inhabitants in a community. They could not endorse
the system whereby every child was by birth a citizen and by

baptism a Christian, and the whole populace was deemed Christian by virtue of a rite accorded to unwitting infants. The Church must comprise only the regenerate. The Church therefore would have to be a select community. But the State should include everybody within a given district. Consequently State and Church could not coincide. The symbol of the Baptist system was the rejection of infant baptism and the repetition of the rite in adult life, though for the Baptists there was no repetition because infant baptism was no baptism at all but only " a dipping in the Romish bath." The question of baptism mattered vastly less in Zwingli's eyes than the disintegration of a Christian society. He foresaw, and rightly, as the outcome of their position the possible secularization of the State. The Church might in the process be purged, but the community would be dechristianized. Such abandonment of the world to the devil he could not abide, and his answer was to invoke at once the arm of the State. The Anabaptists were subjected to a law that originated in the Christian Roman Empire against the ancient Donatists, who claimed that baptism was invalid unless practiced by themselves and therefore repeated baptism in case any Catholic joined their ranks. Against this practice the death penalty was decreed in the Code of Justinian. Not the canon law of the Church of Rome, but the civil law of the Empire of Rome provided the legal basis for Protestant persecution. The Anabaptists were drowned in mockery of adult immersion. This was in the year 1525.

Luther did not approve, and in 1527 he wrote: " It is not right, and I am deeply troubled that the poor people are so pitifully put to death, burned, and cruelly slain. Let everyone believe what he likes. If he is wrong, he will have punishment enough in hell fire. Unless there is sedition one should oppose them with Scripture and God's Word. With fire you will accomplish nothing."

But in the year 1525 another incident occurred that shook Luther powerfully. It was a further coincidence of religion and social disturbance. The Peasants' War alarmed him tremendously. Yet the Peasants' War by itself would never have disposed him to become a persecutor had it not been for the injection into it of a highly explosive religious idea by that firebrand Thomas Müntzer, the first Protestant theocrat. The great difference between Müntzer and Luther was that Müntzer believed in the possibility of the Kingdom of God on earth. Luther claimed that this is entirely unrealizable. The world is and remains a devil's pigsty, which can be restrained from outrageous villainy by the sword of the magistrate but can never be converted into the Garden of Eden. Not even the Church is a Garden of Eden, because the Church is a field in which the tares are mingled with the wheat. But Müntzer asserted that the wheat can be segregated from the tares because now is the time of the harvest. The wheat are the elect and they can be known. This is another point that Luther denied. He believed very strongly that there are elect and nonelect, but he saw no means by which they can be infallibly distinguished. Müntzer had a test, and it was the new birth, the descent of the Spirit, a radical, datable conversion. People who have had such an experience know very definitely that they have had it and are in a position to form a Church. More than that, they can form a society. Here is the idea of a holy commonwealth, the Kingdom of God realized upon earth. For Müntzer the hour had struck for the saints to reign. Into their hands had been placed the sword to smite the ungodly. Here is a form of intolerance staggering in its dimensions, if a little handful of saints are to put all the uncircumcised to the edge of the sword. Müntzer tried to recruit his saints from among the princes and failed, from among the humanists and failed, then from among the peasants, who were already on the rampage. Thus religious and social revolution coincided. Müntzer unfurled the banner of the Peasants' Revolution in the very sanctuary and then went out to lead the hordes to slaughter in the name of the Lord of Hosts.

Luther was stupefied and then infuriated. He believed in the elect, but also that their identity is known only to God. He believed in the Kingdom, but that God would give it in his own good time. He believed in the use of the sword, but only in the hands of the magistrate ordained of God. Under no circumstances did he believe that each man should be his own avenger, and for social revolution to clothe itself with the slogans of the gospel was to him utterly monstrous. He called upon the princes for a ruthless suppression of the rebellion.

When it was all over, he was left in a state of distraught nerves and ready, for the future, to suppress persons like Thomas Müntzer before the situation got out of hand. Then the Anabaptists began to infiltrate into his district. They did not agree with Thomas Müntzer's program of revolution, but they did believe in the segregation of the saints and the establishment of holy communities. They did disintegrate the Church-State relationship, and in Luther's Thuringia there were among their leaders some who had been associated with Thomas Müntzer. Luther's position gradually veered. For a time he was silent. When the Diet of Speyer in 1529 decreed death for the Anabaptists throughout the Holy Roman Empire, Luther made no immediate comment. But in 1531 he was ready to countenance death for blasphemy and sedition. Faith he would not constrain. Heresy in the form of an incorrect opinion he would not molest. But open reviling or overt rebellion must be suppressed. For a long time there was no open rebellion on the part of the Anabaptists. They were as sheep for the slaughter. But in 1534 the worm turned, and a little group of fanatics reverted to the program of Thomas Müntzer and forcibly seized the city of Münster in Westphalia. Their entire coup failed. But the episode branded all Anabaptism with the suspicion of revolution, however unjustified. In the year 1536 Melanchthon drafted a memorandum on the treatment of the Anabaptists, in which he distinguished the peaceful from the revolutionary and demanded death for both varieties, and Luther signed. He still held to his formula that only blasphemy and sedition should be punished, but he interpreted as blasphemy a rejection of an article in the Apostles' Creed and as sedition a mere refusal to participate in war or to serve as a magistrate. Yet in later life Luther came back to his earlier statement that banishment was sufficient as a penalty, and of course imprisonment. There was an Anabaptist, Fritz Erbe by name, who suffered incarceration for nine years in the Castle of the Wartburg, where Luther himself had been for a year in exile. Erbe died in captivity but Luther never expressed one word of sympathy, respect, or regret.

The year of the Anabaptist memorandum was the year when John Calvin published his *Institutes*. That is, his career began when the Protestant position was already formulated, and that explains in part why he never went through the liberal period as Luther had done. The lines were already sharply drawn as between Catholic and Protestant. Calvin came from France at a time when one could no longer be a liberal Catholic reformer, neutral as between Wittenberg and Rome. In France the king and the high ecclesiastics would march in solemn procession to the cathedral to attend the celebration of the Mass, then dine sumptuously and top off the day by watching the burning of heretics. John Calvin escaped such a fate by flight. He came as a refugee to the Protestant cities of Strasbourg and Basel, where also the lines were sharply drawn as to the varieties of Protestantism and dissenters could no longer expect here to find an abiding place. John Calvin was twenty-six. He became the formulator of an entrenched Protestantism and the inaugurator of a militant Protestantism. His manifesto, published in Basel in the year 1536, was the *Institutes of the Christian Religion.*

Calvin's Protestantism was more activist than Luther's, partly because of the point of departure. Luther started with the grace of God in Christ, which we cannot earn but can only accept. Religion entails an initial act of passivity. Calvin opens the *Institutes,* not with a proclamation of justification by faith, but with the disclosure of the sovereignty of God. He is the only Lord, the Everlasting, the Eternal, the Creator of the ends of the earth, before whom the nations are as a drop in the bucket. Here and throughout his writings Calvin never flagged in lauding the majesty of the Eternal. " Our souls are but faint flickerings over against the infinite brilliance which is God. We are created, he is without beginning. We are subject to ignorance and shame. God in his infinite majesty is the summation of all virtues. Whenever we think of him we should be ravished with adoration and astonishment. . . . God has made the sun our servant and the moon our chambermaid, and the very creatures will rise against us in the judgment because we, having been irradiated by the sun and the moon, nourished from the fowls of the earth and enriched by all bounty, have by our ordures sullied the glory of God. The chief end of man is to enjoy the fellowship of God and the chief duty of man is to glorify God. Observe," remarked Calvin, " it is not that we may be kept alive on this earth that God saves us from our enemies, but that we may be sustained by his grace. What is this life but a passing shadow? Let us then recognize God as our eternal Saviour and let us so walk in his fear that we may expect from him not only guidance for a brief moment but reception at the last to himself. The blessings of this life may be enjoyed in so far as they minister to our salvation. Otherwise they are a curse."

Ours it is to glorify God, to accept his judgments, not to murmur at his dispensations, to receive without repining whatever he may give. " The children of God must put a check upon their affections so that they desire nothing which is not pleasing to him. All our prayers should be grounded in faith. We must fully accommodate our requests to the will of God, and if in a burst of fervor we exceed this rule, then we should add, ' My God, thy will be done! ' Take the example of a man who has a sick wife or child. He may cry vehemently, ' O my God, wilt thou not have pity on me? ' Such a man is at fault and should hasten to add: ' Alas, my God, it is true that this is my desire, nevertheless thou requirest that I render unto thee absolute obedience, that I be humbled in thy hands. Therefore, Lord, dispose of me and of all things mine according to thy will. It suffices me to know that there is nothing better than to be held by thy hand.' "

Such a view of God and man might end in absolute quiescence. The paradox of Calvinism is that the utter malleability of man in the hands of God makes for an adamantine rigor over against men, and the reason is that God is not quiescent. He has a work to do. He will accomplish it on earth within the historical process. Here is the point at which Calvinism, with all its pessimism as to man, becomes optimistic as to history. Not that men are good, but God is great and God has a plan. He will not achieve it through the immediate return of Christ to set up his Kingdom. Here again Calvin diverged from Luther, and curiously at this point Luther was closer to the Early Church and Calvin to the medieval Church after Augustine. For the early Christians, and Luther after them, expected the imminent return of the Lord, but

Augustine, and Calvin in his wake, projected the coming indefinitely into the future. In that case the historical process becomes the field of God's operation. Here in religious form is the doctrine of progress.

In what way and through what instruments is God's purpose to be accomplished? Through human instruments, through his chosen, through the elect. Calvin was not hopeful because of any roseate picture of men, whom often enough he compared to dogs and swine, but rather because the elect, even though imperfect, are nevertheless chosen by the Eternal to achieve a stupendous work on earth.

There arose once more the problem of how the elect are to be known. Luther denied that they can by any means be recognized. Müntzer found the distinguishing mark in the new birth. The Anabaptists fastened on an upright life. Zwingli discovered a test in the possession of a sound faith. Calvin agreed with Luther that there is no absolutely infallible test. Nevertheless there are presumptive signs adequate for practical purposes. He selected three, and he did not include the new birth. This was to return as a test in New England Calvinism and to prove very much of a torment to sensitive spirits. Calvin did not suffer himself to be distraught in this fashion. His tests were all comparatively external and realizable. They consisted in (1) a confession of faith; (2) a disciplined life; (3) participation in the sacraments. Creed, deed, and sacrament — these were the three.

If anyone qualified by these standards, he should assume his election and stop worrying. To be constantly anxious over one's salvation is unworthy and devastating. He who is perpetually troubled about his destiny can never worship God aright.

This was the faith that forged heroes — to accept without a murmur as God's will whatever should befall, to be utterly unconcerned about oneself, to be wholly committed to the implementing of God's program on earth. This ends in the cry, " Onward, Christian soldiers! " " God with an outstretched arm delivered Israel of old and his arm is no whit weakened today. God says to us, ' My children, you are weak and your enemy is strong, but nothing laid upon you will exceed your strength. Though the devil and the world rage I will curb them. I will help you. Fear not.' " " Fear," said Calvin, " can never be entirely overcome, but fear should never impede us from calling upon God. How else shall we confront the world and the infinity of devils raging like lions? "

This stupendous dream could not be realized simply by writing an *Institutes of the Christian Religion*. It called for concretion among men here on earth. The place proved to be Geneva. The city was at the moment independent, having thrown off the yoke of the duke of Savoy and the bishop, and not yet having joined the Swiss Confederacy. William Farel, the vociferous, had converted the city, but felt himself unequal to curbing the turbulence of the unyoked bullocks, and commandeered the young theologian, John Calvin, much against his inclination, to leave his studies in order to head the incipient holy commonwealth. To recount here the whole story of Geneva is beyond our limits. Suffice it to say that after invitation, exile, and reinvitation, Calvin was able in the end to fire a populace with his dream. Greater than Torquemada, he imposed a grandiose concept, not on an impressionable girl, but upon a hard-boiled citizenry, who became quite as much imbued with the vision of a holy commonwealth as himself. Geneva became *une ville église,* a city that was a Church.

This end was attained through a selective process. Those who did not subscribe to the constitution of the holy commonwealth had to leave. The Catholic religious orders departed at the outset. The Mass of course ceased, and all public practice of Catholicism. Catholics accepted the new regime or migrated. Those excommunicated from the Church, if not reconciled within six months, left the city. In the meantime hordes of refugees flocked in, fleeing from persecution in France, Spain, Italy, and even England. Geneva became by inclusion and exclusion a city of the saints. Thus the Anabaptist ideal of a pure Church of convinced believers was combined with the Catholic-Lutheran-Zwinglian pattern of the Church coincident with the community. Only convinced believers belonged to the Church. Everyone in the community belonged to the Church because only convinced believers stayed in the community. Thus was the Church both holy and catholic, comprising all within the walls.

But what should be done with dissenters who arose within the midst of the holy commonwealth — not those whose lives were impure so much as those who despised the sacraments or rejected some article of the creed? Recall that for Calvin the creed admitted of no uncertainty. It was the epitome of the will of God as revealed in the Holy Scriptures. To be sure, not everything declared by God is entirely clear, for the mountain was shrouded with thick darkness when God declared himself unto Moses. But the Ten Commandments admit of no obscurity, and the saving articles of Christian redemption are neither dubious nor obscure. To reject one of these is to give the lie to God.

What Calvin would do to such people nobody could doubt who had read his commentary on the thirteenth chapter of Deuteronomy, which presents the stoning of false prophets. "This law," comments Calvin, "at first sight appears to be too severe. For merely having spoken should one be so punished? But if anybody slanders a mortal man he is punished and shall we permit a blasphemer of the living God to go unscathed? If a prince is injured, death appears to be insufficient for vengeance. And now when God, the sovereign emperor, is reviled by a word, is nothing to be done? God's glory and our salvation are so conjoined that a traitor to God is also an enemy of the human race and worse than a murderer because he brings poor souls to perdition. Some object that since the offense consists only in words, there is no need for such severity. But we muzzle dogs, and shall we leave men free to open their mouths as they please? Those who object are like dogs and swine. They murmur that they will go to America where nobody will bother them.

"God makes plain that the false prophet is to be stoned without mercy. We are to crush beneath our heel all affections of nature when his honor is involved. The father should not spare his child, nor the brother his brother, nor the husband his own wife or the friend who is dearer to him than life. No human relationship is more than animal unless it be grounded in God. If a man be conjoined to a wife without regard to God, he is worthy to be cast out among the brute beasts. If friendship is contracted apart from God, what is this union but sheer bestiality? God wishes to denude you of all love for your wife if she seduces you from him."

This language of Calvin's sounds appallingly like that of the Communists, who place the party above every human tie. The difference is that Calvin made the demand, not in the name of a human institution or party, but in the name of the Author of our being, whose will is our law and his glory the end of our existence. If we would rise above the level of the beasts, every human tie must be contracted only in loyalty to him. Therefore no matter how dear, no matter how near, we must cast off and chastise all who blaspheme the name of the Creator. "He who has trampled under foot the majesty of God is worse than a brigand who cuts the throat of a wayfarer." And the God who spared not even the babies of the Amalekites requires that we be inexorable. If this demand appear to us cruel, "we must rest assured that God would suffer only those infants to be destroyed whom he had already damned and destined to eternal death." Thus the doctrine of predestination was summoned to steel men against any tenderness of feeling, for why should man be more compassionate than God?

One wonders whether Calvin would have been quite so obdurate if his holy commonwealth had not been so imperiled. It was like the apex of a triangle jutting into Catholic territory, perpetually menaced with extinction by a military coup from the king of France or the duke of Savoy, continually replenished by those who had only just escaped with their lives, who left goods behind and often martyred loved ones. And there were those who came for a period of training before returning to probable death. Geneva lived in all the tension of a wartime psychology. Those men steeled themselves by taking as their model that Abraham who, at the behest of God, refused not to lift his knife even against his only son through whom he had been promised to become the father of a great nation. In the Biblical story, as Abraham raised his knife, the voice of an angel arrested him and a ram appeared in the thicket. All too often in Calvin's case there was no ram.

Chapter Three

THE VICTIM OF PROTESTANT PERSECUTION:

Michael Servetus

The most celebrated case of Protestant persecution is the burning of Michael Servetus at the stake for heresy at Geneva. He was a Spaniard, born in the early years of the sixteenth century (1511), when the work of Torquemada was done and the Inquisition had in a measure mitigated its rigors. There were, indeed, still converted Jews and converted Moors to be watched, but they had learned either to conform or to be exceedingly discreet and the Inquisition was content to tread softly. The *conversos* had their revenge by cultivating mystical illuminist tendencies within Christianity. The Alumbrados were later to suffer, after Protestantism had occasioned a rekindling of inquisitorial fires, but for the moment they were indulgently treated.

Michael Servetus

Even more significant was the wave of Erasmianism which flowed over the Pyrenees. There was a particular reason for the vogue of Erasmus in Spain, apart from his general European reputation. It was that the king of Spain, Charles, the grandson of Ferdinand and Isabella, had been reared in the Spanish dependencies, the Low Countries. He spoke Flemish by preference and surrounded himself at court with persons

from The Netherlands. These circles were addicted to the
cult of the great Hollander, Erasmus of Rotterdam, and carried with them their devotion when, in the train of the
monarch, they entered the Iberian peninsula. The popularity
of Erasmus was a part of the cultural interchange between
Spain and its dependencies. The views of Erasmus have already been noted — his undogmatic piety, his rational and
ethical emphasis, his decrying of contention over the subtle-
ties of theological speculation.

Among the liberals at the Spanish court was the king's
confessor, Quintana, a Franciscan, who at one time had expected even more from Luther than from the pope. To the
service of this man Servetus was attached. The reason could
hardly have been the liberalism of the king's confessor, because the family of Servetus appears to have been distinctly
orthodox. A brother was a beneficed priest, who joined with
his mother in the erection of an altar in their native town.
But any sort of post at court no doubt appeared advanta-
geous, and the family probably thought to facilitate the son's
advancement. The position was not onerous, and did not pre-
clude a period of university study. Servetus was permitted to
go to the University of Toulouse for the study of juris-
prudence.

That he had imbibed something already from the illumin-
ism of Spain and the Erasmianism of the court may be
inferred from tendencies manifest in his later work. A Spaniard he remained, and was deeply preoccupied with the problem that had so long agitated his country of what to do with
the Moors and the Jews. The Inquisition had been tried, and
the problem had diminished in intensity but was not wholly
at an end, and certainly was not solved for Europe as a
whole. Servetus addressed himself to the more fundamental
question of why the problem existed at all. If God has revealed himself in Christ and through the sacred Scriptures,

why should the Jews and the Moors be so obstinate in refusing to accept God's gracious declaration? The obvious
answer was that the monotheism alike of Judaism and Mohammedanism was offended by the Christian doctrine of the
Trinity: that God is of one substance, differentiated in three
persons. The unbelievers interpreted the doctrine as plain
tritheism, and some warrant was at hand for their assumption in the artistic representations of the Trinity which portrayed God sometimes with one head and three faces and
sometimes even as three indistinguishable old men.

Servetus, revolving this problem, came to the University
of Toulouse, renowned for its orthodoxy, only to discover
that the very citadel of doctrinal rectitude harbored evangeli-
cals. Student groups were poring over the Scriptures. Servetus discarded Justinian for the Gospels, and thereby to his
amazement discovered that the one essential tenet of Christianity required of the Moors and the Jews was not so much
as mentioned in the Bible. To be sure there is something
about the Father and the Son and the Holy Ghost, but the
word " Trinity " does not occur. There is nothing of the one
substance and the three persons. The relationship of the Son
to the Father is not described as consubstantial. There is no
reference to the procession of the Holy Ghost. Servetus was
perfectly right in his observation, because the Council of Nicaea had been driven reluctantly to the conclusion that the
teaching implicit in the New Testament could be safe-
guarded against Arian misinterpretation only if extra-Biblical
language were used, since the Arians would accept any Biblical terminology and place upon it their own construction.

The whole history of the matter was not apparent to Servetus. The one point of crucial importance to him was this,
that the Moors and the Jews should not be alienated from
the fold by requiring of them subscription to a formula that
is absent from the Bible. At the same time Servetus was con-

cerned to know for what reason the doctrine had originated and whether it could be defended. To answer these questions he addressed himself to the whole history of Trinitarian speculation. He read mostly the late Scholastics, without properly sensing their relation to previous periods of thought. The earliest phase was that of the primitive Church, when the need was felt to satisfy the Hellenistic theological urge to explain the relation of Christ to God. The primitive Christians had experienced in Christ redemption from guilt, sins, sinfulness, death, and the power of the devil. They were clear that the Redeemer must have been man, to provide a moral example, and at the same time God, if he was able to overcome sin, death, and hell. At first they were content to call him simply the Word of God or the Son of God. More precise formulation came at the Council of Nicaea in 325, with the teaching that Christ so participates in the being of God that he may be described as of one substance or essence with God. With the Father and the Son was associated the Spirit, all participating in the being of God. In this sense all are God, yet all are at the same time in a measure distinct. They are not sufficiently separate to constitute three Gods, nor sufficiently one to obliterate all differentiation. The doctrine of the Trinity was a formula devised to express the complexity within the unity of God by defining the relationship of the Son and the Spirit to the Father.

After the doctrine had once been formulated, schools of thought arose in the West in the Middle Ages with regard to the degree to which it can be established as true. Saint Augustine gave the first and the dominant answer, that the doctrine cannot be demonstrated but can be illustrated, because man, having been made in the image of God, although corrupted by the fall, yet retains at least analogies to the Trinitarian structure of God in that the mind of man can be differentiated psychologically into intellect, memory, and will. The analogy is not conclusive proof, but if the doctrine has already been revealed, we are able then in a measure to comprehend by virtue of these comparisons. This line of thinking runs from Saint Augustine straight through Saint Thomas Aquinas.

The second view arose in the high Middle Ages, according to which the doctrine can be not only illustrated but even demonstrated. Richard of St. Victor in the twelfth century originated this view. The demonstration was discovered through the Neoplatonic conception of God as expansive being continually throwing off emanations. The problem is to stop them at three. Saint Richard here had recourse to the Christian picture of God as love, and love, he said, requires at least two persons, one to love and one to be loved. And perfect love requires a third, to provide the possibility of excluding jealousy. All this doubtless sounds very farfetched. Servetus certainly thought so. What it amounts to is this, that the philosophic doctrine of God as expansive being was checked by the Jewish-Christian view of God as personality. In the whole process the Victorine school found an undergirding for the orthodox doctrine that God expands up to but not beyond the limits of personal life. This type of thought is characteristic of those with mystical leanings in the Middle Ages.

A third view held that the doctrine of the Trinity can neither be illustrated nor demonstrated, but only believed. The reason was the adoption of the nominalist philosophy, according to which reality consists, not of great entities called universals, but only of unrelated particulars. There is no such thing as " chair " apart from this chair or that chair. Extreme nominalism reduces reality to atoms. When this philosophy is applied to the Trinity, the three persons, being deprived of any relating universal, must of necessity become three Gods, and this, said the nominalists, is precisely what the doctrine entails from the philosophical point of view. The Trinity therefore cannot be proved and cannot even be illustrated but only accepted on the basis of the authority of the Church. Philosophy and theology are thus considered to be conflicting disciplines. Not that there are two varieties of truth, but there are two sorts of logic, which end in contradictions to be resolved only by an act of credence. This was the type of thinking inaugurated by William of Occam in the early fourteenth century and prevalent in Servetus' day. Erasmus and Luther alike agreed that, philosophically speaking, the doctrine of the Trinity entails tritheism.

At this point Servetus made his contact with Trinitarian thinking. He accepted avidly the Occamist criticism without appreciation of the philosophical background and interpreted all the earlier development in terms of this outcome. But he was not content like the Occamists to rest with double logic and accept the authority of the Church, because the repercussions of the Reformation had shaken him even in orthodox Toulouse, and presumably also because he was relieved to discover a valid way of facilitating the conversion of the Moors and the Jews by removing an unnecessary impediment. A doctrine that is neither Biblical nor philosophically defensible, argued Servetus, ought not to be made a *sine qua non* of Christianity.

When he came to the reconstruction of his own view of God and of Christ, he landed in a state of rich confusion, because he considered the fall of Christianity to have occurred at the Council of Nicaea in 325, and consequently would accept only the Scriptures and the ante-Nicene writers as normative for his own thinking. But they were not clear. That was exactly why Nicaea had essayed a more precise definition. Servetus developed a view compounded of the ideas of Tertullian and Irenaeus and highly reminiscent of a position that we now know to have been that of the heretic

Paul of Samosata. Servetus destroyed immediately the doctrine of the Trinity by declaring that the Holy Spirit was not a person at all, but simply the spirit of God indwelling in man. With regard to Christ, a distinction, he contended, was to be made between the pre-existent Word and the incarnate Son. The Word was forever with God, but the Son was produced by the union of this Word with the man Jesus. The Son therefore had a beginning of existence in time. The Word was eternal but the Son was not eternal. Yet after the union the Father and the Son were scarcely to be distinguished save as modes of divine activity.

But the terminology of Servetus was often inexact as he moved from theology to lyrical rhapsodies about Christ. "With Daniel," he said, "I see Jesus Christ coming on the clouds of heaven. I see him in the chariot of Ezekiel and riding among the myrtles of Zachariah. I see him on the throne of Isaiah. He is more than the effulgence of the glory, as Paul speaks of the Lord of glory crucified, he is the glorious star of the morning, he is the light of God, the light of the Gentiles. The splendor of his countenance illumines the whole heaven and will illumine the worlds in generations to come. He is the power of God by which the worlds were made, and although the Word of Christ is to some foolishness, to others it is the power of God. With marvelous power he has subjected the world to his sway and will subdue it. Without clamor of arms he leads captive the minds of men."

The position of Servetus could scarcely commend itself to the orthodox because he had denied the affirmation so fundamental to Athanasius of the eternal, timeless generation of the Son of God. If there were any change in the Son, then, according to Athanasius, our salvation would be imperiled. There was another point at which Servetus was even more to offend John Calvin. It was in the appropriation from the Greek theologians of the view that humanity is capable of participation in divinity. Men can so share in the being of God as themselves to become divine, and the significance of the incarnation is that in Christ God and man were fully conjoined. The significance of the sacrament of the bread and wine is that by feeding upon Christ we can through him attain divinity and immortality. " What is the mystery of the incarnation," exclaimed Servetus, " other than the mingling of man with God? Unless I believe this with regard to the flesh of Christ I should have no hope, for we shall be made sharers in the divine substance even in the flesh as now in the spirit we are partners of the divine nature."

The combination of this view of the possible deification of man with the current Catholic belief that man is capable of doing good sufficient to merit reward at the hands of God went far to complete the Renaissance doctrine of man. There was one other ingredient, namely, the idea of the full-orbed personality, the master of all skills and learnings. And this Servetus well-nigh accomplished in his own person, for he was a theologian, Biblical scholar, geographer, anatomist, and physician. His picture of man alienated Calvin even more than his view of Christ. The union of humanity and divinity was for Servetus an elevation of humanity, but for Calvin a degradation of divinity.

Servetus was recalled in 1529 from his studies at Toulouse by his master, Quintana, who himself had been summoned to accompany Charles at his coronation as Holy Roman Emperor by the pope at Bologna. The withdrawal of the court from Spain in the wake of the emperor was fraught with consequences that contemporaries little divined. This marked the end of the Erasmian period in Spain, though no doubt it would have passed in any case, as it did elsewhere, under the impact of the wars of religion. The works of Erasmus were to be placed on the Index in Spain, and the censors vented their spleen on his woodcut portrait by crisscrossing with a pen and blackening the eyes to suggest a skull.

Yet even the Erasmians in the train of the emperor would scarcely tolerate the position developed by Servetus. Consequently he slipped away and went to the Protestant cities of Basel and Strasbourg, there to publish his views. His book on *The Errors of the Trinity* appeared near Strasbourg in the year 1531. He had chosen wisely. Basel was the city where Erasmus had spent his last days and where he was buried. He had left behind him there a circle of liberals. And Strasbourg was still extremely lenient toward Anabaptists. Yet Servetus was to experience that not even these, the most broad-minded of the Protestant cities, would harbor him. At Basel he was told that if he were to be received as a Christian brother, he must confess Christ as the eternal Son of God, consubstantial with the Father; and Strasbourg, after a period of hesitation, became equally firm. Melanchthon studied his views and concluded that they were utterly unacceptable. Servetus had hoped that the Erasmians might be favorable, but Quintana was thoroughly shocked. After all, Erasmus had only taught that so abstruse a doctrine as the Trinity should not be discussed until the Judgment Day. He had not said that it might be rejected.

Servetus would have been highly naïve if he expected a sympathetic hearing among the more orthodox Catholics. When Aleander, Luther's old opponent at the Diet of Worms, saw the book on *The Errors of the Trinity,* he declared that he had never read anything more nauseating. He proposed to notify the authorities in Spain to burn the book and the effigy of the author *al modo di Spagna.* They scarcely needed this instigation, for Servetus had the temerity to send a copy of his book to the bishop of Saragossa, who denounced him to the supreme council of the Inquisition. An order was issued that a notice should be placarded in Servetus' native place, summoning him to appear. But a postscript added that the summons should be posted only at an hour when no one would read it, lest he be warned not to return. Rather let a confidential agent be employed to entice him back to Spain. The one selected for this office was his own brother. A record five and a half years later indicates that this envoy actually made a trip to Germany but came back without success.

Portrait of Erasmus
Censored by the Inquisition

Where, then, should Servetus go? The Protestant and the Catholic lands alike were closed to him. For the first time perhaps in history he thought of America as a possible place of refuge for victims of religious intolerance. "With Jonah," he said, "I longed to flee *ad novas insulas,* to one of the new isles." Were he to leave, however, he would be recreant to a mission. He decided instead to preach repentance to the people of Nineveh, yet only under an assumed name. He went to France with the pseudonymn of Michael Villanovanus or Villeneufve.

Of course he had to support himself and nearly everything he did got him into further trouble. For a time he was established at Lyons as a corrector of proof and an editor. In this capacity he brought out a new edition of the Bible, earlier edited by Pagnini. Servetus in the preface explained his theory of prophecy, namely, that the prophets were not predictors but were simply describing the events of their own time. To be sure the Holy Spirit placed in their mouths language too rich for the occasion in hand. And thus the link between the Old Testament and the New Testament is not dissolved. Yet the argument for the truth of the Christian revelation from the fulfillment of prophecy is undercut. Likewise Servetus eliminated the allegorical chapter headings of The Song of Songs, which turned an Oriental love poem into a rhapsody of the Christian soul and Christ the bride.

Next he edited the geography of Ptolemy. In typical humanist fashion he was interested in men rather than in fauna, flora, or topography. Unhappily, however, at one point he did deal with the external features of the land and that was in the description of Palestine, which he declared to be indeed a promised land but not a land of great promise. Servetus, as a matter of fact, was not the author of this passage which he borrowed from a prior edition, but he was accused of giving the lie to Moses. To clear himself in the next edition he left the page completely blank, but even so he was not to hear the last of this unfortunate remark.

Perhaps the vexations of publishing disposed him to seek another means of livelihood. He turned to medicine and studied in Paris, where he was a fellow dissector of cadavers with Vesalius. In the course of his studies Servetus became the discoverer of the pulmonary circulation of the blood. This does not mean of course the complete circulation, which was fully grasped only by Harvey, but only the circuit in the lungs. The older view of Galen was that the blood originates in the liver and is used up in feeding the body without ever returning to the point of origin. The blue blood seeps through the wall of the heart and, having done so, changes in color. Only a trickle goes to feed the lungs. Servetus made three important observations. The wall of the heart is impermeable. The artery that carries the blood to the lungs is large enough for the entire blood stream, and the change in color through aeration takes place in the lungs. Thus he discovered the pulmonary circulation. This point is, strictly speaking, irrelevant in a consideration of Servetus as a heretic, but it is worthy of note to impress the point that persecution may often enough liquidate a highly gifted and serviceable individual.

After his medical training Servetus for twelve years practiced in the neighborhood of Lyons. He had not lost interest in theology. The old ideas still filled him with missionary zeal, but they were reinforced by two new currents. While in Strasbourg he had come in contact with the Anabaptists and had imbibed from them the concept of the Church as composed only of convinced believers. He agreed with them that baptism is desecrated by application to infants. He pointed even to the example of Christ, who was not baptized until his thirtieth year. Since the orthodox gave baptism to children in order to wash away original sin, Servetus held that no unforgivable sin could be committed, at any rate not until after the twentieth year.

From the Anabaptists he received also a belief in the imminent return of the Lord to set up his Kingdom. All speculations as to the date employ the figure 1260, the number of days spent in the wilderness by the woman in the book of Revelation. The common procedure is to make the days into years and add them to some date in early history that will project the coming shortly ahead of one's own time. Servetus selected the year 325, the year of the Council of Nicaea, which marked for him the fall of the Church, and, by adding 1260 to this, arrived at the date 1585, within his own generation, as the time of the great renewal. Then would come the complete restoration of the Church, the "restitution," another favorite Anabaptist term.

The second influence profoundly to bear upon Servetus was that of the Neoplatonism of the Italian Renaissance, then enjoying a great vogue among humanist circles in France. The current fashion in this school to seek confirmation of Christianity by precarious borrowings from the esoteric lore of the East disposed Servetus to copious citations from the Jewish cabala, the Sibylline and Zoroastrian oracles, and the wisdom of Hermes Trismegistus. Even more significant for the thinking of Servetus was the interpretation of light in terms, not of physics, but of metaphysics, as a form infused into all objects rendering them capable of luminosity. Servetus combined these ideas with Christology: Christ is the light of the world. It is he, then, who confers the light forms which transform clay into resplendent stones and water into lustrous pearls, which in regeneration transform the spirit of man and in the resurrection will transform also his body. Christ, thus infusing all reality with the luminous, becomes himself a universal presence. One is reminded of Luther's doctrine of the ubiquity of Christ. To Calvin such thinking was completely alien. For him God is utterly transcendent and Christ is seated at his right hand.

Servetus entered into correspondence with Calvin. The two men were both profoundly religious. From the standpoint of a secularized generation they appear highly similar, but within a common framework of ideas the differences were so great as to be resolved in that day only by death. Servetus was drawn by the austere magnetism of Calvin and sought to reassure himself by convincing this trenchant intellect. Servetus initiated the correspondence and made no secret of his identity, which he could scarcely have concealed since he repeated in a measure the views already known through the publication of his earlier work. Calvin at first courteously replied until Servetus became both galling and demanding. Calvin regarded him as an emissary of Satan to waste his time, and to answer all questions with a single throw sent him a copy of the *Institutio* which Servetus adorned with insulting marginalia and returned. He sent also a manuscript copy of a work entitled *Restitutio,* possibly a play upon Calvin's title. Calvin retained the manuscript, broke off the correspondence, and confided to a friend in Lyons that if Servetus came to Geneva he would not get out alive if Calvin's authority prevailed. This was in 1546.

Servetus reworked his manuscript, and in 1553 published it secretly at his own expense through a concealed press near Lyons. One thousand copies were struck off. One fell into the hands of a Protestant in Geneva who had a Catholic cousin living in Lyons. They had often debated the relative merits of their faith, and the Catholic had reproached the Protestant with destroying the discipline of the Church. The arrival of Servetus' book provided an opening too good to miss. The Protestant wrote to his Catholic cousin that whereas he reproached the Protestants with a lack of discipline, the Catholics in Lyons were tolerating a heretic who compared the Trinity to Cerberus, the three-headed hound of hell (this was true), and disgorged all possible villainies against the eternal generation of the Son of God. Such views were not only heresy but such detestable heresy as to abolish the entire Christian religion. This man wrecked all the fundamentals of the faith. He denied infant baptism. The man was Michael Servetus, masquerading under the assumed name of Villeneufve. The printer was named Arnollet.

This was news in Lyons, because the *Restitutio* appeared only with the initials " MSV," standing for Michael Servetus Villanovanus but cryptic to the uninitiated. In the circle of Calvin, who had the manuscript, the identity of the author was not difficult to decipher. How the printer was known eludes us. The Catholic cousin promptly laid the disclosure before the Inquisitor, who conducted an examination, but fruitlessly because Servetus had already disposed of all incriminating evidence. The informer then wrote back to Geneva requesting some tangible proof. The following letter from the Protestant cousin discloses the sequel and brings John Calvin into the affair:

" My dear cousin:
" When I wrote the letter which you have communicated to those whom I charged with indifference, I did not suppose that the matter would go so far. I simply meant to call your attention to the fine zeal and devotion of those who call themselves the pillars of the Church, although they suffer such disorder in their midst, and persecute so severely the poor Christians, who wish to follow God in simplicity. Inasmuch as this glaring instance had been brought to my notice, the occasion and subject seemed to me to warrant mentioning the matter in my letters. But since you have disclosed what I meant for you alone, God grant that this may the better serve to purge Christianity of such filth, such deadly pestilence. If they really want to do anything, as you say, it does not seem to me that the matter is so very difficult, though I cannot for the moment give you what you want, namely, the printed book. But I can give you something better to convict him, namely, two dozen manuscript pieces of the man in question, in which his heresies are in part contained. If you show him the printed book he can deny it, which he cannot do in the case of his handwriting. The case then being absolutely proved, the men

of whom you speak will have no excuse for further dissimulation or delay. All the rest is here right enough, the big book and the other writings of the same author, but I can tell you I had no little trouble to get from Calvin what I am sending. Not that he does not wish to repress such execrable blasphemies, but he thinks that it is his duty rather to convince heresies with doctrine than with other means, because he does not exercise the sword of justice. But I remonstrated with him and pointed out the embarrassing position in which I should be placed if he did not help me, so that in the end he gave me what you see. For the rest I hope by and by, when the case is further advanced, to get from him a whole ream of paper, which the scamp has had printed, but I think that for the present you have enough, so that there is no need for more to seize his person and bring him to trial. . . .

"Geneva, March 26."

What actually was sent was a body of the manuscript letters of Servetus and a copy of the *Institutio* containing Servetus' contemptuous comments. Thus Calvin collaborated with the Inquisition. Servetus was again summoned and confronted with his handwriting. He examined it closely. It had been written so long ago he was not sure whether it was his. But on a more careful examination he thought that it was. Then he admitted that when he had been in Germany some twenty-five years ago a book was published near Strasbourg by a certain Spaniard named Servetus. His views appeared plausible, and, being curious as to their validity, Villanovanus had submitted them for criticism to Calvin, who, perceiving the questions to be those of Servetus, assumed his correspondent to be Servetus, to which the correspondent replied that although he was not, yet for the sake of the discussion he was willing to assume the role. "On those terms," said Villanovanus, "we interchanged until the correspondence became heated and I dropped it. For the last ten years there has been nothing between us, and I affirm before God that I have no desire to dogmatize or to assert anything contrary to the Church and to the Christian religion."

But Servetus well realized that his position was becoming precarious, and, committed to prison, promptly sent a valet to call in his debts outstanding. For exercise and the needs of nature he was permitted access to a walled-in garden on application to the jailer for the key. One evening Servetus carefully surveyed the terrain. At the far end of the garden was a flat roof abutting on the edge of the wall. The next morning Servetus rose at four as the jailer was starting out to dress his vines. The prisoner wore his velvet nightcap and fur bathrobe, which in the dusk concealed a full costume beneath. The jailer, though he was to be gone for several hours, confided the key. Servetus, when he was sufficiently distant, disposed of the velvet nightcap and bathrobe in the garden, scaled the roof and thence the wall, and let himself down without mishap on the other side. Before the alarm was given, some two hours later, he was well beyond the city gate.

Two months subsequently the secret press at which his book had been printed was brought to light. The printers, on being examined, professed complete ignorance of the Latin language, which they had set letter for letter. The Inquisition closed the case by confiscating all the available property of Servetus and by consigning all recoverable copies of the *Restitutio* to the flames. Only three survive today. One is at Vienna, one at Paris, and one at Edinburgh. The author was condemned to be burned at a slow fire until his body was reduced to ashes. In his absence all details were executed upon his effigy, which was first strangled and then consumed.

Some four months after the flight certain brothers from Lyons attending church at Geneva on a Sunday morning recognized Michael Servetus in the congregation and reported his presence to John Calvin, who immediately lodged against him with the town council a capital charge of heresy. Why had Servetus thus walked into the mouth of the lion? This question, which is genuinely puzzling, has provided the ground for a conjecture which seeks to exonerate Calvin from religious intolerance on the ground that the menace of Servetus was political: He had come to Geneva because he feared nothing since he was in league with Calvin's political opponents, the so-called party of the Libertines, who were plotting a coup for his overthrow and exile. Servetus before his detection had actually been in Geneva for a month conniving with the conspirators. He chose a most auspicious time for his arrival, inasmuch as Calvin's position at the moment was highly tenuous. He had excommunicated a leader of the Libertines and a trial of strength was pending. If Calvin failed, he would undoubtedly again go into exile.

Contemporary evidence for this interpretation is extremely scant. There is nothing to support the claim that Servetus had been ambushed in Geneva for a month, and his own statement went unrefuted in the courtroom that he had arrived on foot the night before, had taken lodging at the Inn of the Rose, had requested the innkeeper to engage a boat that he might sail to Zurich, whence he proposed to make his way to Italy and practice medicine at Naples.

Calvin's position actually was precarious, but if Servetus had really understood the situation, he would have derived from this little comfort because the town council in matters of heresy had been rigorous enough during Calvin's previous banishment. One can only infer that Servetus did not understand the situation, and if he misjudged the council, in all likelihood he may also have misjudged Calvin, never dreaming that he would go to such lengths.

This much may be conceded with regard to his relations with the Libertines, that some of the conflicting contemporary testimony indicates that the Libertines did seek the release of Servetus after he had been brought to trial. But this they might well do in order to embarrass Calvin, without having been engaged in any previous machinations or collusion with Servetus for the overthrow of the Genevan regime. One further argument is adduced, that during his trial Servetus was at times brazen to the point of recklessness. Why should a man who had dissembled in France have been so impudent at Geneva if not that he counted on help? The question admits of no easy answer, but this must be taken seriously, that Servetus was passionately earnest in his expectation of vindication from heaven. He had indeed set the date for the Second Advent in the year 1585, but, as he felt the power of Antichrist closing in upon him, he may have forgotten his chronology, and perhaps even he may have believed his death to be a necessary prelude to the denouement, for he had written earlier in a private letter: " I know that I shall die on this account, but I do not falter that I may be a disciple like the Master. He will come, he will certainly come. He will not tarry." One thing is plain. Calvin brought no political charges against Servetus and the public prosecutor sought to convict him only of immorality, not of sedition, and in any case failed. The counts on which Servetus was condemned were entirely theological.

Calvin's action certainly calls for as much explanation as that of Servetus. One can understand why he would not tolerate dissent within Geneva, but why should he detain a man who was simply passing through and had hired a boat to depart the next day? Geneva frequently disposed of the unassimilable by banishment. Why not let this man banish himself? The answer could only be that Calvin did not equate Christendom with Geneva. He still thought in universal terms, and it is significant that the statute under which Servetus was condemned was of course not that of the canon law of the Catholic Church; but neither was it, save for details, the law of Geneva. It was the law of the Holy Roman Empire, the Code of Justinian, that proscribed the penalty of death for a denial of the Trinity and a repetition of baptism.

During the trial all Servetus' indiscretions and misdemeanors were adduced to discredit him. The description of Palestine was interpreted by Calvin as giving the lie to Moses. Servetus replied that he had not composed the passage, and in any case it was simply a description of the present-day condition of the Holy Land. Calvin believed his denial of the authorship to be a plain lie. Calvin was perfectly outraged by the treatment of the Old Testament prophecies. Even the great fifty-third chapter of Isaiah, so commonly referred to Christ, was by Servetus interpreted as applying to Cyrus. Calvin characterized this view as " a bold corruption of a signal prophecy."

Much more serious was the clash over the doctrine of man in relation to God. Servetus believed that Calvin's doctrine of original sin, total depravity, and predestination reduced man to a log and a stone. Calvin believed that Servetus' doctrine of the deification of humanity degraded God and made deity subject to the vices and infirmities of the flesh. Here more than anywhere else was the conflict between the Renaissance and the Reformation.

On the subject of the Trinity, Servetus was inclined to be somewhat concessive. He said that he did believe in the Trinity, that is, in the Father, the Son, and the Holy Spirit, three persons in God. But he interpreted the word " person " differently from the moderns, by which he meant that he took " person " to mean simply a mode of the divine manifestation. He went on to say that he applied the terms " Trinitarian " and " atheist " only to those who placed a real distinction in the divine essence, which is of course precisely what the orthodox doctrine does. In other words, Servetus admitted that he repudiated the teaching of the Nicene Creed.

On the subject of infant baptism he was positively abusive: " It is an invention of the devil, an infernal falsity for the destruction of all Christianity." He freely admitted that he could not regard as mortal any sin committed before the twentieth year.

The trial on both sides was conducted without amenities. When Servetus asked for a lawyer, which the Inquisition would not have denied, he was told that he could lie well enough without one. Servetus often railed at Calvin, whom he called Simon Magus, on the supposition that Simon originated the doctrine of predestination. Servetus petitioned the court for a change of raiment, declaring that his clothes were torn and the lice were eating him alive. He remonstrated against being judged by the law of Justinian, for Calvin would concede that in the days of Justinian the Church was already degenerate. Servetus was even bold enough to demand that Calvin himself be brought to trial for having betrayed him to the Inquisition, and on the charge of being a false accuser and as a magician following Simon Magus. " Let Calvin be not merely condemned but exterminated and driven from your city. His goods should be adjudged to me as compensation for what he has caused me to lose." The council did not deign a reply.

During the course of the trial a courier came from France requesting that Servetus be surrendered to the Inquisition. Servetus fell on his knees, begging to be judged in Geneva. He exonerated the jailer from any complicity in his escape.

The council evidently felt a measure of insecurity as to its course because advice was sought from the Swiss Protestant cities. All recommended severity. Zurich felt that Servetus' denial of the possibility of a mortal sin before the twentieth

year was subversive of morality, " especially in these days
when the young are so corrupted." But none recommended
the death penalty. The reason was that every city had at
least a small dissenting minority. Yet the general tenor was
so severe that Geneva felt warranted in proceeding.

One must remember that the sentence was pronounced,
not by John Calvin, who was only an accuser and not even
a prosecutor, but rather by the town council, a body of lay-
men. The verdict dropped all the charges save two, and those
two are exactly the ones visited by death in the Code of
Justinian, namely, the denial of the Trinity and the repudiation of baptism. The sentence read:

" And we syndics, judges of criminal cases in this city, having
witnessed the trial conducted before us at the instance of our
lieutenant against you ' Michel Servet de Villeneufve,' of the
country of Aragon in Spain, and having seen your voluntary and
repeated confessions and your books, judge that you, Servetus,
have for a long time promulgated false and thoroughly heretical
doctrine, despising all remonstrances and corrections, and that
you have with malicious and perverse obstinacy sown and divulged
even in printed books opinions against God the Father, the Son,
and the Holy Spirit, in a word, against the fundamentals of the
Christian religion, and that you have tried to make a schism and
trouble the Church of God by which many souls may have been
ruined and lost, a thing horrible, shocking, scandalous, and infec-
tious. And you have had neither shame nor horror of setting your-
self against the divine Majesty and the Holy Trinity, and so you
have obstinately tried to infect the world with your stinking
heretical poison. . . . For these and other reasons, desiring to
purge the Church of God of such infection and cut off the rotten
member, having taken counsel with our citizens and having invoked the name of God to give just judgment . . . having God
and the Holy Scriptures before our eyes, speaking in the name of
the Father, Son, and Holy Spirit, we now in writing give final
sentence and condemn you, Michael Servetus, to be bound and

taken to Champel and there attached to a stake and burned with your book to ashes. And so you shall finish your days and give an example to others who would commit the like."

On receiving the news Servetus was at first stunned, then cried out in Spanish, "*Misericordia, misericordia!*" When he recovered his composure, he sent for Calvin, who came to him in prison. Servetus begged his pardon for the scurrility used during the course of the trial. Calvin told him to beg God's pardon. If he would but return to reason, Calvin offered to do everything to reconcile him to the servants of God. When Servetus proved unamenable to remonstrance, Calvin withdrew from the heretic. Servetus addressed to the council a request that he might be executed by the sword rather than at the stake, lest in the extremity of his anguish he should recant and lose his soul. Calvin supported this request, which was denied.

William Farel, who happened at the moment to be in Geneva, accompanied Servetus to the stake, exhorting him on the way to repudiate his errors. Servetus was silent. He was bound to the stake with an iron chain, his book was attached to his arm, a stout rope was wound four or five times about his neck. From the flames he was heard to pray, "O Jesus, thou Son of the eternal God, have pity on me!" Farel said that if he had been willing to confess Jesus, the eternal Son of God, he might have been saved. He put the adjective in the wrong place.

We are today horrified that Geneva should have burned a man for the glory of God, yet we incinerate whole cities for the saving of democracy.

PART

2

THE TOLERATION CONTROVERSY
OF THE SIXTEENTH CENTURY

Chapter four

THE REMONSTRATOR:

Sébastien Castellio

The case of Servetus became a *cause célèbre*. Some feel that its significance has been grossly exaggerated. Why should the execution of one man be regarded as so much worse or so much more important than those of thousands who suffered equally and quite as cruelly? The answer is simply that the Servetus case became more celebrated because it was the point of departure for the toleration controversy within Protestantism. Hitherto the voices raised on behalf of liberty had been

Sébastien Castellio

few and little regarded. Sébastien Castellio by his attack brought the issue into prominence, provoked replies and counterreplies, and set going an agitation that runs in a direct line to the English Act of Toleration.

Castellio exemplifies within himself the conflicts of Protestantism. He was enough of a Calvinist to migrate on his own volition from France to Geneva and to place himself at the service of the Reform. He was at the same time in many respects more of an Erasmian. From collaboration with Calvin he passed to acrid criticism, yet he never ceased to have the clear-cut decisiveness that was more characteristic of Calvin than of Erasmus.

Castellio had spent his youth at Lyons, before the period of Servetus' activity. He was one of those exuberant humanists who reveled in the classical revival and so distinguished himself in Latin and Greek composition that his comrades altered his name of Châteillon to Castalio, after the nymph Castalia, whose fountain flowed from the foot of Parnassus. The form Castellio came, however, to be preferred and is that by which today he is commonly known. His formative years fell like those of Servetus in the liberal interlude when a Catholic could still laud the Bible as " fairer than ' The Romance of the Rose ' " without incurring the suspicion of Lutheranism. But the days of ambiguity were abruptly ended when Cardinal de Tournon burned three Lutherans at Lyons in the year 1540. Some of the Catholic liberals submitted to the Church with a formal gesture and a shrug and thereafter went neither to Mass nor to prison. Like Montaigne, they believed that either to die or to kill for an idea is to place too high a price upon a conjecture. Others like Margaret of Navarre, the king's sister, solaced themselves by mystical piety which could allegorize the superstitions of the crowd.

Some were so converted to the Reform that for them the only choice lay between death or exile. Of such was Sébastien Castellio. As to what moved him, we know even less than we do in the case of Calvin. The sight, perhaps, of some hardy spirit refusing to uncover or bow at the passing of a Catholic procession, the fervor of Huguenot psalm-singing, some word from the Bible that refused to be dislodged, or perhaps the cry of a Lutheran martyr at the stake forever reverberating in memory. Whatever the occasion, Castellio made the choice and fled from the confines of France.

The place to which he directed his steps was Strasbourg. The reason can hardly have been the same as in the case of Servetus ten years earlier. At that time Strasbourg was renowned for liberalism toward dissent, in 1540 rather for liberalism restricted to mediation between the Lutherans and the Zwinglians. Quite possibly the greatest attraction was the presence of John Calvin, at the moment himself an exile from Geneva. In Calvin's home Castellio found lodging. He was then twenty-five years of age. When the plague smote the city, Castellio acquitted himself manfully in caring for the sick, and received from Calvin a tribute of praise. In 1541, Calvin, having been invited to return to Geneva, requested Castellio to accompany him and to assume the headship of the academy. He accepted with enthusiasm.

Calvin had lofty views of education. He desired to establish a school where Protestant boys would be educated in the ancient tongues as tools, but not primarily in the ancient literature, pagan as to its content. Castellio was heartily in accord with the plan that would combine classical Latin with Biblical stories, lest youth be corrupted by the obscenities of Terence, Plautus, or Ovid. Here was another example of the perennial conflict of Christianity with secular culture. Castellio sought to meet the situation by composing a booklet entitled *Sacred Dialogues,* consisting of dramatizations of the Bible stories in Latin and in French in parallel columns. The work was to enjoy an immense vogue, less probably in France than in Germany, England, and the United States — there, of course, in the Latin version. One hundred and thirty-three editions have been identified. There is a copy in the Yale Library with the inscription, " Bought at Boston, 1759, David Eli, his book."

A collection of Bible stories retold for children is scarcely the place to which one would naturally turn for a manifesto of religious liberty. Yet here it was that the themes subsequently so dear to Castellio were first voiced. He was particularly fond of those episodes in the Bible that exhibited kindness, such as Abraham's entertaining of the angels, and was especially indignant over any manifestation of cruelty, as in the case of Pharaoh's attempt to exterminate the male children of the Hebrews, or the plot of Joseph's brethren to dispose of their brother. Here, in English translation, is Castellio's version of these two themes. The first is entitled " Moses in the Bulrushes ":

MOSES' MOTHER: Thus far we have escaped and reached the river. Now we must expose the little boy so that Pharaoh will not know that we have kept him against his order and will. We have run great risk in hiding him these three months, but it is better to incur danger and even to lose one's life than to let such a beautiful child be killed. Oh, the cruel king, to command that they destroy all the boy babies! How many have been killed by his order just as they came into life! Who has ever heard of such cruelty? To strangle the babies on the threshold of life! O my darling little boy, your poor mother must leave you here in the papyrus! I carried you, bore you, and hid you these three months. I would hide you longer if I could. How bitter! Must I leave you without hope of seeing you any more? What will become of me and of you, my boy, whom I leave here? But since we cannot do what we wish, we have to wish what we can. I did right to hide you. Now I leave you to the mercy and care of God. Good-by, my darling, good-by, my little son.

THE SISTER: Mother, I will stay here, if you like, to see what will happen.

MOTHER: That is good, and I will return home.

PHARAOH'S DAUGHTER: Here is the river where we have come to bathe. Maidens, you stay here while I will go with the attendant to that lovely little hiding place. But what is that papyrus? Maid, go and see. It looks like an ark.

MAID: So it is, and it is covered with pitch.

PHARAOH'S DAUGHTER: Bring it here. Open it. Oh, the poor little fellow, and he cries! It goes right through me. This is one of the Hebrew children.

THE SISTER (to herself): I begin to have good hope of saving the baby. I will go near. (To Pharaoh's daughter) God bless you.

PHARAOH's DAUGHTER: What did you say?

THE SISTER: Would you like a Hebrew nurse for the baby?

PHARAOH's DAUGHTER: I should. Go and bring her.

THE SISTER: She will be here at once.

PHARAOH's DAUGHTER: How fortunate that I came! I have a boy whom I will bring up for my own. Nothing better could have happened. I am not afraid to offend Father in something so kind and good. It is a crime to strangle the little babies. Isn't he a darling! How well-formed! Isn't it wicked to kill such boys!

THE SISTER: Here is the nurse.

PHARAOH's DAUGHTER: Will you take care of this boy and bring him up for me? I will pay you.

MOTHER: That I will.

The second example is " Joseph and His Brethren ":

SIMEON: Here comes that dreamer. Let's kill him and throw his body into some cave.

LEVI: But what shall we tell Father?

SIMEON: That a wild beast ate him. We will see what will come of his dreams.

REUBEN: It is a crime to stain our hands in the blood of a boy, and a brother at that. Don't do it. You cannot suggest anything worse for us or for our father.

SIMEON: When did you begin to be so tender? Do you want us to let him live who predicts in his dreams that all of us, even Father and Mother, will bow down to him? Doesn't he deserve rather to go to hell with his dreams?

REUBEN: Brother, if it's going to be, who are you to stop it? And if it is not going to be, why are you afraid? [Observe the arguments against persecution drawn from predestination.] Does it seem to you so wicked that a callow lad should dream? What harm is there in dreams? [In other words, the points controverted are not so important after all.] But if you are so set and will not yield, here is a dry well. At least do not lay hands on him. Put him down the well. That will not be quite so bad. [Just as banishment was often to be proposed by the liberals because not quite so bad as death.]

SIMEON: You mind your own business. We are going to make away with him.

JOSEPH: God bless you, brothers.

LEVI: We'll show you how God will bless you. You dream that your brothers worship you and then you salute them so politely. Let's strip the pet of his rainbow coat.

JOSEPH: What are you going to do to me?

LEVI: Kill you.

JOSEPH: Don't.

SIMEON: We will.

JOSEPH: My brothers, for God's sake, for Father's sake! He will die of grief. Don't. What have I done? What has taken hold of you?

SIMEON: You waste time. Let him down.

REUBEN: I am leaving. I can't stand this.

JOSEPH: Where am I going? I shall die! Father, Father, what sad news will you have of your boy! In what grief will you drag out your days! Judah, help me, pity me, pity Father!

LEVI: Let's sit down and have a bite to eat.

JUDAH: I see some merchants coming. What good shall we have of our brother's blood? Let's sell him to the Ishmaelites over there, and lay no hands on our brother, shed no blood, for he is our brother of the same seed. Come, listen to me.

LEVI: He is right.

SIMEON: But perhaps —

JUDAH: Don't worry. You will be rid of him as well by sale as by slaughter.

LEVI: True, and we shall make something on the sale which we shall lose if we kill him.

JUDAH: Merchants, want to buy a fine boy?

MERCHANTS: Let's see him.

JUDAH: Pull him up. They'll take him.

JOSEPH: Now I am going to die. They are bringing me up to kill me.

JUDAH: Don't be so frightened. You aren't going to be killed but sold. Merchants, look at him. He is well built.

MERCHANTS: Yes, he is handsome and bright. How much do you ask for him?

JUDAH: Thirty pieces of silver.

MERCHANTS: Done. Here is your money

Very instructive is a comparison of the way in which Calvin handles these passages. He scathes, of course, the unparalleled severity of Pharaoh, not because killing babies is itself so monstrous, for Calvin fully condoned the slaughter of the babies of the Amalekites at the divine behest. Pharaoh's deepest offense lay in his intent to frustrate God, and the moral of the whole story is that Providence and not chance directed Pharaoh's daughter to the very spot that enabled her to rescue the savior of his people. Likewise in the case of Joseph's brethren. They were unquestionably incited by diabolical fury, and had they been possessed of a grain of humanity could not have sat down to eat after putting their brother down the well. But the main point is that unwittingly and unwillingly the brothers were instruments of Providence for their own ultimate salvation.

Why should men react so differently to the same Biblical passage? Why should one center on the wickedness of cruelty and the other on the power of God to circumvent its effects? Why does one shudder at inhumanity as such and the other inquire for what purpose it is being exercised? One wonders whether it is ultimately a matter of temperament, and that is only another way of inquiring whether after all it may not be predestination. Some are tough and some are tender. Some shrink not only from bloodshed but from any infliction of pain, and would sooner dissimulate than hurt. Others are of stouter fiber. If this be true, the arguments used by this side or that are immaterial. One fights against this conclusion, and with reason, because sometimes arguments have made converts, and the periods of history do exhibit such advances and

such retrogressions in the practice of liberty as to suggest
something more at work than merely temperament.

But to come back to Castellio. The plague broke out in Geneva. The town council requested the ministers to send as a
chaplain to the hospital one of their number other than Calvin. One went, and died. A successor was requested. The ministers replied that they recognized this service as their duty,
" but God had not given them the grace, the courage, and the
constancy to go to the hospital and they begged to be excused.
They prayed God would give them greater strength for the
future." Sébastien Castellio volunteered, but his offer was not
accepted because he was needed at the school and in any
case was not ordained.

Then arose a circumstance that gave him a particular reason for seeking ordination. He married and his stipend was
insufficient. The Council, unable to raise his wages, proposed
that in addition to the school he assume a church, to which
a salary would be attached. For this ordination was necessary.
But the ministers rejected him on two counts: because he
denied Calvin's allegorical interpretation of the descent of
Christ into hell, and because he repudiated the inspiration of
The Song of Songs in the Old Testament. Castellio thereupon resigned from the school and asked for a letter of rec-
ommendation to a post elsewhere. Calvin gladly acceded,
and in the name of the ministers gave him a letter testifying
that he would have been unanimously elected to the pastorate save for the two points of doctrine.

" The chief dispute," the letter continued, " was about The
Song of Songs. He said that it was a lascivious love poem in
which Solomon described his indecent amours. We told him
that he should not be so rash to despise the perpetual con-
sensus of the Church Universal. There was no book of doubtful authenticity that had not been debated, and those books
that we now receive without a question were at first dis-

puted. But this book had never been openly rejected by any-one. We told him that he should not trust to his own judg-ment, especially when he advanced nothing that had not been obvious to everyone before he was born, and we pointed out the similarity of this book to the Forty-fifth Psalm.

" When this did not weigh with him, we consulted what we should do. We were all agreed that it would be dangerous and would set a bad example if he were admitted to the min-istry on this condition. To begin with, people would be not a little offended if they heard that we had ordained one who openly rejected and condemned a book accepted as Scripture by all the churches. Further, the door would be opened to adversaries and detractors who seek to defame the gospel and disrupt the Church. Finally, we should be without an answer for the future to any who wanted to repudiate Ecclesiastes or Proverbs or any other book, unless we wanted to debate whether or no the book were worthy of the Holy Spirit.

" That no one may suppose there was any other reason for Sébastien's leaving, we wish to attest wherever he goes that he gave up his position as schoolmaster of his own free will. He has so conducted himself that we deemed him worthy of the ministry. He has been rejected, not because of any blem-ish in his character, nor because of any failure to accept the fundamentals, but simply for this reason that we have men-tioned. The ministers of Geneva signed in the name and by the mandate of all, John Calvin." And Calvin showed a genu-ine concern to find a place for Castellio somewhere else.

Here, then, was a man possessed of more courage than any of the ministers, yet denied ordination to the ministry on ac-count of two admittedly minor doctrinal points. The contrast was all the more glaring because the ministry at Geneva re-tained some who in matters of sex were undisciplined and in matters of finance irresponsible. Calvin was greatly exercised over the situation, but not disposed to go to extremities of discipline when he had none better with whom to replace the offenders. The task of building up a reputable Protestant ministry within one or even two decades was formidable. The alternatives were either to tolerate the tares or to reduce the Church to a winnowed conventicle. When the need for trained and upright candidates was so acute, the marvel is the greater that Castellio was turned down. The explanation is simply that a religious community built around an idea can less readily tolerate a rejection of the idea than a failure to live up to it.

Castellio went to Basel, still redolent with the spirit of Erasmus even if Servetus had been dismissed. The problem of ordination, which had occasioned the departure from Geneva, was not again raised. Castellio remained for life a layman. But the problem of financial support was all the more stringent. He tilled the earth, carried water for the gardeners, harpooned the logs that drifted down the Rhine, and engaged in tutoring and in correcting proof for Oporinus, the famous publisher of Basel.

The residue of time and strength was devoted to classical and Biblical studies, with the aim of rendering the Bible into a Latin not offensive to the humanists and into a French savoring of the soil. The vernacular version should wherever possible avoid words of immediate Latin derivation because foreign terms obscure the stark vigor of Christ's demands. He calls upon a would-be disciple to take up his cross. If the Latin word " cross " be used, many will readily consent because the term has so familiar a ring. But render the passage, " If anyone would come after me, let him carry the rope for his own lynching " — that strikes home. Castellio went rather far, however, in making the Bible indigenous when he turned the officers of Israel into marshals, seneschals, bailiffs, and gendarmes. All in all, his work was marked by high competence and distinction. The Latin version has necessarily become a curiosity because Latin has ceased to be a spoken tongue, and the French, of course, has been superseded.

Only the preface to the Latin version is still read. It was in the form of a dedicatory epistle to Edward VI, the boy king of England, and constituted a plea for religious liberty. Here again a comparison with Calvin is instructive. The *Institutes* begins with a dedication to Francis I, the king of France, who was besought to exercise clemency in religion, not because constraint as such is wrong, but because the Calvinists were right. Castellio adduced other considerations. The Scriptures, he claimed, " are full of enigmas and inscrutable questions which have been in dispute for over a thousand years without agreement, nor can they be resolved without love, which appeases all controversies. Yet on account of these enigmas the earth is filled with innocent blood. We certainly ought to fear lest in crucifying thieves justly we crucify Christ unjustly. If we suffer Turks and Jews to live among us, the former of whom scarcely love Christ and the latter dearly hate him, if we suffer detractors, the proud, envious, avaricious, immodest, drunkards, and like plagues, if we live with them, eat with them, and make merry with them, we ought at least to concede the right to breathe common air to those who confess with us the same Christ and harm no one, who are indeed of such a temper that they would rather die than say or do anything other than that which they think they ought to say and do. Of all men this sort is the least to be feared because he who would rather die than say what he does not feel is not open to bribery and corruption. I venture to say that none are more obedient to princes and magistrates than those who fear God in simplicity and obey him to the extent of their knowledge. On controverted points we would do better to defer judgment, even as God, who knows us to be guilty, yet postpones judgment and waits for us to amend our lives."

Castellio's achievements in the field of scholarship were not without their recognition. In the month of August of the year 1553 he was made a Master of Arts at the University of Basel and thus became eligible for a teaching post which shortly thereafter was conferred upon him. He was thirty-eight years of age, a humanist with an international reputation, and now so comfortably situated that he might look forward to another quarter of a century of tranquil literary labors. So might it have been if in October of that same year Geneva had not burned at the stake Michael Servetus.

Castellio, profoundly indignant, took counsel with like-minded spirits on how best to launch an effective protest. The decision was to issue an anthology of opinions, ancient and modern, against persecution, in which the earlier or incautious utterances of contemporary persecutors were skillfully interlaid between the statements of genuine and persistent liberals in order to create at once an appearance of unanimity and to provide an occasion for embarrassment. Luther and Calvin were side by side with Sebastian Franck and Sébastien Castellio. But Castellio's name did not appear save at the head of the excerpt from the dedication of his Bible to Edward VI. The collection as a whole was attributed to Martin Bellius, who signed the dedicatory epistle. Other pseudonyms were Basil Montfort and George Kleinberg. The recent discovery of a lost manuscript of Castellio puts to rest at last all the conjectures of his contemporaries and of the moderns as to the authorship of these portions. He was responsible for the whole. The place of publication likewise was fictitious, ostensibly Magdeburg. Beza surmised that it was Magdeburg on the Rhine and he was quite right, for the title of the book has been discovered in a list of the publications of Oporinus of Basel. The identity of the author was not so readily determinable, and although Castellio was speedily suspected, the pseudonym was accepted and the term Bellianism was used to denote the advocates of religious liberty. The work bore the title *Concerning Heretics, Whether They Are to Be Persecuted.*

A lively duel ensued, the more so because Calvin had already entered the lists. Murmurs of disapproval prompted him at once to essay a justification in the tract, *A Defense of the Orthodox Faith Against the Errors of Michael Servetus.* To this work Castellio replied in the *Contra Libellum Calvini* ("Against Calvin's Book"), which, however, was not published until 1612, in Holland, long after his death. Beza at once undertook to refute *Concerning Heretics* in a work with the same title appearing in the same year, 1554. Castellio wrote a rejoinder both in French and in Latin, but that work has not yet been published and was only recently discovered by a Russian refugee among the papers of a Dutch Bellianist in the Library of the Remonstrants at Rotterdam. A collection of theological tracts entitled *Four Dialogues* was permitted in Basel, but not until 1578, after the author had long been dead. One of the most significant of his works, the treatise *On the Art of Doubting,* has found itself curiously involved in the struggles of our own time. A Frenchman intended to edit it but was deterred. An American entertained plans of doing it, but delayed. An Italian wrote to the American of his own purpose to undertake it until he learned that a German professor in Heidelberg was about to begin. Then came word to the American that a young woman in Berlin had the task actually in hand. The American informed the professor in Heidelberg and the young woman in Berlin of their mutual plans. The professor withdrew in her favor, but when she had finished, she was unable to publish because of Hitler's racial laws. Then the Italian came to the rescue and brought out the work on the other side of the Alps just before Mussolini succumbed to Hitler.

Castellio's days were embroiled in controversy. The min-

isters at Basel were not eager to molest him, yet were not desirous of any open breach with Geneva. One of them wrote
to Beza advising him not to stir up Castellio, who was in-
nocuously engaged in editing classics. The advice went unheeded, and he was at last brought to trial in Basel. The outcome would scarcely have been worse than banishment, and
in all likelihood he would have migrated to Poland had not
death intervened in 1563.

Concerning Heretics begins with the parable of the White
Robe. It is couched in the form of a dedicatory epistle to Duke
Christoph of Württemberg, and opens:

"Most Illustrious Prince, suppose you had told your subjects that you would come to them at some uncertain time
and had commanded them to make ready to go forth clad in
white garments to meet you whenever you might appear.
What would you do if, on your return, you discovered that
they had taken no thought for the white robes but instead
were disputing among themselves concerning your person?
Some were saying that you were in France, others that you
were in Spain; some that you would come on a horse, others
in a chariot; some were asserting that you would appear with
a great equipage, others that you would be unattended.
Would this please you?

"Suppose further that the controversy was being conducted, not merely by words, but by blows and swords, and
that one group wounded and killed the others who did not
agree with them. 'He will come on a horse,' one would say.

"'No, in a chariot,' another would retort.

"'You lie.'

"'You're the liar. Take that.' He punches him.

"'And take that in the belly.' The other stabs.

"Would you, O Prince, commend such citizens? Suppose,
however, that some did their duty and followed your command to prepare the white robes, but the others oppressed

them on that account and put them to death. Would you not
rigorously destroy such scoundrels?

"But what if these homicides claimed to have done all this
in your name and in accord with your command, even
though you had previously expressly forbidden it? Would
you not consider that such outrageous conduct deserved to be
punished without mercy? Now I beg you, Most Illustrious
Prince, to be kind enough to hear why I say these things.

"Christ is the Prince of this world, who on his departure
from the earth foretold to men that he would return some
day at an uncertain hour, and he commanded them to prepare white robes for his coming, that is to say, that they
should live together in a Christian manner, amicably, without controversy and contention, loving one another. But consider now, I beg you, how well we discharge our duty.

"How many are there who show the slightest concern to
prepare the white robe? Who is there who bends every effort
to live in this world in a saintly, just, and religious manner
in the expectation of the coming of the Lord? For nothing
is there so little concern. The true fear of God and charity are
fallen and grown cold. Our life is spent in contention and in
every manner of sin. We dispute, not as to the way by which
we may come to Christ, which is to correct our lives, but
rather as to the state and office of Christ, where he now is and
what he is doing, how he is seated at the right hand of the
Father, and how he is one with the Father; likewise with regard to the Trinity, predestination, free will; so, also, of God,
the angels, the state of souls after this life, and other like
things, which do not need to be known for salvation by faith
(for the publicans and sinners were saved without this knowledge), nor indeed can they be known before the heart is pure
(for to see these things is to see God himself, who cannot be
seen save by the pure in heart, as the text says, 'Blessed are
the pure in heart: for they shall see God'). Nor if these are

known do they make a man better, as Paul says, ' Though I understand all mysteries, and have not love, it profiteth me nothing.' This perverse curiosity engenders worse evils. Men are puffed up with knowledge or with a false opinion of knowledge and look down upon others. Pride is followed by cruelty and persecution so that now scarcely anyone is able to endure another who differs at all from him. Although opinions are almost as numerous as men, nevertheless there is hardly any sect that does not condemn all others and desire to reign alone. Hence arise banishments, chains, imprisonments, stakes, and gallows and this miserable rage to visit daily penalties upon those who differ from the mighty about matters hitherto unknown, for so many centuries disputed, and not yet cleared up.

" If, however, there is someone who strives to prepare the white robe, that is, to live justly and innocently, then all others with one accord cry out against him if he differ from them in anything, and they confidently pronounce him a heretic on the ground that he seeks to be justified by works. Horrible crimes of which he never dreamed are attributed to him, and the common people are prejudiced by slander until they consider it a crime merely to hear him speak. Hence arises such cruel rage that some are so incensed by calumny as to be infuriated when the victim is first strangled instead of being burned alive at a slow fire.

" This is cruel enough, but a more capital offense is added when this conduct is justified under the robe of Christ and is defended as being in accord with his will, when Satan could not devise anything more repugnant to the nature and will of Christ! Yet these very people who are so furious against the heretics, as they call them, are so far from hating moral offenders that no scruple is felt against living in luxury with the avaricious, currying flatterers, abetting the envious and calumniators, making merry with drunkards, gluttons, and

adulterers, banqueting daily with the scurrilous, impostors,
and those who are hated of God. Who, then, can doubt that
they hate not vices but virtues? To hate the good is the same
as to love the evil. If, then, the bad are dear to a man, there
is no doubt but that the good are hateful to him.

"I ask you, then, Most Illustrious Prince, what do you
think Christ will do when he comes? Will he commend such
things? Will he approve of them?"

This passage comes close to epitomizing Castellio's whole
position. It brings to the fore the idea destined to play an
enormous role in the entire struggle for religious liberty,
namely, the distinction between the essentials and the nonessentials of Christianity. Fundamentalism arose in the sixteenth century in the interests of reducing the number of the
fundamentals, that persecution might be allayed. Castellio
in the above passage did not enumerate what they were, but
he definitely indicated what they were not. His refusal to include any judgment with regard to the location of Christ's
body after the resurrection touched upon a moot point between the Lutherans and the Calvinists, for Luther regarded
the body of Christ as ubiquitous, needing only to be disclosed, not to be conjured upon the altar, whereas Calvin
held that Christ, being at the right hand of the Father, can
be present only spiritually in the sacrament. The assigning
of the Trinity, predestination, and the nature of the afterlife
to nonessentials, elicited a blast from Théodore Beza, who
ejaculated: "Bellius says that publicans and sinners were
saved without these beliefs. O unheard-of impudence! Saved
by him on whom they had not called. Did they call on him in
whom they did not believe? Did they believe in him whom
they had not known? If Christ is not in heaven, how can he
be our high priest? If he be not coeternal and consubstantial
with the Father, how can he be our Saviour?"

The question of the essentials entailed, of course, the prior question, essential for what? And the answer was always that essential referred to salvation. Here Castellio, with the Erasmians, introduced a rational consideration, that nothing can be essential for salvation that cannot be known, and much in Christian teaching cannot be established with absolute certainty, particularly the matters that are most controverted. Calvin and Beza promptly dubbed Castellio an academic, that is, a skeptic, and charged that he would reduce the whole of Christianity to conjecture. He replied by reviving an ancient distinction between faith and knowledge as representing two levels of certainty. In accord with a venerable tradition associated with the name of Thomas Aquinas, Castellio held that faith and knowledge are mutually exclusive. That which is known is no longer believed and that which is believed by definition is not yet known. Another and equally persistent tradition, congenial especially to the mystics, held that, since the vision of God is possible in this life, he may be at the same time known and believed, because faith and knowledge are not mutually exclusive but are rather variant modes of apprehending God at the same time. Calvin stood perhaps unwittingly in this line, and went even beyond his predecessors in equating faith with knowledge, assurance, and certitude. That was why he could not be deterred from constraining others through the fear of making a mistake. Under such circumstances to take no action to curb death-dealing error appeared to him to be culpable negligence. And Beza declared religious liberty to be "a most diabolical dogma, because it means that everyone should be left to go to hell in his own way."

Such assumptions of certainty Castellio flatly challenged. In the preface to his Bible he had already contended that Scripture is fraught with enigmas. The very fact of controversy is itself the proof of uncertainty. "All sects hold their religion according to the Word of God and say that it is certain. Calvin says that his is certain, and they, theirs. He says they are wrong and wishes to be judge, and so do they. Who shall be judge? Who made Calvin the arbiter of all the sects, that he alone should kill? He has the Word of God and so have they. If the matter is certain, to whom is it certain? To Calvin? But why does he then write so many books about manifest truth? There is nothing unknown to Calvin. He talks as if he might be in paradise and writes huge tomes to explain what he says is absolutely clear.

" In view of all this uncertainty we must define the heretic simply as one with whom we disagree. And if, then, we are going to kill heretics, the logical outcome will be a war of extermination, since each is sure of himself. Calvin would have to invade France and other nations, wipe out cities, put all the inhabitants to the sword, sparing neither sex nor age, not even the babes and the beasts. All would have to be burned save Calvinists, Jews, and Turks, whom he excepts." At this point Castellio was not fair, because Calvin did not contemplate a crusade and did not insist that every Church conform to the pattern of Geneva. He too distinguished the essentials and the nonessentials and would correct a slight superstition with patience and only when religion was shaken to the foundations would have recourse to the extreme remedy.

But Castellio returned to the charge that the points at which the extreme remedy was invoked were precisely the least certain because the most controverted. " No one doubts that there is a God, whether he is good and just, whether he should be loved and worshiped, whether vice should be avoided and virtue followed. Why? Because these points are clear. But concerning Baptism, the Lord's Supper, justification, predestination, and many other questions there are capital dissensions. Why? Because these points are not cleared up in Scripture."

The moral is to wait. "We should imitate Judas Mac-
cabaeus who, not knowing what to do with the altar of sacrifice, laid aside the stones until a prophet should arise to tell.
Let us wait, lest we pull up the wheat with the tares, which
has so often happened when the martyrs and the Son of God
were put to death under the color of religion. Let us wait,
just as, when night falls upon the field of battle, fighting
ceases lest by striking at hazard friends be killed instead of
foes. Since, then, so much is doubtful and entangled, with-
hold fire until the day dawns and the forces are better disen-
gaged, that in the darkness and confusion you do not that
of which you will have afterward to say, 'I did not intend to.'"

Castellio, as a matter of fact, was not a skeptic, but he was
a rationalist. In his judgment there are two sources of knowledge. One is sense experience and the other is revelation.
Neither is beyond the need of correction, and the office falls
to human reason. The senses obviously are not infallible, because a stick half immersed in water appears bent and a
mountain in the distance seems to be blue. Reason therefore
must interpose control and it is competent to do so because
not vitiated by the Fall of man. The tree from which Adam
ate was the tree of knowledge, and we are not to turn it into
a tree of ignorance. Thus Castellio turned the story of the
Fall into a myth of progress. After the manner of the Enlightenment he waxed lyrical in praise of reason: "She is, so
to speak, the daughter of God. She was before letters and
ceremonies, before the world was, and she is after letters and
ceremonies, and after the world is changed and renewed, she
will endure and can no more be abolished than God himself.
Reason, I say, is a sort of eternal word of God. According to
reason Jesus Christ himself, the Son of the living God, lived
and taught. In the Greek he is called Logos, which means
'reason' or 'word.' They are the same, for reason is a kind

of superior and eternal word of truth always speaking."

Reason thus became for Castellio a principle of continuous revelation, and this explains why he had no sense of departing from the Christian revelation when he called upon reason to resolve Scriptural riddles. Nor was he an apostate in distinguishing different levels within Scripture or even in admitting positive discrepancies. When told that if these were true the authority of Scripture would be undermined, he replied that if the inference were correct the statements were not therefore false, but he would not admit the inference, because authority does not reside in a few passages pressed into a rigid conformity, but in the tenor and body of the whole. "My confidence," he said, "in the authority of sacred authors is confirmed when I see them so intent upon the salvation of men as to be unconcerned for words. Their reliability is thereby manifest. Those who tell the truth do not strain at words. It is precisely liars who aim at a particular verbal consistency to hide their deception." Castellio did not fully perceive that he was undoubtedly introducing a subjective factor into Biblical interpretation, and no doubt this was why he was the more ready to repudiate the passages condoning persecution in the Old Testament as contrary to the mind of Christ.

Alongside of the rational in Castellio lay a strong ethical emphasis:

"Now I know well that my detractors are accustomed to say that one must look not at the life, but at the doctrine, and that my life is hypocrisy. There are even some who say that to live well is the peculiarity of heretics. . . . I answer that it is a great shame for those who wish to condemn others to so live that their life is worse than that of those whom they condemn. . . . Shall it be said that the spirit of the heretics has more power than that of the Christians?

"This man you say is a heretic, a putrid member to be cut

off from the body of the Church lest he infect others. But what has he done? Oh, horrible things! Yes, but what? Is he a murderer? an adulterer? a thief? No. What then? Does he not believe in Christ and the Scriptures? Certainly he does, and would rather die than not continue in his belief. But he does not understand them correctly, that is, he interprets them differently from our teachers. . . . This is a capital offense to be expiated in the flames."

Castellio would say not merely that deeds are more important than creeds, but that deeds must be the test of creeds. The layman cannot pass judgment on the arguments of the medical sects, but he can tell which one cures the most. So he can evaluate the theological sects by observing which one best cures vices, and changes the greatest number from drunk to sober, from intemperate to continent, from greedy to generous, making them patient instead of impatient, kind instead of cruel, instead of impure, chaste. Sound doctrine is that which makes men sound. The doctrine of the persecutors must be bad because their lives are bad.

Good deeds, moreover, are the condition of right creeds. These obscure religious matters can be known only by the pure in heart. The Scriptures can be rightly understood only by Christ's disciples, and they are his disciples who obey him and have love. This point was made all the more insistently by Castellio because he believed in the possibility of moral perfection. He did not claim to have attained it, but he did demand that the gospel be taken seriously, and he held that the new man in Christ is able to overcome sin, provided he strive as assiduously as he would to learn German or French, music, dancing, or cards. When critics scornfully demanded, "Show us a perfect man," Castellio witheringly retorted, "Such men are generally obscure and unknown, but if I knew one I would not point him out, because the question is like that of Herod who asked the Wise Men to report to him the whereabouts of the newborn King of the Jews that he also might worship him."

A controversy with Geneva over the moral requirements of Christianity must appear anomalous in view of the repute of the Calvinists for rigorism comparable to that of monastic asceticism. The difference was in part the one already noted between the relative weight of the doctrinal and the moral. But there was also a divergence as to the outward and the inward in morality. A religious society that exacts from its members a pattern of behavior is almost bound to center on that which can be readily determined. Thus the Genevan consistory declared that " a minister should be deposed for heresy, cardplaying, and dancing, but a fraternal admonition would suffice were he guilty of scurrility, obscenity, and avarice." To this scale of vices Castellio applied the test of inwardness. "Why," he asked, " does Calvin not bring about the death of hypocrites and the avaricious? Or does he think that hypocrites are better than heretics? He claims that heretics destroy souls. So do the envious, the avaricious, and the proud. But if Calvin wished all the proud to be punished by the magistrate, none would be left to punish the magistrate himself."

Because righteousness for Castellio was so inward, the criterion of morality became subjective. He defined conscience as loyalty to that which one believes to be right, even though objectively one may be in error. If a boy follows a man supposing him to be his father, the intention need not be corrected but only the opinion. To say what one believes is to tell the truth, even though one may be mistaken. Servetus was put to death for telling the truth. Had he been willing to recant and speak against his conscience, he might have escaped. He was executed because he would not lie. He perished because he said what he thought.

Scarcely anything in the teaching of Castellio was more

radical than this. He relativized conscience. Few in his day agreed or even understood. Not until the late seventeenth century on the eve of the Enlightenment did his position come to prevail. In his own day the almost universal view was that conscience, to have any validity, must be grounded on truth. Error had no rights. Castellio did not counter by saying that mere conviction makes one correct, but he did insist that loyalty to conviction is an elemental necessity, because " I must be saved by my own faith and not by that of another." If a man recant, his soul is destroyed and his moral fiber undermined. Castellio could cite examples of men who lived blamelessly so long as they were loyal to their convictions, but who, after recantation, suffered a complete moral disintegration. Therefore, " to force conscience is worse than cruelly to kill a man."

Castellio's position at this point has come to be the common coin of liberalism. The danger implicit in such relativism is that truth itself will follow the way of conscience. The slogan has frequently come to be that one idea is as good as another so long as it be sincerely held. Not until recent decades have we been brutally taught that sincerity in the service of a pernicious idea only makes it all the more frightful. How hard it is to remedy one abuse without incurring another!

A further element in Castellio's thinking, likewise Erasmian in tone, was a sharp distinction of the spiritual from the carnal. The reason why the sword of the magistrate is inappropriate in religion is that religion is spiritual and the sword carnal, and incapable therefore of creating or even understanding religion. " Religion resides not in the body but in the heart, which cannot be reached by the sword of kings and princes. The Church can no more be constructed by persecution and violence than a wall can be built by cannon blasts. Therefore to kill a man is not to defend a doctrine. It is simply to kill a man." Certain things persecution can do, but they are the wrong things. The magistrate can constrain men to recant and thus turn heretics into hypocrites. The number in the Church is thus increased, but the quality is not improved. " I say that those who have regard to numbers, and on that account constrain men, gain nothing, but rather lose, and resemble a fool who, having a great barrel and a little wine in it, fills it up with water to get more, but instead of increasing the wine, he spoils what he had." The gospel was forced on England under Edward VI, but the accession of Mary revealed how few were genuinely persuaded. " The Jews in Spain, who have been baptized by force, are no more Christians than before."

Again, coercion may completely defeat its own end by simply advertising heresy. Calvin complains that the views of Servetus are spreading. " He has only himself to blame. There was no mention of the first book of Servetus and the later could be sold like the others without disturbance, but now that the man has been burned with his books, everybody is burning with a desire to read them." Castellio knew a man who had been converted to the views of Servetus by the extracts from his works that Calvin included in the refutation. The Protestants flourished " like drops of dew at break of day " when they suffered persecution, which served merely to make seven for one.

Another and still more serious consequence of persecution is that it may provoke sedition. The common claim was that heresy would disturb the body politic. On the contrary, answered Castellio, " seditions come rather from the fact that they want to force and kill heretics rather than to let them live without constraint, for tyranny engenders sedition."

Closely akin to the spiritual is the mystic approach, according to which the way of salvation is the bearing of the cross, the crucifixion of the old man. The way to God is the way of suffering. It follows of necessity, therefore, that although those who suffer may not be martyrs, certainly those who inflict suffering cannot be saints. Castellio declared that to " assert one's faith is not to burn a man, but rather to be burned." Calvin and Beza called the heretics wolves. Castellio replied: " The mark of the wolf is to eat raw flesh. Therefore they are not the wolves who are killed, but rather those who kill." " The just have always been killed." " From the foundation of the world the truth has always been persecuted by the great and renowned." " He who is according to the flesh persecuted him who is according to the Spirit." Christ, the apostles, and the martyrs were persecuted, and such has always been the fate of simple and true Christians.

Castellio's spiritualization of religion had unhappily also its pitfalls. His fear of the externalizing of Christianity brought him to the verge of dissolving the visible Church. In a tract as yet unpublished he declared: " They are of the true Church who have heard the voice of the Shepherd and obey, who have the true sacraments, who have gone into the laver of redemption and experienced the new birth. They are new creatures, baptized with fire and in the Spirit. They have truly eaten of the flesh of Christ and drunk of his blood, having put off the old man of sin and put on the new. This Church is unknown to the Calvinists because, being taken up with their visible and carnal Church and impeded by its visible marks, they are not able to consider and see the spiritual Church. In this regard they are like the ancient Jews who were so immersed in the shadows and ceremonies of the law that they could not see the end of the law in Christ. But the children of this celestial Church recognize it just as children recognize their mother, and they know no less their brothers than the carnal know their own. And not only do they recognize each other, but strangers also mark them by the fruits of charity and of the spirit which are proper to those who fear God. Thus they are discerned as the disciples of

Christ, and not by exterior sermons and sacraments, which are common to the good and to the bad. Our Lord said, ' By this shall all men know that ye are my disciples, if ye have love one to another.' Those who are in this Church recognize it as a musician recognizes music and sings in accord."

In this passage Castellio comes close to reducing the Church to an invisible fellowship. Surely that is a high price to pay for liberty! The centuries have demonstrated that it is an unnecessary price, but radical diseases require drastic cures. Perhaps in his day no lesser word would have sufficed.

Finally, in Castellio there was an element of abiding validity rooted in his faith in the mercy of God and the compassion of Christ. The Christian God is a God of mercy and forgiveness. If, argued Castellio, " before the sacrifice of Christ God had compassion on guilty Nineveh, how much more now on innocent babes! God draws, attracts, urges, invites, and persuades. The imitation of this heavenly Father leads us to love our enemies and to err on the side of mercy. Christ likewise was so meek that to seek a warrant from his example for putting to death heretics with the sword is like trying to discover a case of a lamb eating a wolf." The preface of the tract *Concerning Heretics* ends with an impassioned apostrophe to Christ:

" O Creator and King of the world, dost thou see these things? Art thou become so changed, so cruel, so contrary to thyself? When thou wast on earth, none was more mild, more clement, more patient of injury. As a sheep before the shearer thou wast dumb. When scourged, spat upon, mocked, crowned with thorns, and crucified shamefully among thieves, thou didst pray for them who did thee this wrong. Art thou now so changed? I beg thee in the name of thy Father, dost thou now command that those who do not understand thy precepts as the mighty demand be drowned in water, cut with lashes to the entrails, sprinkled with salt, dis-

membered by the sword, burned at a slow fire, and otherwise tortured in every manner and as long as possible? Dost
thou, O Christ, command and approve of these things? Are
they thy vicars who make these sacrifices? Art thou present
when they summon thee and dost thou eat human flesh? If
thou, Christ, dost these things or if thou commandest that
they be done, what hast thou left for the devil? Doest thou
the very same things as Satan? O blasphemies and shameful
audacity of men, who dare to attribute to Christ that which
they do by the command and at the instigation of Satan!"

Chapter five

THE HERETIC AS HYPOCRITE:

David Joris

Bellianism as a term would never have gained currency had there not been Bellianists. Castellio had disciples and collaborators. Two of them will be noticed here because they represent variant emphases in the theory of liberty and because they exemplify in their lives certain of the fruits of persecution. The first, David Joris, was a Hollander and an Anabaptist of a very eccentric variety. He is of interest chiefly as an example of the mystical approach to tolerance and likewise because in his behavior he demonstrated the thesis of Castellio that persecution can all too readily turn a heretic into a hypocrite.

David Joris

Joris was born in Holland in the early years of the sixteenth century (1501–1502) when the Low Countries were a Spanish dependency. The political tie between Spain and The Netherlands made possible mutual influences in reverse directions. Through the Flemish court at Madrid the liberalism of the Brethren of the Common Life and Erasmus was disseminated in the Iberian peninsula. Through the Spanish court at The Hague heresy was closely watched and severely restricted in the Low Countries. But thereby a rift was created between the occupying power and the native administration which out of national resentment would often abet heresy. In consequence at the same time auto-da-fés multiplied and heresy increased. From the point of view of the Catholic powers the variety mattered little. Lutheranism and Anabaptism were alike subject to fire and water. The first burning of Luther's books began in the Low Countries and the first Lutheran martyrs were here to suffer. Coincidentally Anabaptism found the way prepared by the simple Biblical humanism of Erasmus and the Brethren, and by the 1530's Holland had come to be a land of three religions, Catholicism, Lutheranism, and Anabaptism, to which Calvinism as a fourth was about to be added.

Joris grew to manhood in a period of exceptional ferment, because only in The Netherlands could one find such a juxtaposition of an intensely orthodox foreign administration in clash with a populace widely addicted to Protestantism of the most radical type. Joris was a strapping young fellow, squarely built, impressive in person, red-bearded, artistically gifted, a painter of stained-glass windows by trade. After commissions in France and England, he married in 1524 and settled in Delft. He was then twenty-two or twenty-three years of age. The Lutheran agitation enlisted his ardor and he began to distribute scurrilous sheets against the pope as Antichrist. He would affix them to church doors or leave them in the confessionals. Once on Ascension Day, when a solemn procession marched from the Church of Our Lady to the New Church, he cried out against the abomination. He was condemned by the local court to a mild penance, which the court at The Hague increased to fine, whipping, tongue-boring, and three years of banishment.

His zeal was only the more inflamed, and he passed speedily from Lutheranism to Anabaptism when one of the Anabaptist martyrs at the stake called out to him by the name of "brother." The Anabaptism of The Netherlands at the time of his adherence had assumed highly ecstatic forms. The movement was already ten years old and the soberer leaders had been liquidated. The direction fell in consequence to less balanced spirits, and in any case placidity does not well survive a decade of the dragnet. Hunted and hounded, the little flock dreamed of vindication at the hands of the Lord, and the Apocalypse provided the imagery for the unfolding of the world drama when Antichrist should be overthrown and the one hundred and forty-four thousand apostles should go forth in the power of the Spirit to usher in the reign of the saints. Human agents were indispensable as precursors and prophets of the great day. Soon the woods were full of Enochs and Elijahs, all of them Spirit-filled, able through dreams and visions to declare the mind of the Lord.

Into this maelstrom Joris was drawn. He was ecstatic over the new day, when, Latin, Greek, and Hebrew having been rejected, the Holy Ghost was talking Dutch. He knew well, however, that tribulation was the prelude to the Great Day and the saints must expect to suffer. In one of his hymns he sang:

"All the godly must drink
 From the chalice of bitterness, 'pure red wine,'
 But the dregs shall God give to the godless to drain.
 They shall spew and shall belch and fall into death without end.
 Understand, 'dear Christian.
 Hold fast. God's honor spread.
 Be ready ever to die.'"

At the same time one should be ready for the Great Day. Joris sang:

"Are you ready?
 O I am ready.
 Are your clothes white?
 Are your feet washed?"

The mood grew ever more tense. In the town of Münster in the year 1535 the saints succeeded in obtaining control of the government. The New Jerusalem was established, with several novel features. One was the avowal of vengeance rather than of meekness toward the Babylonian abomination. Now was the hour to gird on the armor of David, who by slaughter should prepare the way for the peaceful Kingdom of Christ. The second innovation was the introduction of polygamy, on the ground that it had been permitted in the Old Testament to the patriarchs and never abrogated in the New Testament. When Paul said that a bishop should be the husband of one wife, he implied that others might have more. A third novelty arose among the Dutch Anabaptists of going naked as a sign. This particular aberration had nothing to do with sex. It was an imitation of the example of the prophet Isaiah, who for six months went naked as a testimony to the doom of Jerusalem. Similar manifestations were later to occur among the early Quakers and in recent times among the Dukhobors. The practice was of one stripe with the act of a Dutch Anabaptist who took a live coal from off the hearth and touched his lips after the manner of Isaiah, except that, unlike the prophet, he was not able to say, "Here am I; send me," because for two weeks he was speechless.

The New Jerusalem at Münster was of short duration. The city fell and the leaders were put to the sword. Then the Anabaptist movement in The Netherlands was confronted by the necessity for clarification. A conference to that end was held in the early fall of 1535 at Bocholt, where Joris proved to be the most influential figure. The discussion brought to light two opposing parties. There were the Covenanters of the sword, who still adhered to polygamy, chiliasm, and revolution. They ravaged the land, carrying off cattle, rooting up trees, trampling grain, plundering churches, burning villages, and hanging the inhabitants. On the other side were a sober group who maintained their persistent repudiation of revolution, polygamy, and millenarianism. They were Anabaptists in their insistence on adult baptism, austere deportment, strict discipline, and the rejection of war and capital punishment. Of this group the leader was Menno Simons, the leader of the Mennonites.

Joris undertook to mediate. He stood with the Mennonites in his complete rejection of revolution. The saints should bear the cross and suffer injustice. The problem of polygamy was handled by a periodization of history. The first period was that of the Old Testament patriarchs marked by polygamy, the second that of the Son in the New Testament characterized by monogamy, and the third would be the age of the Spirit distinguished by celibacy. Thus the patriarchs were not condemned and polygamy was not condoned. As for nakedness, Joris averred that he had no urge to make of himself a spectacle before the lewd but, if one were impelled by the Lord, he could not gainsay him. In other words, this was a form of testimony to be adopted only under direct inspiration. Joris was at one with the Covenanters, however, in his vivid expectation of the imminence of the Great Day of the Lord. He differed from all the parties in displaying already certain mystical tendencies that were to enable him in the end to spiritualize and allegorize the beliefs and programs of all the parties. Perhaps that was why he was able at Bocholt to reconcile for the moment groups so diverse. The agreement between such irreconcilables was, however, of necessity but short-lived. The significance of the conference was rather that it marked a parting of the ways and that it brought Joris into prominence.

Shortly thereafter he received a prophetic call to come forward himself in a messianic role. The immediate occasion was a rhapsodic letter from a female admirer, who addressed him in these terms: " May the Lord who inhabiteth eternity

. . . increase and fulfill in thee that which he has begun. I thank my Father and glorify my Saviour for the gift of grace in thy wisdom which comes down from above through an exalted spirit and a wonderful counsel of God to the honor and glory of his most holy name and the sanctification of his people. Blessed be thou in the Lord, my brother. Faint not to complete what thou hast begun in the house of the Lord. Be thou the fan in his hand to prepare for him an acceptable people that he may speedily come to his temple. . . . Therefore, O valiant knight of Israel, beloved of the Lord, look well to his vineyard. The Lord will increase thy strength and wisdom in whom he is well pleased. He has made thee a watchman in his house, a shepherd for his flock. Thou art the most godly among those whose names are written. As the rain refreshes the earth and the dew the flower of the field and makes the scent sweet to man, so do thy warnings, teaching, and instructions, though simple and plain, give men life, showing them the way to the perfect wisdom of God in which they grow up to the full stature of the man in Christ Jesus our Lord. O how excellent art thou among others!"

On the receipt of this letter, Joris declared: " The glory of the Lord shone round about me eight or ten days thereafter. The brilliance in my eyes I cannot describe. It was no outward light, but with inward vision I saw the children of God coming in radiance, and before them and before me the ungodly princes and the mighty fell down in great anguish. . . . Then I came to myself and saw that I stood on my feet. I heard many voices and saw dreams and visions. From that moment I had to write furiously, for the words would come to my mouth three or four times more rapidly than I could pen them."

The result of these visions was the assumption of a new messianic role. " Hitherto," said Joris, " I have been ashamed of everyone. Now I am ashamed of none, be he kaiser or king." For himself, he claimed to be the third David. The first was David the king; the second, Christ the Son of David; and the third, David Joris. The greatest is he who is in the middle, who has already killed Goliath so that nothing remains for the the third David but to cut off his head. The first David was a type, the third an ambassador.

Yet Joris was accused of exalting himself above Christ. He certainly indulged in some high-flown pretensions, as, for example, when he wrote: " Come hither and hear me. Come, I say, you who thirst for the water of life. Come to the fountain of wisdom in the highest. Behold I, David, who have been awakened by God's grace in the last time in the faith, shall set before you the eternal truth and declare the righteousness of my God according to the promises from heaven upon earth before the face of the firmament. The truth shall abide firm and unchangeable in eternity and be found from death unto life. Consider this." And again: " I, David, have power with my spirit to judge you in the Lord according to the Spirit and to bless and curse according to the truth . . . to forgive or retain sins, to bind and to loose by the Lord in heaven. Yes, at the right time to slay with the rod of my mouth, which is the eternal word of the power of God. These are hard thunderclaps, are they not? " A good many thought they were. Precisely what was meant is, however, difficult to assess since Joris may have been laying claim to nothing more than the word of the apostle (I Cor. 6:3), " Know ye not that we shall judge angels? " At the same time Joris did demand of fellow Anabaptists that they give him implicit credence, and they found themselves driven to insist on testing the prophets by the norm of the written Word. To this Joris opposed the inward word, and there his mysticism came into play, so that the role of the third David was transmuted into that of the purgative stage of the mystic and resembled therefore greatly the mission of the Suffering Servant of Isaiah.

"The victory," he wrote, "or the resurrection in spirit and truth is against no flesh and blood outwardly, but inwardly against the unrighteous and perverted spirit and all lying, which brings forth through enmity of God nothing but evil, death, and darkness, which must become naught. . . . Wherefore the struggle and the victory are spiritual and can neither begin nor end save in love and through love and with love. . . . This victory seems at first to be defeat, this power to be weakness. The reason is that he who has deserved no enmity, disquiet, trouble, or labor, must suffer in the strife, and must endure disquiet, trouble, and labor. He must pay what he does not owe. He must be weak and despised although he is godly, strong, and worthy of honor, for he cannot receive the name until he has shown himself a servant to those in need. Therein must his glory, honor, power, victory, and truth appear and be found."

Soon for Joris the blowing of the trumpets in the last day was reduced to an inner experience and "death, the devil, hell, and damnation," he said, "take place in a man and not outside." If such mystical tendencies had been dominant at the beginning, he could scarcely have founded a sect. But even at the outset he was vague. His fulsome language attracted tender spirits who discerned in him a seer and prophet, a new David in the spirit of Elias. A following gathered and a sect was formed.

Blesdijk, a lad of sixteen, later to be Joris' son-in-law, testified: "Among the writers from the time of the apostles until now there is none who has so touched my heart, so powerfully drawn me from the love of vanity, self-wisdom, arrogance, and impurity to the true wisdom which is the fear of God, to simplicity, chastity, and righteousness as this one writer has done. Many others can testify that we have been led through the service of this man from darkness to light, from the love of ourselves to the love of God." Some of the disciples were men of means, who placed their substance at Joris' disposal and thus enabled him to bring out his first extensive publication, the massive *Wonder Book* of 1542. The title page bore the combined figure of a lion and a lamb, designed no doubt by Joris himself. The reference was to the book of Revelation 5: 5, 6, where the book sealed with seven seals is opened by the Lion of the tribe of Judah and by the Lamb that was slain.

Joris' activity all this time, one must remember, was clandestine and every movement fraught with danger. Those who attended Anabaptist conferences did not expect to die in bed. After the birth of his first son in 1535 he sought refuge for wife and child in Strasbourg, but in vain. An attempt to reach England was frustrated by a storm. When his wife

David Joris' Lion and Lamb

again became pregnant, he left her with his mother in Delft and sought employment here and there, suffering several near betrayals at the hands of travelers. Sometimes he found no shelter and walked throughout the night. Once he escaped from a town through the kindness of a servant, who packed him in a basket like a dog, covered him with skins, and dropped him into a boat. Worry, privation, and severe fasting weakened his health.

In 1538 the court of The Hague decreed that should he be caught he should be hanged before his own door, and a price of one hundred gulden was placed upon his head. In that same year his own mother was beheaded because of her confession that her son was as true in his teaching as were the prophets and the apostles. His wife and daughter were banished from Delft and thirty-one followers were executed. Joris himself continued as a fugitive, saved on one occasion by the descent of a heavy fog and on another by the failure of a servant in an inn to provide a candle.

One is not amazed that the head of an underground religious association, wandering for five years with a price on his head, should have been an advocate of religious liberty. The arguments that he adduced in favor of liberty differed in their emphasis from those of Castellio, with whom the ethical and rational considerations predominated rather than the mystical. With Joris the reverse was true. Occasionally he could say that we " ought not to strive and condemn one another over the relation of the persons in the Trinity about which we do not have perfect light and assurance of the truth." And there was at times an ethical note as when he protested against the incongruity of shedding the innocent blood of those who have committed no offense other than to reject war and the oath, " Whereas nothing is done against the idle, frivolous, drunkards, adulterers, double-dealers, gamblers, swearers, and revilers."

The approach of Joris was, however, prevailingly mystical. Basic was his picture of God as impartial and unrestricted, extending his grace to all creatures and refusing to be bound by all man-made lines of land or sect: " How may we recognize those who truly follow Christ? Are they a nation called and separated from a city or land in Europe, Asia, Africa, or the New World? Are they a particular sect or order? To this I would answer: They are neither a nation nor sect nor people from any city or land. Christians were called from Christ, religious orders from their founders such as Augustinian, Franciscan, Dominican, et cetera. But the way is not here. Rather, it consists in a firm faith in love and patience." The object of the religious quest was union with this boundaryless God, to be God with God himself. And the way of union is the way of inward transformation through a re-enactment in personal experience of the incarnation and passion of Christ, neither of which is of any avail unless thus inwardly appropriated. " What does it help me to know that Christ was conceived of the Holy Ghost, and born of the Virgin Mary, if he be not born in me? " " If you have missed the nature and spirit of the love of Christ, all the outward physical blood of our Lord Jesus will not help you, however firmly you believe that it has been shed for you. Listen to this, you slaves of the letter, who teach that we are justified by a faith which consists in holding firmly that Jesus Christ died for us."

That being the case, faith cannot be assent to an article, but only an experience of the spirit. " The faith of Jesus Christ is in no word spoken with the tongue, but in the eternal, true, pure, and divine work and spiritual nature of God against all flesh and is intelligible only to him who has received it. Faith does not consist in any special articles or spoken words, but in the true, eternal, living God and his Christ. No one can speak of the true faith if he is not found in it. Can anyone witness of that which he has not seen and heard?"

If faith is thus defined, the customary tests of orthodoxy are demolished, the common objects of religious controversy are eliminated, and the competence of the magistrate in religion is destroyed.

The customary tests are the Creeds, the Bible, and the Spirit. With regard to the Creeds, Joris wrote: " Faith is displayed by the power of the Spirit and the truth, not by the recital of Biblical history, nor by the miracles of the apostles and prophets, nor by the outward cross of Christ, nor by his incarnation, death, resurrection, and Second Coming for judgment. The devil believes all this. But what good is it apart from the Spirit of Christ? If a man believes in the Holy Trinity, is baptized in outward water in the name of the Father, Son, and Holy Ghost, if he believes in the twelve articles of the Holy Creed and can recite the larger and smaller catechisms like an angel, yes, if he can remove mountains, gives his goods to the poor, and his body to be burned, apart from the love of the truth it profits him nothing." There is no value in repeating the Lord's Prayer and the Creed according to the letter, no, not even in Dutch. Joris had ceased to be exuberant because the Holy Ghost was talking Dutch.

The Bible became nebulous as a test because its value resides only in the eternal Word. " This book which is so wonderfully written inwardly and outwardly is no visible book written by the hand of man, but it is living, eternal, and potent. No one is worthy to discover, open, teach, confess, or read it. Yet this book of life is not in itself obscure or hidden, but it is a sevenfold light shining in the faces of men and angels. No one can open the seals save the Lamb, the Lion of the tribe of Judah. The eternal living word lies not in the power of men but of God. Otherwise men could save themselves through the Bible, the written Scripture which is called the word of God, though Paul called it the dead letter. He who has the eternal word of God in his heart needs nothing else. If we had not only the whole Bible, but also all the words delivered by the Holy Ghost through the fathers, apostles, and prophets from the beginning of the world, these could not make a new creature."

Joris himself very frequently appealed from the Creeds and the Bible to the Spirit and thereby introduced the possibility of a new intolerance such as that of the Münsterites, who grasped the sword under divine inspiration. But Joris had checks for the extravagances of the Spirit and they were derived in Erasmian fashion from the mind of Christ as well as from the prevalent teaching of the mystics that suffering is the way to God. Persecution, said Joris, " is contrary to the holy faith of Jesus Christ and to the apostolic teaching of the Holy Church, for the Holy Church is not that which persecutes but that which suffers persecution." Religious controversies were cited by Castellio to prove that the issue must be uncertain, but by Joris to demonstrate that the disputants must have a bad spirit. " Some claim," he wrote, " that Christ is a human God, others that he is a divine man; some give him two natures, some one; some believe that Christ became flesh spiritually from the Spirit; others that he received his flesh from Mary, and others hold both to be true; some believe that he ascended to heaven with the same body which he had on earth and they condemn any doubter as a heretic worthy of death, but others say that Christ rose with a glorified body. In a word they are all divided and persecute one another with bitterness. What does it all prove? Simply that they do not have the true faith and love, but a bad spirit."

Then who is a heretic? Castellio had said that according to the current definitions the heretic would be simply the one with whom we disagree. Joris undertook to define the real heretic as the one who lacks the new birth, " who is proud toward God, who for a single error in an article of belief will deprive another of his goods and honor and even his life." The objects of religious controversy were relegated by Castellio to the nonessentials, because uncertain and unimportant in comparison with a good life. Joris arrived at the same conclusion by contending that for the most part the controverted points dealt with externals, whereas the inward alone mattered. For Joris neither water baptism nor exile and martyrdom were of avail without the spirit: " One may observe Baptism and the Lord's Supper, preaching, marriage, and all the rest of the sacraments and miss the eternal truth. Why? Because the Kingdom of God does not lie in outward things." The church does not consist of wood and stone, but the Lord Almighty is their temple and the Lamb is their light. Those who serve God worthily are themselves a holy temple or house of God in the spirit according to the truth. They have no need for outward sacraments. The outward is of so little importance that it is permissible even to attend the papist churches, though we should do so only with a heavy heart, for " how shall we sing the Lord's song in a strange land? "

The inwardness of religion destroyed likewise the competence of the magistrate in matters of faith. Joris' political theory was very similar to that of Luther save for the stronger emphasis on the separation between the two kingdoms. The sphere of the magistrate is restricted by Joris much more exclusively to the external. " Wherefore," exclaimed Joris, " you noble and elect men in Christ Jesus, consider in what faith consists. If it is in earthly temporal outward things, you are right to permit the magistrate to drag men in or drive them out, but if faith consists in heavenly eternal things, then the heart cannot be forced. Let the magistrate confine himself to goods and houses and leave faith to the proper judge and to the proper time. Better to die a thousand deaths than to kill a believing Christian or a righteous soul. If it be said that only heretics are destroyed I answer that the upright have always suffered along with Christ as heretics. Leave the tares. God alone has jurisdiction in the spirit over soul and body. Men have jurisdiction only over the body, but the new-born man of God from heaven judges and knows all things and is judged of none."

Constantly Joris reverted to the theme so congenial to the mystics that suffering is a part of the purgative stage in the process of union with God. Hence the true Christian must expect to suffer, and although the deepest suffering is inward, the outward may be an aid and may definitely be expected. " No one can have a real true faith, love, and firm trust in Christ who has not suffered and died to himself." The Christian must expect to follow Christ " in his shame as well as in his glory, in his cross as well as in his exaltation, outwardly as well as inwardly, according to the flesh as well as according to the spirit."

Joris made more continuously than Castellio the point that the true Church is bound to be a persecuted Church. " The true Church kills no one, but rather suffers. The persecutors kiss costly crosses while in their hearts they affix Christ to the cross. God's chosen people will be found as roses among thorns, as sheep among wolves. There is one Church that slays without mercy or consideration of conscience, and another that is scattered to the four winds, banished, condemned, and downtrodden as most abominably heretical and unworthy to mingle with the good. Are there then none who love the Lord? Oh, yes. And who may they be? They are those who are despised and rejected, publicans, sinners, and Samaritans, who love their neighbors."

The negative mark of the Church for Joris was suffering; the positive mark was love which finds expression in meekness, gentleness, and lowliness. This spirit excludes not only persecution but even abusiveness: "Let us stop reviling the pope and the monks, and if the end cannot be attained without contention, leave it to God." What words are these from one who in his youth had had his tongue bored because of scurrility against the pope and the monks! Joris was in part reproving himself when he exclaimed: "What makes men so bitter against one another? The cause is a false heart and a proud spirit. No one ought to take offense at another, despise and judge, let alone persecute and kill in the name of Christ. I have in mind the various sects as of Cephas, Barnabas, Apollos, Paul, Peter, and James as well as the Papist, Lutheran, Zwinglian, Philipist, Calvinist, and Anabaptist, not to mention the hundreds of Catholic orders. There are diversities of gifts, but the same spirit. If anyone knows more than others he ought not to curse them. He who has the most love, grace, peace, and mercy has the best faith.

"How comely and beautiful is love! How excellent is she before God and his angels as she comes in her majesty in festive peace on the last day, as she appears more radiant than the sun! Then shall she be praised and honored above all others, for in her is the world redeemed and all men made blessed. Who understands this? Consider love, for she is known neither by angels nor devils nor men. Her children are without father and mother in the flesh, like the Son of God in eternity. They are brought forth by the living word of faith in the will of God by the Holy Spirit to his glory and to a vision of eternal truth. Be mindful of this.

"God himself is love, for love is his life, his desire, his honor and glory, a crown of exaltation and beauty from his eternal holy wisdom for a light to the angels. She is the most holy and beautiful tabernacle of God's eternal unseen being, his holy heaven, the seat or throne of the honor of his high majesty, his own glorious being and body, adored and crowned, blessed above all, triumphant in eternity.

" O how beautiful is her generation, how noble, how excellent are her children, obtained through love and affection! Her memory is imperishable, for she is known by God and by men. When she is present she attracts all loving hearts through the affectionate glow of her being, and draws them to follow her, and when she is absent men have a desire and yearning for her. In eternity is she crowned and held in honor for in the strife of the pure she has overcome. Love is among the first, yet is she the last of the three. God has made faith for a way. Hope leads through Christ to the truth, but for life the Holy Spirit has revealed love, the most beautiful and abiding being of God in eternity, for whom through the glory of his countenance all things were made, both seen and unseen, for joy and eternal happiness in heaven and peace on earth."

Joris was very far from enjoying peace on earth. Word reached him that his wife had been arrested and his daughter was left alone in a strange city. He was prompted to give himself up in the hope of saving them, but the wife through the sudden death of a magistrate obtained release and found her daughter. Under cover of a heavy fog early one morning Joris joined them.

" How long, O Lord, how long? " he must have exclaimed. Death, perpetual hiding, or exile were the only possibilities, and even exile was not available to a place which would suffer an open profession of the cult of the third David. Why not, then, go into hiding? The inward cross after all is more important than the outward. Noah hid himself in the ark, Jacob put on the clothes of Esau, the Lord told his disciples to go into the chamber and shut the door and forbade casting pearls before swine. Why not make a cloister of one's own heart, and seek to win by persuasiveness and meekness rather than by bluster and controversy? Thus persecution without and mysticism within induced Joris to abandon an open witness.

But where should he go? An inquiry revealed that Anabaptists at Basel were not molested if they kept quiet and did not disturb the peace or disseminate strange doctrines, if they attended church and conducted themselves in a Christian manner. In April of the year 1543, David Joris presented himself, accompanied by his large family and a considerable colony of followers. He announced himself as Jan van Brugge, a fugitive for the gospel. Which gospel he did not say. He was imposing of person, with sparkling eyes and a reddish beard. His deportment was grave and pleasing. Both he and his companions were dressed with taste. Basel accepted them and even conferred citizenship upon several, including Joris himself. The refugees were no doubt the more cordially received because they were not beggars but brought with them considerable household goods, beds, towels, pillows, red Catalonian blankets, elegant clothes of divers colors, feather hats and caps, caldrons, kettles, silver platters, bowls, tankards and pitchers, and some thirty or forty thousand liters of wine. And there was enough in coin to purchase no little property in Basel.

The household lived comfortably. Joris himself was occupied in turning out innumerable mystical meditations in Dutch which continued to be printed in The Netherlands. The earlier part of the day was devoted to writing and the remainder to romping hilariously with the children, visiting the somewhat scattered members of the colony, and painting the charming landscapes about Basel. Joris was reported to be fervent in prayer, unwearied in exhortation, captivating in teaching. Relations with the Baselers were on the whole friendly. Two of Joris' children married into Basel families. The Netherlanders ingratiated themselves by their generosity.

Among others Joris came to know Sébastien Castellio, who submitted to him for criticism the preface to the Latin translation of the Bible.

Then came the news of the execution of Michael Servetus. When Geneva asked the counsel of the Swiss cities, Joris undertook to compose his own reply. It was written in Dutch and in all probability never so much as reached the court. Here is a portion:

"Most noble, just, worthy gracious, dear Lords, now that I, your friend and brother in the Lord Jesus Christ, have heard what has happened to the good, worthy Servetus, how that he was delivered into your hands and power by no friendliness and love but through envy and hate, this news has so stirred me that I can have no peace until I have raised my voice as a member of the body of Christ, until I have opened my heart humbly before your highnesses and freed my conscience. I trust that the learned, perverted, carnal, and bloodthirsty may have no weight and make no impression upon you, and if they should ingratiate themselves with you as did the scribes and Pharisees with Pilate in the case of our Lord Jesus, they will displease the King of Kings and the teacher of all, namely, Christ, who taught not only in the Scripture according to the letter, but also in divine fashion, that no one should be crucified or put to death for his teaching. He himself was rather crucified and put to death. Yes, not only that, but he has severely forbidden persecution. Will it not then be a great perversion, blindness, evil, and darkness to indulge in impudent disobedience through hate and envy? They must first themselves have been deranged before they could bring a life to death, damn a soul forever, and hasten it to hell. Is that a Christian procedure or a true spirit? I say eternally no.

"Noble, wise, and prudent Lords, consider what would happen if free rein were given to our opponents to kill heretics. How many men would be left on earth if each had this power over the other, inasmuch as each considers the other a heretic? The Jews so regard the Christians, so do the Saracens and the Turks, and the Christians reciprocate. The papists and the Lutherans, the Zwinglians and the Anabaptists, the Calvinists and the Adiaphorists, mutually ban each other. Because of these differences of opinion should men hate and kill each other? . . . 'Whoso sheddeth man's blood, by man shall his blood be shed,' as Scripture says. Let us, then, not take the sword, and if anyone is of an erroneous and evil mind and understanding let us pray for him and awaken him to love, peace, and unity. . . .

" And if the aforesaid Servetus is a heretic or a sectary before God . . . we should inflict on him no harm in any of his members, but admonish him in a friendly way and at most banish him from the city, if he will not give up his obstinacy and stop disturbing the peace by his teaching . . . that he may come to a better mind and no longer molest your territory. No one should go beyond this. . . ."

The advice, of course, went unheeded, and in the meantime Joris himself was insecure even at Basel because dissension was breaking out in the colony and threatened to reach such proportions as to incur exposure.

His son-in-law, Blesdijk, became disquieted by Joris' abandonment of an open witness. Blesdijk had been intrigued by the flaming outlaw in The Netherlands, living in cellars and garrets and holds of ships and proclaiming great wonders from before the face of the Lord. Now the austere prophet had become the genial patriarch, painting pictures and romping with the children beyond the decorum befitting his age. Worst of all, the third David was basking under his vines and fig trees while his followers still confronted the Philistines in The Netherlands. Was all this in accord with the teaching of Scripture? Was Joris after all the Lord's anointed? And if he were not, had Blesdijk deceived converts? Their souls weighed heavily on his conscience. He confronted " the old gentleman " with the question of his messianic role. Joris freely conceded that he had claimed too much, and in the second edition of the *Wonder Book* he had already softened the expressions that had given offense because of personal pretensions. These admissions spelled for Blesdijk the dissolution of the sect. Other members of the colony, however, still regarded Joris as the Messiah biding his time. Neither party shared the mysticism of Joris which enabled him to spiritualize all the externals of the Great Day of the Lord. Among his following the strife was acute.

In the meantime a traveler from The Netherlands, staying at Inn of the Stork, reported that Joris was no nobleman but a heretic. The news reached the Baseler mother-in-law of Joris' son and she went straight to Frau Joris, who had been ill for some time. The shock hastened her death within a few days. Joris too was in a critical condition and outlived his wife but briefly. His last hours were filled with lamentations. " No one is true. If only the in-laws would agree . . . What wonders I have gone through this night! I have traveled through the heights of heaven and the depths of hell. The Lord strengthen you." Then the apocalyptic note returned: " The day, the day, the day will reveal all things. Every heart, every heart shall be made manifest. Oh, it is too much you do to me! It is too much."

After his death the dispute in the colony became more rife. Van Schor, who had been Joris' secretary for fifteen years, sided with Blesdijk and was banned by the rest. He left and took service with a doctor in the city, who naturally desired to know the reason for his leaving. Then Van Schor " let the bung out of the barrel," claiming that he had left because Joris had concubines. Van Schor was then asked why in that case he had stayed so long, and he replied that he had only

just found it out, which seems odd in the case of one who had
been a member of the family for fifteen years. Some thirty
years after Joris' death the story had become quite circum-
stantial that he had a bigamous wife Anna and by her two
children. Strange that in all the investigation that followed
the disclosure of the sect, none of this came to light. Anna
was, however, a real person, and is known to have married
someone else in 1548. And there is among the Joris papers a
letter to her husband saying that the father would not be
satisfied with the provision made for the children. The
father in question may be Joris. But still it remains strange
that Blesdijk, when examined, did not make this accusation
and that the story, if true, should have been so long in coming to light.

Van Schor removed the bung very completely from the
barrel by informing not only his employer but also two members of the town council, one of the ministers, and several
others. But no one was disposed to take any energetic action.
As a matter of fact, several persons in Basel had long known
or suspected the truth and refrained from troubling such excellent and generous people. The ministers called in some of
the Jorists, but could learn nothing from them, and the case
lagged from spring until fall. Then the Honorable Boniface
Amerbach, sworn advocate of the city of Basel, intervened.
An odd person was he to prosecute heresy, for he was the
executor of the estate of Erasmus, and on earlier occasions
had shielded liberals from fanatical pressures. But now he
was exercised " for the honor of Christ and for the honor of
Basel," whose reputation would suffer abroad were it indifferent to so notorious a case of heresy.

This was in November, but not until March of 1559 was
any serious action taken. Then eleven of the men in the
colony were imprisoned and their quarters searched. A chest
of papers was discovered and two portraits of Joris. The pa-

pers yielded enough to warrant the arrest of Blesdijk, who admitted that Jan van Brugge was Joris. The other suspects feigned ignorance of anything amiss. One son-in-law said that to be sure he had married Joris' daughter, for she was pretty and he was twenty-two. One of the sons pleaded ignorance and youth. He was thirty-five. The women were examined at home and all averred that they had come to Basel simply because the gospel was there better preached.

But the charge of Van Schor and Blesdijk that Joris was the outlawed Anabaptist, the third David, the head of the sect of the Davidists, was all too abundantly confirmed by the discovery of the books and papers. The university faculty were consulted as to whether Joris might be exhumed and whether relatives should be punished. The answer was that in accord with the Roman law a dead heretic should be disinterred and burned, but relatives if innocent were not to be molested. All the members of the university were required to attest their abhorrence of Joris' errors. Castellio wrote that he repudiated " the articles which are said to be excerpted from the works of David Joris."

The auto-da-fé took place on the thirteenth of May. The crowd was so huge that one would not have supposed the city could hold so many. Sébastien Castellio stood among them. A box $9' \times 5' \times 6'$ was filled with Joris' books. A pole carried his portrait. His body was removed from the coffin and affixed to a stake. " The old gentleman " was still recognizable with his red beard. On his head was a velvet bonnet trimmed in red as well as a crown of rosemary. A long toga covered his body. The flames reduced all to ashes.

The action against the Jorists was mild. They were required to make public abjuration in the cathedral of the errors of David and to subscribe to the Basel confession. The church was packed. The minister preached on the parable of the Good Shepherd, and the congregation sang the 130th

Psalm. The Jorists sank upon their knees as the absolution was pronounced and the minister extended to each the right hand of reconciliation. After the singing of the Apostles' Creed the assembly was dismissed in peace.

When one of the ministers reproached Bern for burning a heretic, the retort was, " If Basel would burn her heretics alive, she would not have the trouble of digging them up."

One can imagine Sébastien Castellio walking home on that thirteenth day of May and reflecting upon the singular demonstration of the truth of his contention that persecution can turn a heretic into a hypocrite.

Chapter Six

THE HERETIC AS EXILE:

Bernardino Ochino

A second associate of Castellio's who was significant for the problem of religious liberty was Bernardino Ochino of Siena. His life illustrates how inadequate was the counsel sometimes proffered by the liberals that banishment be substituted for death as the penalty for heresy. Joris had made this suggestion to the Genevans. In that particular instance Servetus would have been well satisfied to be released. But in cases where the fox had no hole and the bird no nest perpetual wandering could make death appear as a release. The case of Ochino was not quite so drastic because his five exiles were distributed with interludes of respite. Yet in the end protracted insecurity beclouded his spirit. He is of interest also for himself as a Franciscan, a representative of that order which in the Middle Ages was most disposed to criticize Crusades and of that branch of the order which derived the rule of Saint Francis directly from the Holy Spirit without papal mediation.

Ochino had turned the half-century mark when he first came into prominence as the general of the Capuchins, a newly founded branch of the Franciscans. The Capuchins were in the tradition of the Spirituals and the Fraticelli, the radical followers of *il Poverello,* insistent on following literally his devotion to Lady Poverty. Like him, they would beg, travel barefoot, sleep in the open or in the crudest of shelters, devote themselves to the care of the lepers, preach the gospel; denouncing vice, warning of impending doom, despising all meretricious rhetoric, yet rising to the level of poetry in lyrical rhapsodies on the wounds of Christ. Ochino had been a member of the Observant Franciscans and at first opposed the formation of the new branch lest the withdrawal of the ardent should impede the reformation of the whole. Only when disillusioned with regard to the possibility of a comprehensive reform did he join the secession. His zeal and his endowments were such that in a few years he was elected as the general of the Capuchins. This was in the year 1538, when he was fifty-one years of age.

Already he had been preaching for twenty-five years, yet only now began his phenomenal career as the Savonarola of his generation. He was the perfect exemplification of the medieval saint, austere, emaciated, frail, and venerable, with the rapt and ethereal look of a Moses descending from the Mount, the glory still haloing his countenance. With a white beard flowing over his coarse brown cowl, and his feet bare, the general tramped the thoroughfares of Italy from the foothills of the Alps to the shores of Sicily. His sermons were marked by chaste diction and vibrant emotion. There was no blatant striving for effect but the artistry of melodious words cumulating in musical crescendos. His ravishing voice and Sienese pronunciation melted his hearers. *Dolcezza* was the word that described his speech.

So great was his popularity that the pope had to regulate his engagements. Huge throngs assembled hours in advance of his coming. On one occasion he requested the sacristan not to ring the bell because he was too ill to preach. The sacristan replied that he had already done so, but in any case the bell made no difference because the church had been crowded since midnight, with some people even perched upon the roof. At Naples, the emperor Charles "particularly delighted to hear Fra Bernardino of Siena, the Capuchin who preached in the Church of San Giovanni Maggiore with such spirit and devotion as to make the stones weep." At Venice, Cardinal Bembo declared that so saintly a man he had never seen. The power of Ochino's word at Naples unloosed purses and collected five thousand scudi for

Bernardino Ochino

charity. At Perugia, a society was founded to care for orphans. At Faenza, feuding factions were reconciled. In Rome, at two o'clock in the morning, an assembly gathered including twelve purpled cardinals. When the service ended at six o'clock, the preacher was scarcely able to finish his sermon because of the tears of the audience.

The popularity of Ochino was certainly not due to flattery. At Venice, he took as his text John 8:59, " Then took they up stones to cast at him: but Jesus hid himself, and went out of the temple." " As I came into the pulpit reciting the Ave Maria I thought to myself of the meaning of this word, that Christ ' hid himself.' I reflected that he has veiled his face in order not to look upon the abominations of false Christians who fifteen days before the celebration of his Passion have not mended their ways. Your pomp and your pride have caused Christ to hide himself. Go to Rome, visit the chancery, and you will find that Christ has hidden himself and gone out of the temple. Visit the district of ill fame in this city, that veritable hell, and you will find that Christ has hidden himself and gone out of the temple. Go up and down the length of poor Italy and you will discover how many in the course of thirty or forty years have died without remorse for wars which have made widows and orphans and demolished cities. Christ has hid himself and gone out of the temple. And you, my Venice, how many preachers and not merely myself have declared in your city, not philosophy or fables, but the pure Word of God and of Christ, alive and true; how many have spoken of your salvation and of the correction of sins, and you are just the same as you were. With what truth, charity, and love, with what labor and vigils have I besought you, and without fruit. I am confident that if in Germany, if in England, yes, if among the Turks and the Jews, I had so spoken there would have been a greater response. Nevertheless I still hope to see good and sincere Christians, and I can tell you this, that if you do not mend your ways I will testify against you at the judgment, and all those on the left hand who have not had your opportunities will rise against you, but I beg you and pray you with all my heart through Christ that in these few days you prepare yourselves by discipline and penitence, by a living love and a firm resolve, no more to offend Christ. Put off the old; put on the new. If you will not be as Nineveh you will be as Sodom. Strive and labor to improve and may God inspire you."

Denunciation and exhortation were not, however, the staple of his preaching so much as the way whereby the creature might be lifted to the vision of the Creator and the Christian dissolved in adoration before the Crucified. " Let us consider the creatures," said Ochino, " how in them as in a mirror are reflected all the divine goodness, wisdom, power and beauty, love, and every perfection. And let us make of the creatures a ladder by which to ascend to the divine beauty. Behold the exquisite loveliness of flowers and fruits, rise to the contemplation of the light of the stars and the celestial bodies, look upon the beauty of the soul when clothed with virtue and adorned with spiritual gifts of light and grace, gaze with the eyes of the mind on the blessed and angelic spirits commencing with the angels, ascending to the archangels, from choir to choir up to the seraphim. And if one can glimpse the Mother of God in her beauty, this will reward every effort. Lift yourselves in loving thought, I will not say to the divinity of Christ but only to his gracious humanity, and behold his sacred wounds and his great love, for although God in creating and conserving the world has disclosed a drop of his power, goodness, justice, mercy, and wisdom, yet by joining himself to man and dwelling among us for thirty-three years in profound humility, conversing in love, teaching the way of salvation, dying for us a shameful death, behold in this not a drop merely of his goodness and mercy but an infinite sea.

" Let us, then, contemplate Christ upon the cross and put away all vanities and hold converse only with persons steeped in the divine love, whose words, when they speak of Christ, are flames of fire which deeply stir. If, then, there enter into you some harmonious sweet and gracious sound, some melodic voice or angelic song, your spirit will lift you up to contemplate the harmony of the celestial hierarchy of the three divine Persons."

Ochino was beloved and cherished by all sensitive spirits, and those who did not model their lives after his words yet loved to hang upon his lips. How much more warmly was he welcomed by the like-minded who in divers ways cultivated the interior life and sought to follow in the footsteps of the Redeemer! Such a circle gathered at Naples at the villa of a Spanish nobleman, Juàn de Valdés. Naples was at that time a Spanish dependency, and the currents which because of the political connections flowed from The Netherlands to Spain were transmitted likewise from Spain to Naples. Valdés was a disciple of Erasmus and the mystics of the North. His *One Hundred and Ten Divine Considerations* are suffused with inward piety. " Is the only difference," he demanded, " between Christians and Moors that we abstain from meat during Lent and that we observe the Sabbath and the holy days? " The monastic vow appeared to him to afford no better way to salvation than the matrimonial. Nor was dogma the distinguishing mark of the Christian for Valdés. When questions were put to him about such problems as free will and predestination, he would reply: " What is that to thee? follow thou me." He was so inebriated with the love of God that he could see no need for any propitiation of an offended deity, and explained the death of Christ as necessitated only by man's faulty notions. For since man is impeded from returning to God through the belief that the sinner cannot be received until after expiation, therefore God, to allay such fears, has made the superfluous sacrifice.

Valdés was a man of great saintliness and charm, whose villa on the island of Ischia in the Bay of Naples was frequented by choice spirits, men and women of the aristocracy.

After his death one of the circle wrote to another: " Monsignor, I confess that Florence is lovely within and without, yet the amenity of Naples, the site, the shores, the eternal spring afford a higher degree of excellence. The entrancing gardens, the laughing sea, a thousand vital spirits which well up within the heart! I well know that you have often invited me to return, but after all where should we go now that Señor Valdés is dead ? " Ochino was drawn to him, and Valdés was the occasion of his first mutation. For in the eyes of Valdés, Christianity did not consist in going barefoot or in drinking only water. Ochino, under his influence, began to preach that true religion is not exhibited in costumes but in customs, not in clipping one's hair but in pruning one's vices, not in prayer with the lips but with the heart, not in obedience to men but to God.

Inevitably a doubt arose in the mind of Ochino as to whether his own literal imitation of the poverty and garb of Saint Francis was after all a genuine following of Christ. And at that moment Protestant works were infiltrating into Italy under pseudonyms. Calvin, for example, was Alcuino. Ochino was given a dispensation by the pope to read and refute such works, a perilous permission because Valdés had not imbued his disciple with that mysticism which could cultivate the interior life within any framework. Ochino, grown dubious as to the pattern of his own behavior, was not so disillusioned as to question the possibility of discovering the correct *imitatio Christi*. The problem was to answer the question, " What doth the Lord require of thee ? " Perhaps Luther, perhaps Calvin, had the answer. Ochino began to relax the rigor of his Franciscan devotions. In his sermons he was noted to be speaking always of Christ and no longer of San Geminiano. In private he was disseminating Lutheran tracts.

Why, then, did he not come out with an open profession

of Lutheranism? Cowardice is not the answer so much as a mingling of uncertainty and hope. He was not yet fully sure of himself, and he entertained the dream that all Italy might be converted to the Reform and a reconciliation effected between Rome and Wittenberg. The very same motive that induced him to remain for some time with the Observants before going over to the Capuchins impelled him to wait in this instance, and his hopes were not entirely fatuous. There was a very imposing body of Catholic liberals who envisaged drastic reform and were willing to make overtures to the Protestants. Cardinal Contarini was the leader of this party. He would subscribe even to justification by faith. His standing was such that in 1541 he was sent as a representative from Rome to the Council of Regensburg, the last occasion when Catholics and Protestants met together in the hope of accord. Calvin was present. But the hope of any mediation collapsed. Contarini returned to Italy, broken in spirit and in body. In 1542 the Roman Inquisition was established and in 1545 the Council of Trent began.

At this juncture a preacher was imprisoned at Venice simply for having expounded Saint Augustine's doctrine of grace. Ochino could not contain himself and broke into an apostrophe: " O Venice, thou queen of the sea! If thus thou dost cast into prison those who declare unto thee the truth, what place is there left for the truth? " The papal nuncio thereupon suspended Ochino from preaching and shortly thereafter he received a summons to Rome. A few years before he might have supposed that he was being invited to the purple. Now he had reason to surmise the stake. He started with foreboding to Rome, and passing through Bologna called upon the dying Cardinal Contarini. Ochino claimed that the cardinal had counseled flight. The accuracy of this assertion has been contested, but whatever the cardinal said, there can be no question that his death marked the end

of the liberal era in Italy. Thereafter the choice for many
of the Reformers lay between making a cloister of their own
hearts after the manner of Joris, or of going to the stake or
into exile like Calvin and Castellio from France. Highly distraught, Ochino continued to Florence, where he fell in with
a fellow friar already resolved on flight. This example was
decisive. Ochino reversed his direction.

From the heights of the Alps he looked back upon his native land, where he had labored for more than half a century. He was fifty-six. Behind him lay the sunlight playing
upon the Bay of Naples, the silhouette of Siena against an
evening sky, daybreak over Fiesole, conversations on heavenly themes with distinguished men and aristocratic women,
churches packed and throngs in tears, the pope, the emperor,
and a dozen cardinals hanging upon his words — all this behind. Before him lay bleaker lands and unknown tongues,
struggling refugee congregations, and all the insecurity of
religious revolution. Never again could he experience the in-
toxication of swaying multitudes.

In 1542 he arrived in Geneva, where he was to be harbored
for the next three years. Calvin was charmed with the venerable exile, and all the Reformers rejoiced in the acquisition
of a celebrity so renowned. The Council at Geneva assigned
to him the Church of the Italian Refugees. Ochino was
equally charmed with Geneva. Here he discovered the pattern of Christian perfection missed by the Capuchins. The
Protestants had abandoned monasticism in order to make
every Christian a monk in disciplined deportment. Geneva
was characterized by preaching of the pure word of God
from the sacred Scriptures, daily prayers, public and private;
instruction for old and young in the catechism; strict repres-
sion of sexual irregularities; prohibition of gambling; such
charity as to eliminate the need for begging; no criminal
prosecutions because no homicides. Here all superstition had

been eradicated. In the churches there were no organs, no candles, no relics. Every trace of idolatry had been purged.

Even the doctrine of Geneva, Ochino found himself able to endorse. The Franciscans had so emphasized the wounds of Christ that to attribute all man's salvation to his suffering and nothing to human merit was not too far a step. In that case predestination naturally followed. To a Franciscan, believing in the possibility of the vision of God while on earth, Calvin's view that God may be both known and believed at the same time was not difficult. Hence faith could be equated with certitude. Ochino testified to the reality of his conversion by emitting a blast against Antichrist, the tone of which may be inferred from the cartoon (page 165) on the title page of the Spanish translation. On the more positive side he averred that there is no need to make a pilgrimage to Rome or Compostela, but only through faith to come to God, and there is no purgatory other than Christ crucified.

In every respect Ochino appeared to be a thorough Calvinist. Yet Calvin mistrusted him. A long examination on the score of doctrine disclosed no deficiency. But when the proposal was made that the sermons of Ochino should be translated, Calvin was of the opinion that they would be more useful if left in the original. Precisely where the difference lay is not too clear, though Calvin may well have had his reservations with regard to Ochino's lyrical exuberance. The chief divergence is probably to be sought in Ochino's view of the operation of the Spirit. Calvin held, of course, that the Scripture must be corroborated and appropriated through the Spirit, but Ochino spoke of the Spirit as if it might be independent of Scripture. He claimed that his flight from Italy had been due to " the counsel of God and the direction of the Holy Spirit." Such an expression savored all too much of Thomas Müntzer and the Münsterites. Calvin did not feel altogether easy.

But no avowed breach was responsible for Ochino's departure from Geneva. The reason appears, as initially in the case of Castellio, to have been financial. Ochino got married. He explained his course in accord with the usual Protestant claim that marriage is a remedy for sin, which sounds fantastic in the mouth of one who had been chaste until nearly sixty. The real reason was that any convert from the Catholic clergy or monastic orders was almost constrained to marry as a demonstration of sincerity. Ochino's wife was a refugee from Lucca who had heard him preach at home in the meteoric days. Financial stringency was increased by the arrival of a daughter. Presumably because Geneva could not support his household, Ochino left for Augsburg in Germany.

On the way he spent some time in Basel and there formed a friendship with Sébastien Castellio.

Augsburg in 1545 received the penniless pilgrims and private benefaction tided over the emergency until the town council assigned to Ochino the Church of St. Ann. Here he resumed in a limited way his dazzling eloquence, preaching in Italian to a congregation of two hundred Germans, who understood him because they were of the great banking houses of Welser and Fugger and had served several years of apprenticeship in the branch offices at Venice. To have now the Savonarola of his time as their private chaplain was a source of gratification. Ochino became the lion of the aristocracy. He was consulted on questions of state and employed to decipher intercepted papal letters.

The religious situation in Augsburg acquainted Ochino for the first time with a pattern of diversity in a single community. The Catholic monastic orders still retained a foothold and the great banking magnates were not eager for a break with Rome drastic enough to imperil financial collaboration. The Lutherans were dominant and the Zwinglians also were represented. More significant for Ochino's de-

velopment was the presence of a fourth group representing
an element in Protestantism still further to the left, namely,
the Schwenckfelders. They took their name from a Silesian
nobleman of courtly manners and Christian demeanor who
spent his life traveling about Germany in the interests of
pietism, within whatever Church it might be. He had even
Catholic adherents. His ideal was to leaven all lumps rather
than to form a new lump. But, being cast out, he came to be
the founder of a sect. With Ochino he exchanged tracts.
They had in common a fear of that learning which quenches
the spirit, a distrust of externalism, and an openness to lead-
ings of the Spirit, together with an urge to revive the apostolic pattern of Christianity. Schwenckfeld complained of
the externalism and the intolerance of the established forms
of Protestantism. Ochino began therefore to wonder whether
Calvinism after all represented the perfect school of Christ
and the apostles.

Then came war. The emperor Charles V, after having
been impeded by conflicts with the French, the Turks, and
the pope from taking action against Luther and the Protestants, at length in the very year of Luther's death, 1546,
found his hands free. The emperor came to Regensburg and
there waited for his Italian and Spanish troops to assemble. The Protestants sprang to arms under a general famed
in the Turkish war, Sebastian Schertlin von Burtembach.
Within eight days 12,000 men were gathered under his ban-
ners. He wished to strike at once, but the Protestant Con-
federation objected to his various proposals lest they provoke
new enemies. The emperor was left to assemble 34,000 foot
and 5,000 horse. Schertlin had in the meantime brought together 35,000 foot and 6,000 horse, but his advantage was
wasted by delay. His forces began to dissolve and the Protestant cities started to make peace separately.

Augsburg prepared for a siege. Ochino justified resistance

along the lines already laid down by Luther, that a lower magistrate may resist a higher. Augsburg manned its defenses and all the people prayed. The Schwenckfelders prayed for the Lutherans. One wonders whether the Lutherans prayed for the Schwenckfelders. But defense proved hopeless. The emperor demanded as the price of milder terms that the city deliver up the general, Sebastian Schertlin von Burtembach, and the preacher in whose words at Naples he had so delighted, Bernardino Ochino of Siena. The Protestant notables and the Catholic magnates tried to purchase his safety, but the emperor was adamant. The city gave the two a chance to escape. Schertlin with thirty horse rode out to Constance. Ochino, leaving behind for the time being wife and child, followed upon his heels. Once more he was an exile.

Basel afforded again a temporary shelter. There was another occasion to talk with Sébastien Castellio. Then came an invitation to go to England. The bill of the English agent in charge of the passage is extant, allowing a pair of hose for Ochino and a nightcap of velvet, garters of silk ribbon, a supper and breakfast in London, and freight for shipping books. The total for Ochino, a friend, and servants was £126 7s. 6d., with a request for more to bring over his wife.

England at the moment of Ochino's arrival was more Protestant than at any other time during the sixteenth century. The king was the boy Edward VI, to whom Castellio had dedicated the preface of his Bible. The real ruler was the boy's uncle, the Duke of Somerset. At no time in that century was England less subject to foreign interference or more open to foreign influence. The refugees for religion were numerous and from many lands — Germany, Spain, Poland, France, Holland, Italy, and Scotland. The German congregation in London numbered 5,000; Lutheran, Zwinglian, and Calvinist influences alike were felt;

and Archbishop Cranmer entertained dreams of an ecumenical Protestantism to be achieved by summoning to London an evangelical counterpart to the Council of Trent. Melanchthon, Bullinger (Zwingli's successor), and Calvin were urged to come.

In such circles Ochino was warmly received. He was made a prebendary of Canterbury for life, without obligation of residence and with an additional stipend from the king. He began preaching again to the Italian colony in London. The imperial ambassador informed Charles V that Ochino's eloquence had deserted him now that he had become a heretic and that soon he would have no adherents save the Duchess of Suffolk and the Marquis of Northampton. The duchess, by the way, an ardent Protestant, was the daughter of a Spanish lady in waiting to Catherine of Aragon. The marquis was the brother of Catherine Parr, the widow of Henry VIII. But these were by no means the only adherents. Ochino was again the lion of the aristocracy. One of his works was translated into English by Ann Cooke, the mother of Francis Bacon. It bore the title: " *Certayne sermons of the ryghte famous and excellente clerk master Barardine Ochine, borne within the famous universitie of Siena in Italy, now also an exyle in thys lyfe, for the faithful testimony of Iesus Christe. Faythfully translated into Englyshe.* . . . Imprinted at London by John Day: dwelling over Aldersgate beneth S. Martins. These books are to be sold at hys shop in Chepesyde, by the Little Loundnit at the sygne of the Resurrection." Another who turned Ochino from Italian into Latin was the Princess Elizabeth. In long discussions over predestination Ochino came to admire her subtle intellect. In after years when the Puritans feared she would suffer in the churches the relics of the Amorites a plea was sent to Ochino, then in Zurich, to remonstrate, since his influence with her was great.

The situation in England confronted Ochino with something new. At Geneva he had seen a Church State, a holy commonwealth, a select community based upon the Word of God. At Augsburg he had witnessed four religions side by side with a moderate Lutheranism in the ascendant. In England he was to watch the birth pangs of a national Church. The prevailing theory was Erastian, that the State might determine the form of religion. The Reformers did not perceive into what dilemmas they would be thrown if the State should return to Rome, nor did Ochino foresee the peril. Without reserve he set himself to the service of the Reform and composed a work which curiously survives only in English and Polish translations. The English bore the title *A Tragedy or Dialogue of the Unjust Usurped Primacy of the Bishop of Rome, and of All the Just Abolishing of the Same, Made by Master Barnardine Ochino, an Italian, and Translated Out of Latin Into English by Master John Ponet, Doctor of Divinity. Never Printed Before in Any Language. Anno Do. 1549.* The work began with a passage that may have provided the model for the opening of *Paradise Lost.* Lucifer and Beelzebub were in conference as to how to regain that shred of dominion left them by the Fall but utterly lost through the redeeming work of the Son of God. They hit upon the " witty invention " of elevating the bishop of Rome into the pope, that Christ might be undone by his own vicar. The realization of this plan through the theocracy of the late Middle Ages was of course recounted. The whole point was, however, that Antichrist was now being overthrown and Christ's Kingdom restored through the reformation commenced by Henry VIII and in process of glorious completion by his son, Edward VI. The question of course then arose as to the means by which the work should be achieved. The very concept of a national Church predicates the assistance of the civil arm, yet the protector Somerset would not go to extremes. There were no executions for heresy under his regency. He has been described as " one of the most obstinate optimists in English history who believed he could almost dispense with the ax and the gallows." Ochino highly approved of so tolerant a policy, and placed in the mouth of young Edward the words: " If we mind to overcome Antichrist in short space we must first go about to drive him off the hearts of men; for as soon as he hath once lost his spiritual kingdom in men's consciences, he shall forgo by and by all the rest of his jurisdiction without any great difficulty. But to drive him out of the hearts of men, it is not needful to use sword or violence. The sword of the Spirit, that is, the Word of God, is sufficient, whereby Christ overcame and conquered his enemy Satan in the desert."

But the protector Somerset did not last long, nor did his successor, because the boy king Edward sickened and died. He was followed by his half sister, the Princess Mary, the daughter of Catherine of Aragon. Then England by the crown was taken back to Rome. The leaders of the English Church went to the stake; the foreigners were suffered to depart. Ochino was again an exile. He arrived at Geneva on October 27, 1553, the day of the execution of Michael Servetus. Ochino protested. Calvin was displeased.

While seeking relocation, Ochino had twice previously found a temporary abode in Basel. For the third time it was true, and for the third time association was renewed with Sébastien Castellio. Ochino was with him in the very year when he brought out the treatise *Concerning Heretics*. But Ochino was busying himself with something else. He was of one mind with Erasmus that satire is a more Christian and more effective weapon than the sword, and for that reason he brought out in Basel a collection of anecdotes designed to ridicule many of the beliefs and practices of the Church of Rome. Here are a few examples:

Two Roman nobles were accused of rejecting prayers to

the saints. The first justified himself on the ground that one should pray only to Christ. He was sent to the stake. The second justified himself on the ground that one should address oneself only to the pope. He was made a bishop.

A village priest once addressed a petition to the cardinals in the form of a litany. They told him to speak distinctly and respectfully. He answered that he was only speaking to them as they spoke to God.

A Roman was asked why Rome is considered the holiest city. " You would admit," he explained, " that the richest city is the one that draws all riches from others to itself. So Rome is the holiest because she deprives all others of holiness."

The pope was asked why he had appointed only one man to three bishoprics. " So that only one will be damned," he retorted.

A converted Jew continued to keep his accounts with

A Cartoon: Ochino's " Image of Antichrist," the Pope, Receiving His Commission from Satan

Christians in Hebrew. When they objected to the use of an unknown tongue, he answered that if he had to trust them to pray for him in Latin, they would have to trust him to keep accounts with them in Hebrew.

A friar declaiming against those who ate meat in Lent pointed out that for having eaten meat on Friday Christ was crucified and the disciples persecuted. If God did that to his own Son, what will he not do to you?

Such persiflage was more diverting than lucrative, and Ochino was relieved when an invitation came to become the pastor of a congregation of Italian refugees in Zurich. The situation there was very tense. These refugees consisted of ninety-three heads of families, and their dependents, who had migrated from the Italian-speaking city of Locarno in southern Switzerland. They had adopted the reform after the decree of Kappel in 1531, which forbade Protestant minorities in Catholic cantons. The entire Swiss Diet was now called upon to enforce the terms and penalize the converts. Zurich absolutely refused. The other evangelical cantons were willing to concur in banishment, lest otherwise the Catholics might inflict the death penalty. Zurich was adamant. The outcome was banishment, and the emigrees then presented themselves at the gates of that city which had so stoutly championed their right to espouse the true faith. Zurich took them in. She was well aware of the risk, but manned her walls and at the same time trod softly to avoid needless provocation. She was soon to discover that to save a lamb from the lion may be easier than to live with him afterward. The Italians were too prolific and too enterprising. They bought grain on the Zurich market, disposed of it at a profit in Italy, used the proceeds to purchase trinkets in Italy, and then sold them at a price undercutting the rate in Zurich. Local merchants were irate. The town council therefore parceled the Italians out among the guilds and con-

ceded to them a church with services in their own tongue
only until such time as they could learn the Zurich dialect.
Ochino was called to be the pastor of this group.

The situation was quite unprecedented for him. He had
been previously the lion of the aristocracy and now he was
the spokesman of unwelcome guests in an atmosphere where
an indiscretion might provoke an open war within the confederacy. For that reason all the ministers in Zurich were
required to act in unison. Such submission to regulation was
difficult for Ochino. He was a prima donna, an incorrigible
individualist, who had just been diverting himself by ribbing
the papacy. Installed in Zurich, he embarked upon a series
of publications, some of them presumably composed earlier,
at any rate quite oblivious of the existing tensions. The first
was a tract on purgatory, in which an interlocutor inquired
why, if the pope were able to release souls from purgatory,
he did not empty the place. The answer was that some eggs
had to be left in the nest. The tract appeared in Italian, Latin,
and German. To the town council these gibes at the pope at
such a juncture appeared irresponsible. Ochino believed that
Antichrist should be resisted only with the pen. The Zurich
fathers were ready in an extremity to resist with the sword,
but they were not minded to have the extremity precipitated
by the pen, and they pointed out to Ochino that his tract
would incense the Catholic confederates. All copies were
called in.

Ochino mended his ways, and sought to do a service to
the Zurichers by defending their view of the Lord's Supper
against a rabid Lutheran, who held that the body of Christ
in the elements is eaten with the teeth even by unbelievers.
Ochino not only refuted this view, but in so doing pointed
out that Luther advanced in many respects from one position
to another and very probably would have arrived at Zwingli's view of the Lord's Supper if Zwingli had not done so first.

This thrust so angered one of the Lutheran princes that he canceled his contribution to the support of Ochino's congregation.

Colleagues were of the opinion that Bernardino had not treated the subject with proper dignity. He tried again, and this time, to relieve Zurich of any responsibility, published his book at Basel. He dealt once more with the sacramentarian controversy, and this time relegated the whole dispute to the area of nonessentials, because " the penitent thief was saved without having taken Communion, without having thought about the Lord's Supper, without ever having considered whether the body of Christ was or was not in the bread, and his blood in the wine. The one thing needful is to believe with a warm faith and in spirit to taste and feel that Jesus is Christ the Son of God, who out of the highest love died for us. God is everywhere but his presence is of no avail if we be not enamored of him. And what good is the presence of the body of Christ unless we feel it in faith which is not attached to places? "

The relegation of the Lord's Supper to the adiaphora was pleasing to no party, and even less were the Swiss pleased by the next tract emanating from Basel, on the problem of predestination. The treatment is suggested by the title, *Labyrinth,* and from the dedication to Queen Elizabeth, who herself was fond of saying that grace may be resisted when it is not irresistible. Ochino set forth four dilemmas involved in predestination and four in free will, and then extricated himself from the first four and then from the second four, and ended just where he began. The difficulties of course with predestination lie in the realm of morals and the difficulties for free will in the area of theology. If man's destiny and, to some extent at least, his behavior are determined in advance, what meaning can there be in morality, but if he is a genuinely free agent, how can God foresee and control the course of events? Ochino made use of the classical explanations that foreordination applies, not to conduct, but to salvation. The point is not that man cannot do this or that, but rather that nothing he does will alter his destiny. The whole discussion was marked by ingenuity and ended again with the theology of the penitent thief, " who was saved without the least thought as to the freedom or the servitude of his will. If it were necessary to believe in freedom, Augustine would be damned, and if in predestination, then Chrysostom would be a heretic. The safest way in view of such doubt is to strive for the good as if we were free and give all the glory to God as if we were not. God has placed us before Christ the crucified, the heavenly bread of life, and the sweet truth of the gospel, with all its riches and benefits. There is no need for us to inquire how these gifts are bestowed. Enough that we thank God and use them well, giving unto him all glory and honor through Jesus Christ our Saviour."

This book too was published in Basel.

Then came a volume of sermons that declared that all Protestants agreed in regarding " the doctrine of the papists as pestiferous. If one looks at the Reformed Churches in Germany, Switzerland, France, and elsewhere, one observes that some call themselves Zwinglians, some Lutherans, and some Anabaptists and some Libertine, and so on. Between them are great dissensions, with discord, detraction, infamy, and calumny, hate, persecution, and innumerable ills, for each Church holds the other as heretical. One can only infer that they do not have the true gospel, because Paul said that God is not a God of division but of peace. These dissensions show that they are anti-Christian and diabolical, for Christ prayed that his disciples might be one. It may be replied that there is agreement as to the essentials, but Paul required of the Philippians that they be of the same mind and love toward each other. These Churches cannot be truly evangelical because the Evangel bears fruit in love."

A committee of the Zurich ministers waited upon Ochino and remonstrated with him for eluding the Zurich censors by publishing at Basel. He should print no more books unless approved by their deputies.

In the year 1563 merchants from various parts gathered at Basel in the Inn of the Ox and began to discuss the religious situation. " The Nürnbergers," said one, " allow everyone to keep his own faith."

" That's because they don't know where they are," said another.

" But at Zurich," charged a nobleman from Baden, " there are most heretical sects."

A Zuricher sprang to the defense and demanded evidence.

" A book," replied the German, " has just been published here in Basel by Bernardino Ochino, who lives in Zurich. It contains most offensive and unchristian things, including a defense of polygamy."

" I am bound in honor," said the Zuricher, " to report that to my lords."

" If you don't believe me," said the German, " I can take you to the printer's. The book is in Latin. Six hundred copies were struck off and a number have gone to Wittenberg. The Basel authorities on learning of it stopped the sale until further notice."

The book was indeed by Bernardino Ochino. It had been translated into Latin by Sébastien Castellio and bore the title *Thirty Dialogues,* and there was one on polygamy. Into the mouth of one of his interlocutors Ochino had placed a defense of polygamy drawn from a German tract originally composed to justify the bigamy of Philip of Hesse. Ochino himself undertook to refute the arguments and did so well enough until he came to the very end, where the conclusion was that polygamy should not be allowed unless in response to a special revelation from God. This was the device commonly used to exculpate the patriarchs in the Old Testament, and would have been innocuous if Ochino himself had not on occasion pretended to divine inspiration. The whole question was rendered the more dubious because this dialogue was dedicated to the king of Poland, who at the moment was in the predicament of Henry VIII of having had no issue, in this instance by his deceased wife's sister. Annulment might have been granted by the pope if not impeded by the house of Hapsburg. Ochino seemed to be hinting at bigamy as the solution.

Other passages also were offensive. There was one on the subject of religious liberty. Ochino, like Castellio, distinguished nonessentials from essentials. No one, he said, should be punished for an error in the nonessentials, and if the Apostles' Creed contains the essentials, then all those who have been punished for heresy in the last forty years have suffered needlessly. But even in the case of the essentials there is the further qualification that the offender must recognize the article in question to be essential. For that reason a denial of the Trinity should not be punished unless the heretic himself first grants the belief to be indispensable. In any case the penalty should not exceed avoidance, for heretics should be corrected by modesty, charity, and long-suffering.

Ochino was more discerning than any of his contemporaries with regard to the problem of conscience. The persecutors contended that no conscience has any right save a right conscience. Castellio retorted that sincere conviction is to be respected. " But what " — the pope is made to ask in Ochino's dialogue — " what of a conscientious tyrannicide ? " There were such in the sixteenth century on both sides of the wars of religion in France and Holland. These men were conscientious and quite ready to die for their convictions provided they could first kill. Could the State respect conscience in such a case? Ochino did not answer the question. His distinction is first to have raised a problem when others did not sense its existence.

Another ground of offense in his book was a disapproval of armed resistance on the part of the Protestants in France. The gleeful announcement is made by one of his characters that the papists had been beaten in France. " And do you rejoice at that? " is the response. " Christians without a special command from God should not fight. I rejoice more to hear that one martyr has been constant in the flames than that the papists have been killed."

Even more galling were direct strictures on the Reformed Churches. " They have rejected prayers for the dead," said Ochino, " and do not pray for the living. Saints' days and Lent have been abolished and now all days are profane. Images have been smashed, but God is not worshiped. The kingdom of Antichrist is overthrown, but the Kingdom of Christ has not been established."

The ministers and the council at Zurich, having examined the book, decreed that Ochino should be banished because he had disregarded the Zurich censorship. He should have three weeks in which to leave. Ochino admitted that he had received a remonstrance from the ministers, but when they said that his books should have the approval of the censor he supposed that the Basel censor would suffice. As a matter of fact, the Italian manuscript of his book had received a cursory examination by the censor of Basel, but the Latin, due to an oversight, had gone to the press without scrutiny. For this, of course, Ochino was not responsible. He added that in any case he regarded the counsel of the ministers as advice and not as law, and wondered whether Zurich had a pope of her own. His remonstrances were unavailing. He was told that appeal to conscience is the cloak of hypocrisy and conscience has no validity unless grounded in the written Word of God.

Nothing was said about the local circumstances, but the surmise is difficult to stifle that the desire of the Zurichers to dissolve the Italian congregation was one of the reasons for hastening the departure of their minister. His request to be allowed at least to wait until spring was not granted. Ochino left with recriminations, not all of them entirely fair.

In the month of December of the year 1563, Bernardino Ochino, at the age of seventy-six, took to the road with four little children. His wife was already dead. The oldest daughter, born while the parents were at Geneva, had stayed and married there. The son born in England was fourteen. The other three were younger, though precisely of what age we do not know. The ministers of Basel would have harbored them for the winter, but the magistrates refused. Ochino was allowed only to pass through. There he was able to take a last leave of Sébastien Castellio, who would have been brought to trial for having translated his book had not death released him from the proceedings.

Ochino started out for Poland. Already there were many Italians in the land because the queen, Bona Sforza, was Italian. The religious situation was more diversified than anywhere in Ochino's previous migrations, including even Augsburg. The king of Poland was Catholic, though flirting with the idea of espousing the Reform. The varieties of the Reform were many. The Germans had introduced Lutheranism. Visitors from Switzerland and France and the many Polish students who had attended the universities of Basel, Zurich, and Geneva, brought back Calvinism. In this Slavic land the Czechs were readily at home and brought with them Husitism. The Italian exiles, when they forsook Rome, found no resting place in any of the varieties of the Reform, and moved in the direction of Anti-Trinitarianism soon to take shape in the Socinian movement. Such extensive diversity was possible because the crown was weak and the feudal nobles, when so inclined, were in a position to offer an asylum to those whom all others regarded as heretics. Poland was the country on which all of the expellees of Europe converged.

Ochino became once more the idol of the aristocracy. The leaders of the Reformed movement vied for his pen. Earlier works were adapted to the Polish situation. *A Tragedy or Dialogue of the Unjust Usurped Primacy of the Bishop of Rome,* which had been rendered into English by Bishop Ponet, was turned into Polish, with the elimination of course of all reference to Henry VIII, Edward VI, and a substitution of discreet hints to King Sigismund Augustus to take over their role. The circumstances of the appearance of this work symbolized the international character of the Polish Reformation. The book was written by an Italian, had previously appeared in English, was now translated by a Pole, subsidized by a German, printed by a Bohemian, and dedicated to a Lithuanian.

The one party in Poland with which Ochino had had no previous acquaintance, save for isolated individuals like Servetus, was the Anti-Trinitarian. The claim was made by contemporaries that Ochino gave to this group his adherence. Nothing in his printed works substantiates the claim, but there was one point at which he did contribute to the theology of the Socinians. It was not with regard to the Trinity but rather concerning the atonement. Nor was he in this respect original. Rather, he was the transmitter of the views of Juàn de Valdés. Like his master, Ochino said that God does not need to be propitiated because he is not angry. Wrath comports neither with his impassibility nor with his love. If the death of Christ had any expiatory value, it was only because God so chose to regard it. The real purpose of the death of Christ was not to change God but to change us.

One notes of course here also echoes of the Scotist view that God might equally well have chosen any other way of saving men. Thus the lines from Scotus and Valdés ran through Ochino to the Racovian catechism of the Socinians.

His period of influence in Poland was speedily cut short. The king was alarmed by the heresies abroad in the land and thought to banish the anti-Trinitarians. His Catholic advisers pointed out that to do so would be to tolerate other varieties of Protestantism. By this time the king had recoiled from any attachment to the Reform, but feared to banish all the Protestants lest an upheaval should be created. The decision was to expel all foreign non-Catholics. The Bohemians, however, were specifically excepted, and the German Lutherans were unaffected because already naturalized Polish citizens. A nobleman of the country sought to provide this way of escape for Ochino by conferring upon him a tract of land and thus making him eligible for citizenship. But Ochino declined to avail himself of the subterfuge, and again with his children took to the road.

On the way the plague overtook them. Two sons and one daughter died. The old man, with the one remaining child, set out for Moravia to find a refuge with a fellow Italian, an Anabaptist, a member of the Hutterian colony. Under the patronage of liberal nobles the Anabaptist communities in Moravia had come to number three thousand. There were Germans, Hungarians, Poles, and not a few Italians. Colonies were restricted to about one hundred and fifty. The religious communism of these groups more nearly resembled the voluntary poverty of Saint Francis than the attempts of modern Communism to raise the standard of living. The fundamental conception of these brethren was the aim to restore primitive Christianity with ascetic living, repudiation of the oath and of war, abstention from all force in religion, and dedication to the way of suffering. Ochino, who began as a spiritual Franciscan, ended in strong sympathy with the Anabaptists.

Would he have been disillusioned with regard to them also? Would he have once more repeated his judgment on the Reformed Churches that the wings of Antichrist are everywhere? We do not know. Had he lived, he would not have stayed. An invitation came from Johann Zapolya, the king of Transylvania, to come to his country, where under the suzerainty of the Turks religious liberty prevailed among Christians. Ochino with his child would once more have taken to the road had he not been intercepted by that last great migration of which Saint Francis sang:

" Be praised, O Lord, for Sister Death
Which none escapes who draweth breath.
Blessed to die in Thy holy will;
Then the second death can do no ill."

THE FREEDOM OF THE INDIVIDUAL
IN THE SEVENTEENTH CENTURY

Chapter Seven

THE BARD OF SPEECH UNBOUND:

John Milton

The survey thus far presented of the toleration controversy as precipitated by the execution of Servetus and as waged by Calvin and Beza on the one side and by Castellio, Joris, and Ochino on the other must have left the impression of liberty in rout. So indeed it was in so far as liberty of the person was concerned. But great gains had nevertheless been made during the course of the century, not so much for individuals as for confessional groups, and individuals at the same time benefited because the penalties for heresy had been mitigated. As the sixteenth century advanced, dissenting religious bodies increasingly attained at least a restricted toleration. First were the Zwinglians, who by the peace of Kappel in 1531 obtained a recognized position and were to be unmolested in those areas where already established. In similar fashion Lutheranism acquired an assured territorial status by the Peace of Augsburg in 1555. Calvinism, apart from Geneva, first obtained toleration in the United Provinces of The Netherlands by the Pacification of Ghent in 1576, later in France by the Edict of Nantes in 1598. Anglicanism became under Elizabeth the partner of the State. Thus four varieties of Protestantism were both

John Milton

recognized and established: the Zwinglian, Lutheran, Calvinist, and Anglican. And although no individual could lay claim to any rights apart from the group to which he belonged, yet the lot of the private dissenter was ameliorated in that the death penalty fell into abeyance even when not formally abrogated. The last execution in Holland took place in 1597. In England there were but two instances of death for heresy after 1600. And on the Continent in general the seventeenth century was to be marked rather by banishments and imprisonments than by death.

This century was to make still further gains in the direction of freedom for the individual, and no country contributed more at this point than England. The reasons were several. England was more favorably situated to make experiments in liberty than was any Continental country at that time, because England enjoyed an island isolation and had therefore less reason to fear that weakening through internal dissension might invite foreign intervention. At all times this was true in a measure, but peculiarly in the seventeenth century, because the power of Spain had been broken when the galleons of the Armada skulked to their base. On the outbreak of the Thirty Years' War in 1618, the great Continental powers were involved in an all-engaging conflict with each other, from which the English with discretion were able, and for the most part did, remain aloof. Thus the English were at liberty to make a venture toward freedom.

Furthermore England was consolidated, and not like the Germany of Luther's day when religious ferment might engender social anarchy. England under the Tudors had experienced a century of centralized government. Feudal anarchy had been overcome. The task had been in fact so well achieved that now Englishmen had become restive under restraints and were for throwing off controls, both economic and political. When the Stuarts attempted to continue the pattern of the Tudors, there were cries of innovation and tyranny. The monarchs rightly retorted that the innovation lay rather on the other side, and for historical precedent the champions of the rights of Englishmen had to construct the myth of Saxon freedom and make of Magna Charta a manifesto of personal liberties. The arguments are of less interest, however, than the situation, where a struggle for civil liberties and democratic controls provided the milieu in which religious liberty could and can best arise and flourish.

The possibility of achieving some understanding in mutual toleration in the field of religion was facilitated in England because the conflict lay between less implacable opponents than on the Continent inasmuch as England was wholly Protestant. The strife was between the varieties of Protestantism, and, bitter as this might be, there were not the long-accumulated grievances that the Middle Ages had piled up against the Church of Rome, nor were the Protestants disposed to hurl at each other all the imagery of Antichrist and the whore of the Apocalypse.

Again, the controversy was not doctrinal because in the area of doctrine the Anglican Church was latitudinarian. Some lessons had been learned from the previous struggles and already it was apparent that force could not deprive men of their convictions. The distinction made by Castellio and many other liberals between the essentials and the nonessentials for liberty had been appropriated by the Anglican divines, who were prepared to concede toleration as to the essentials over which men would be damned if they believed incorrectly. This, of course, is not to say that there were no doctrinal demands. The Thirty-nine Articles were employed as a test, yet they were ambiguously couched and mildly enforced. Queen Elizabeth was no bigot. Her desire was to minimize dissent. Her successor, James I, averred that " no religion or heresy was ever extirpated by violence or the

sword, nor have I ever judged it a way of planting truth."
And Archbishop Laud, who so largely determined the policy
of Charles I, could discover in Scripture only one doctrinal
requirement, namely, the belief that " God . . . is, and that
he is a rewarder of them that . . . seek him " (Heb. 11:6).
The line, he held, should not be drawn so narrowly as to shut
even the meanest Christian out of heaven.

The controversy centered rather on points that admittedly
were not essential for salvation. They had to do with the externals of the Church, with polity and liturgy. The main
reason for this was a political union of two countries with
different Established Churches. Under James I, England and
Scotland came together, and in England the State Church
was the Anglican and in Scotland the Presbyterian. There

A Cartoon: Puritans Demolishing Crosses on Canterbury Cathedral

might have been no problem at all if each had been satisfied with a territorial solution whereby Presbyterianism should remain the Church of Scotland and Episcopalianism the Church of England. But the idea was not yet extinct that, in the interests of national unity and civil peace, one country must have one religion. Presbyterianism therefore aspired to be the religion of England and Anglicanism endeavored to enforce itself upon Scotland. The debate became warm as to the relative merits, the divine ordination, and the Scriptural warrant of prelacy, prayer books, and vestments.

The matter was further complicated by the proliferation of Protestantism into a multitude of sects. The pattern that Germany had exhibited a century earlier was, by a fortunate time lag, postponed in England until it coincided with the conditions of political and social stability already described. The sects were numerous. Among those that have survived were the Congregational, Baptist, Unitarian, and Quaker. In that day there were in addition the Muggletonians, Ranters, Family of Love, Fifth Monarchy Men, not to mention social and political parties with a strong religious ideology, such as Levelers and Diggers. With the death penalty in abeyance, the problem of religious diversity could not be solved by general extermination. Banishment was possible, but England would be seriously impoverished by an extensive migration of enterprising citizens. Wholesale imprisonment was a great strain upon penal accommodations. Toleration, then, alone remained. For the wisdom of this solution the example of Europe during the preceding century afforded irrefutable arguments: France had been decimated by wars of religion, whereas Holland was thriving under religious liberty.

In all this ferment Calvinism, which had been persecuting on the Continent in the sixteenth century, came to be the ally of liberty. The reason was of course in part that Calvinists were immalleable and would not leave off agitation, civil disobedience, and even armed revolution until they had achieved recognition for themselves. This had always been true, and in this sense John Calvin himself had sponsored liberty. Calvinist intransigence had wrung from France the Edict of Nantes. But the England of the seventeenth century presented a new situation. Calvinist theology was shared by a number of the contesting groups. The Presbyterians, the Independents, and many of the Baptists were Calvinists, not to mention the Puritan wing in the Anglican Church. If Calvinism was not to devour itself, some measure of mutual recognition must be accorded. And this was only an extension of the principle already espoused by Calvin himself, that not every church need exhibit the pattern of Geneva and " tolerable ineptitudes " could be suffered. The seventeenth century need only enlarge the area of the ineptitudes deemed to be tolerable. But to do so immediately opened the door to some of the considerations adduced by Castellio as to degrees of importance and relative incertitude of religious doctrines. Thus in the 1600's Calvinists not infrequently employed arguments that earlier would have ranked them with Calvin's opponents.

The men chosen to epitomize the struggle in Britain in the Puritan period are two, John Milton for England and Roger Williams for the colonies. One may question whether Milton should be considered a Calvinist at all. On some doctrinal points he would have been anathema in the Geneva of John Calvin. Yet in his general justification of the ways of God with men he is the poet of Puritanism and the bard of Calvinism. Some would question whether he is the best single figure to select in order to illustrate the struggle for religious liberty, because his pleas were never timed to strike the most decisive moments. Sometimes he did no more than voice in nobler language what others had abundantly declared, and sometimes he raised his voice only after the cause was lost. The reason is that Milton was never satisfied with any party in power and was always torn within himself and moving from one camp to another. In his allegiances he was almost as migratory as Ochino. For that reason Milton is a poor representative of any single position or group but an admirable mirror of his age.

He might be described as a Renaissance Puritan, a scholar amazingly versed in all the learning of antiquity whether classical or Christian, and profoundly lured by the quest of all knowledge and the enjoyment of all loveliness. He was a son of England by birth and of Italy by adoption. While in college, he had made the acquaintance of a young Italian, and from him had acquired the rudiments of the tongue. A visit to Italy enabled him to indulge his passion for the new science, when he called upon the aged Galileo, who through his glass perused the craters of the moon and pursued the satellites of Jupiter. Here was a living symbol of the unconquerable human spirit despite the censures of an obscurantist Inquisition. By another aspect of the Renaissance Milton was enthralled. He went to Rome and attended the presentation of an opera. Here he heard the singing of Leonora Baroni. She was twenty-seven years old, with golden hair and flashing eyes. She composed, and played several instruments. Her voice was an echo of the song of pure conceit, sung in the morn of endless light before God's sapphire throne. Hers was an Orpheus voice, which could move forests and lure the moon to earth. Careful, Milton! She was reputed to be of questionable morals. This was the pagan Renaissance, the cult of beauty divorced from ethical restraints. Already Milton was an inharmonious spirit, for at that very moment he made his stay in Rome almost untenable by his frankness in identifying the papacy with Antichrist. Never to the end of his life did he cease to berate the Church of Rome as the whore of the Apocalypse. Never would he concede toleration to Catholics in England. Yet he was a child of beauty, who quivered at the memory of Leonora's voice and had no mind to subject England to a regime of dour rigidity. He had no sympathy with a Puritan like Prynne, who in the index to his book on stage playing defined actresses as whores, and that at the very moment when the queen was playing in a masque. For this offense Prynne lost his ears, and Milton again was outraged by lopping ears to penalize indecorous indexes. No wonder that he could not bring himself to issue clarion calls when those with whom he mainly and yet not entirely sympathized came into power!

Milton returned to England from Italy in 1639. He was then thirty-one. To what should he devote himself? He had considered the Church. The oath stood in his way. A life of literature appealed to him, that he might " imbreed and cherish in a great people the seeds of virtue and public civility, celebrate in glorious and lofty hymns the throne and equipage of God's almightiness, and sing the deeds and triumphs of just and pious nations." He thought to become the bard of Arthur and the Table Round, but this had to be left for Tennyson, because too much history was in the making to be singing of Arthur just then. England was seething. What had been commended as a firm hand under the Tudors was considered tyranny when practiced by the Stuarts: the levying of taxes on inland districts to support a navy superfluous after the debacle of the Armada, the quartering of troops on the civilian population in time of peace, above all, the enforcement of religious uniformity — these were not to be endured. The Stuarts did believe in uniformity and it was to be Anglican uniformity. James I, though his mother had been a Catholic, did not propose to return to Rome and subject Britain to papal vexations. Neither, though Scottish, did he intend to impose Presbyterianism on England. He had had his belly full of Presbyterians who called him " God's silly vassal." The Anglican Church, decorous and amenable to royal control, best suited his taste. But the Anglican Church, as the Church of England, did demand something of Englishmen. If they were allowed to believe as they liked, they must behave as they were told, in the interests of seemliness, decorum, and good order. Charles I thought so too, and even more was this the position of Archbishop Laud.

A Cartoon: Archbishop Laud Dining on the Ears of Prynne, Bastwick, and Barton

Had he gone no farther than to enforce his program on England, there would have been trouble with the Puritans, but when he attempted to impose it also upon the Scots, there was war. English Puritans and Scottish Presbyterians joined to resist Laud and Charles and all the mitred bishops and hireling priests parading in the rags of Antichrist.

Milton, not always in terms more decorous, devoted his pen to the service of the Puritan cause. His first tract was a defense of the repudiation of any prescribed form of prayer, including, of course, *The Book of Common Prayer*. Why, he inquired, should they who can " learnedly invent a prayer of their own to the Parliament still ignorantly read the prayers of other men to God? " Where did this English prayer book come from if not from the " abomination of the anti-Christian temple? " Essentially it is the Mass. " Is this to magnify the Church of England " that it should have recourse to the Church of Rome? Strange that John Milton who had such an ear for speech should not have been enthralled by the solemn cadences of *The Book of Common Prayer!* Perhaps it was because he knew so well how to compose prayers of his own. The following is an example, not only of his incomparable style but of his ardent hope, essentially Calvinist, that God would establish his Kingdom upon earth and in England:

" Come, therefore, O Thou that hast the seven stars in thy right hand, appoint thy chosen priests according to their orders and courses of old, to minister before thee, and duly to dress and pour out the consecrated oil into thy holy and ever-burning lamps; thou hast sent out the spirit of prayer upon thy servants over all the land to this effect, and stirred up their vows as the sound of many waters about thy throne. Every one can say that now certainly thou hast visited this land, and hast not forgotten the utmost corners of the earth, in a time when men had thought that thou wast gone up from us to the farthest end of the heavens, and hadst left to do marvelously among the sons of these last ages. O perfect, and accomplish thy glorious acts; for men may leave their works unfinished, but thou art a God, thy nature is perfection: shouldst thou bring us thus far onward from Egypt to destroy us in this Wilderness? Though we deserve . . . yet thy great name would suffer in the rejoicing of thine enemies, and the deluded hope of all thy servants. When thou hast settled peace in the Church, and righteous judgment in the Kingdom, then shall all thy saints address their voices of joy and triumph to thee, standing on the shore of that Red Sea into which our enemies had almost driven us. And he that now for haste snatches up a plain ungarnished present as a thank offering to thee, which could not be deferred in regard of thy so many late deliverances wrought for us one upon another, may then perhaps take up a harp and sing thee an elaborate song to generations. In that day it shall no more be said as in scorn, ' This (or that) was never held so till this present age,' when men have better learned that the times and seasons pass along under thy feet to go and come at thy bidding: and as thou didst dignify our fathers' days with many revelations above all the foregoing ages, since thou tookest the flesh, so thou canst vouchsafe to us (though unworthy) as large a portion of thy Spirit as thou pleasest: for who shall prejudice thy all-governing will? seeing the power of thy grace is not passed away with the primitive times, as fond and faithless men imagine, but thy Kingdom is now at hand, and thou standing at the door. Come forth out of thy royal chambers, O Prince of all the kings of the earth, put on the visible robes of thy imperial majesty, take up that unlimited scepter which thy almighty Father hath bequeathed thee; for now the voice of thy bride calls thee, and all creatures sigh to be renewed."

Next Milton undertook to support the Presbyterian attack on prelacy, by which he meant the Episcopal system. At this point his defense of liberty commenced. The argument in favor of prelacy was that without its strict control England would teem with sects. Milton replied that if all sects were to be suppressed, then England might as well imitate Italy and

Spain. Then he turned to an analogy from nature. If the chief end were to have no weeds, then " winter might vaunt itself " as the season that keeps down " all noisome and rank weeds." To this the reply would be that winter destroys also " all wholesome herbs " and confines all " the fresh dews in hidebound frost." For the destroying of weeds there is no need of such " imprisonment and bondage." Let rather " the gentle west winds open the fruitful bosom of the earth." Let " the sun scatter the mists." Then when " the flowers put forth and spring . . . the hand of the tiller shall root up all that burden the soil without thank to " winter's " bondage. But far worse than any " such " frozen captivity is the bondage of prelates."

The conclusion is not only that the tares should be left to grow with the wheat, but that in some measure the tares may be regarded as useful to the wheat. " Sects and errors it seems God suffers to be for the glory of good men, that the world may know and reverence their true fortitude and undaunted constancy in truth." Virtue that wavers is not virtue. The English people, being a hardy nation, should be left to exercise themselves in the field of truth. The magistrate should not step in save to concern himself with the body and its outward acts. " His general end is the outward peace and welfare of the Commonwealth and civil happiness in this life." The purity of the Church is to be guarded solely through its own discipline by means of excommunication.

In this defense Milton far overshot what was expected or desired of him. The Presbyterians objected to prelacy, not on the ground that it would curb the sects which they were of no mind to encourage, but because the system in their judgment was not ordained of God and enjoined in Scripture. They were quite as eager to impose their system on England as were the Anglicans to accomplish the reverse for Scotland. And neither one would tolerate sects. The Presbyterians were soon to have their turn. The fortunes of war cast down the king and exalted the Westminster Assembly. There followed the ejection of ministers and the licensing of books.

And that was the point at which Milton fell foul of their regime. He had some tracts to publish for which he could not well expect the approval of any Presbyterian licenser because the subject was a defense of divorce solely on the ground of incompatibility. Behind the tracts lay an urgent personal dilemma. In the summer of 1643, Milton had visited the country estate of a loyalist squire, Richard Powell, in order to collect a debt of five hundred pounds. Milton came away without the payment of the debt, but married to the squire's daughter Mary. She was seventeen and he was thirty-five. They went up to live in London. Milton considered the whole duty of a wife to be ministering to her husband. Mary, who had been used to the bustle and convivialities of a country house, did not care to be a maid in waiting to a grave and sedentary scholar. After a month she returned home.

Milton a year thereafter eluded the censors and brought out a tract on the legitimacy of divorce for reasons other than adultery. Knowing that he would have difficulty in obtaining a hearing, he began with a plea that " the womb of teeming truth " be not closed. Then he addressed himself to the argument. In so doing he delineated a view of marriage that was peculiarly the product of Puritanism. Previously there had been, broadly speaking, two Christian attitudes toward marriage. The first may be called the sacramental. This was the position of the Catholic Church prevalent throughout the Middle Ages, according to which marriage is a sacrament instituted mainly for progeny and property. There was no touch of romance, because marriage was esteemed inferior to virginity. Unions were commonly made by families. Against this view arose the romantic revolt in the Courts of Love, which exalted love as an ennobling passion rather than as a sickness. The beloved became the object of almost a religious devotion, but this cult in its beginnings was extramatrimonial, on the ground that love freely given is impossible within the marriage bond. Only in the age of the Renaissance was romanticism transferred to marriage, and only then of course could it be accommodated to a Christian view. A third position entered with Puritanism, and Milton expounded it with singular persuasiveness. It is the position that marriage is primarily a companionship in a common endeavor, calling for mutuality of taste and conviction. Companionability is a prime requisite. The center of common interest for the Puritan was, of course, religion. Secularized versions have later stressed common interests, intellectual, artistic, and the like.

Milton commenced his tract by saying that the first command of God was not, " Be fruitful and multiply " (the favorite text for the Catholic sacramental view), nor was it that " To marry is better than to burn " (the chief proof text of the Lutherans), but rather this, " It is not good for man to be alone." " In God's intention a meet and happy conversation is the chiefest and noblest end of marriage." " The chief society thereof is in the soul rather than in the body, and the greatest breach thereof is unfitness of mind rather than defect of body." " Since we know it is not the joining of another body will remove loneliness, but the uniting of another compliable mind; and that it is no blessing but a torment, nay a base and brutish condition to be one flesh, unless where nature can in some measure fix and unite the disposition." " Loneliness is the first thing which God's eye named not good." " There is a peculiar comfort in the marriage state beside the genial bed, which no other society affords. No mortal nature can endure either in the actions of religion or study of wisdom, without sometime slackening the cords of intense thought and labor "; therefore we " have need of some delightful intermissions wherein the enlarged soul may leave off a while her severe schooling; which as she cannot well do without company, so in no company so well as where the different sex in most resembling unlikeness and most unlike resemblance cannot but please best, and be pleased in the aptitude of that variety." So fundamental indeed is community of taste, interest, and conviction for such a spiritual interchange that in Milton's judgment it were better both parties should be irreligious than that one should be religious and the other not.

If these conditions be not fulfilled, there is no real marriage. " What a violent and cruel thing it is to force the continuing of those together whom God and nature in the gentlest end of marriage never joined." He who misses the true end of marriage " by chancing on a mute and spiritless mate remains more alone than before." " Suppose he erred. It is not the intent of God or man to hunt an error so to the death with a revenge beyond all measure and proportion." The magistrate is not the one to decide whether a marriage be successful. When a Roman was asked why he had put away his wife, he pulled off his shoe and said, " This shoe is a neat shoe yet none of you know where it wrings me." The magistrate should take care only that the conditions of the divorce be not injurious. If two such spiritual persons as Paul and Barnabas found it wise to separate, shall the married be held " to the most intimate and incorporating duties of love and embracement . . . if unfitness and disparity be not till after marriage discovered? "

The difficulties that Milton had experienced in eluding censorship for three tracts on divorce prompted an eloquent plea for the freedom of the press. The treatise was entitled *Areopagitica,* from Areopagus, the hill of Mars, where the Athenians exercised freedom of speech. Not one word was said about divorce. The greatness of Milton was that he could rise above some particular and personal circumstance to an overarching principle, and in tones majestic plead for all time the cause of truth in free encounter. The *Areopagitica* appeared in the year 1644, and opened with an unparalleled apologia for the printed page. " Books are not absolutely dead things but do contain a potency of life. . . . They do preserve as in a vial the purest efficacy and extraction of that living intellect that bred them. . . . As good almost kill a man as kill a good book; who kills a man kills a reasonable creature, God's image; but he who destroys a good book kills reason itself — kills the image of God, as it were, in the eye. Many a man lives a burden to the earth; but a good book is the precious lifeblood of a master spirit, embalmed and treasured up on purpose to a life beyond life. 'Tis true, no age can restore a life, whereof perhaps there is no great loss; and revolutions of ages do not oft recover the loss of a rejected truth, for the want of which whole nations fare the worse. We should be wary therefore what persecution we raise against the living labors of public men, how we spill that seasoned life of man preserved and stored up in books; since we see a kind of homicide may thus be committed, sometimes a martyrdom, and if it extend to a whole impression, a kind of massacre, wherein the execution ends not in the slaying of an elemental life but strikes at . . . the breath of reason itself; slays an immortality rather than a life."

Then the argument soars from books to truth itself, which is not a deposit recorded or committed to a Church, but rather the object of a quest. " To be still searching what we know not by what we know, still closing up truth to truth as we find it, this is the golden rule in theology as well as in arithmetic." Milton was no skeptic — not, indeed, as much of a skeptic as Erasmus or Castellio, who insisted that certain theological tenets can never be known in this life and discussion should be deferred until the Judgment Day. Milton welcomed discussion because of his confidence that truth could be reached provided inquiry were unimpeded. His assurance rested upon pessimism as to licensers and optimism as to Englishmen. No individual is sufficiently inerrant to be trusted with the responsibility of suppressing a book. If it come to prohibiting, nothing is more likely to be prohibited than truth itself. If there be found in an author " one sentence of venturous edge, uttered in the height of zeal, and who knows whether it might not be the dictate of a divine Spirit, though it were Knox himself they will not pardon him their dash; and the sense of that great man shall to all posterity be lost, for the fearfulness or the presumptuous rashness of a per-functory licenser. . . . What is it but a servitude like that imposed by the Philistines, not to be allowed the sharpening of our own axes and coulters, but we must repair from all quarters to twenty licensing forges." When I " visited the famous Galileo, prisoner of the Inquisition," Italians vaunted the liberty of England.

Licensers cannot be trusted but Englishmen can. The judg-ment of the entire people will fall upon the side of truth. Nor is licensing " to the common people less than a reproach; for if we be so jealous over them that we dare not trust them with an English pamphlet, what do we but censure them for a giddy, vicious, and ungrounded people? " " I cannot set so light by all the invention, the art, the wit, the grave and solid judgment which is in England." " Lords and commons of England, . . . why else was this nation chosen before any other, that out of her as out of Sion should be proclaimed and sounded forth the first tidings and trumpet of reformation to all Europe [that is, under Wycliffe]? " And why did God when he desired a reforming of reformation show himself first to his Englishmen? " Behold now this vast city; a city of refuge, a mansion house of liberty, encompassed and sur-rounded with his protection."

Nor would Milton restrict soundness of judgment to the

English. All mankind are, if not equally, at any rate similarly endowed, and truth itself has a potency that compels recognition. " Let truth and falsehood grapple; whoever knew truth put to the worst in a free and open encounter. . . . For who knows not that truth is strong next to the Almighty; she needs no policies, nor stratagems, nor licensings, to make her victorious. . . . Give her but room, and do not bind her when she sleeps."

The triumph of truth is, however, contingent upon the process of a co-operative quest in which the insights and the findings of each are subjected to the scrutiny and criticism of all. Clash is an indispensable ingredient in the emergence of truth, which can be discerned only through its ability to withstand the onslaughts of falsehood. Here it is that error itself performs a useful function, so that one may speak of " the knowing of good by evil." Truth requires a sparring partner. " I cannot praise," exclaims Milton, " a fugitive and cloistered virtue unexercised and unbreathed, that never sallies out and sees her adversary, but slinks out of the race." " Our faith and virtue thrive by exercise. . . . Truth is compared in Scripture to a streaming fountain; if her waters flow not in a perpetual progression, they sicken into a muddy pool of conformity and tradition. A man may be a heretic in the truth; and if he believe things only because his pastor says so, or an assembly so determines, without knowing other reason, though his belief be true, yet the very truth he holds becomes his heresy." Milton here enunciates a far-reaching principle. He has gone beyond the customary definition of truth as that which is objectively correct and has made it also that which is inwardly appropriated. Truth, then, is almost a synonym for faith, and all the arguments for the inviolability of faith then become pertinent for truth.

When at last truth is attained, one is not to suppose that it will necessarily exhibit a single face. " Is it not possible that she may have more shapes than one? What else is all that rank of things indifferent, wherein truth may be on this side or on the other without being unlike herself? . . . What great purchase is this Christian liberty which Paul so often boasts of? His doctrine is, that he who eats or eats not, regards a day or regards it not, may do either to the Lord. How many other things might be tolerated in peace and left to conscience, had we but charity, and were it not the chief stronghold of our hypocrisy to be ever judging one another! I fear this iron yoke of outward conformity hath left a slavish print upon our necks." This passage is fraught with vast implications because in it Milton espouses the ideal of variety rather than of uniformity. He was but voicing an idea grown prevalent in his day that variety is the glory and the gift of the Creator, who in nothing so much displayed his beneficence to man as in fashioning the world with such rich diversity. The same principle applies to marriage, when companionability is enhanced by " most resembling unlikeness and most unlike resemblance." Variety had become also a principle of aesthetics, and some hold that Milton deliberately introduced certain apparently inharmonious styles into *Paradise Lost* in order to exhibit a greater variety. When, then, this thesis was applied to religion, the death knell tolled for the *Corpus Christianum,* the Christian society based upon one form of religion. Milton was not an originator at this point. Some of the Remonstrants in Holland and the Baptists in England had declared variety and competition to be wholesome for the Church. What earlier centuries had deplored as a calamity and compared to the rending of the seamless robe of Christ was hailed by the sectaries as an ideal and as a state of health for Christendom. Uniformity for Milton was symbolized by vegetation dormant in the grip of ice, but diversity by all the profusion of the variegated flowers of spring.

Plainly at this juncture Milton did not belong with the

Presbyterians. He transferred to the Independents, as the Congregationalists were then commonly called, and became in time the secretary of their champion, Oliver Cromwell. His greatest historical significance lies in this, that he substituted a national religion for an Established Church. Cromwell was a profoundly religious figure, a Gideon, a Joshua fighting the battles of the Lord of Hosts, a man of prayer who would adjourn a council of officers in order to seek the leading of the Spirit. Cromwell aspired to rear in England a holy commonwealth, much after the Genevan model but with this great difference, that a larger diversity would be allowed. Milton's ideal of variety had laid hold on him, and he compared the several sects to the trees mentioned by the prophet Isaiah, the myrrh and the olive, the cypress and the plantains of Israel, all different and all alike affording shade. Diversity, however, should not be permitted endless ramifications. Here the distinction between the essentials and the nonessentials determined the lines, and the essentials were so defined that the Catholics and the Unitarians were excluded; the Presbyterians, Congregationalists, and Baptists constituted the core. The Episcopalians and Quakers might be unmolested if devoid of political threat. Cromwell hoped to disestablish the Anglican Church and to erect instead a commonwealth of the saints recruited from the central three.

But the saints were able to collaborate only up to a point. In opposition to the bishops and the king the three groups were one. In the first stage of the civil war the Presbyterians of Scotland and the Puritans of England, of whatever complexion, were allied. The intent was not to destroy the king but only to dislodge the bishops. The theory eloquently expounded by Milton was that the Roundheads were not fighting the king at all, but only the "Malignants" by whom he was surrounded and beguiled. The war was designed to liberate His Majesty, but when His Majesty refused to be thus liberated and made abundantly plain that he was responsible for the policy attributed to the Malignants, then either the war must stop or else frankly be directed against his person. At this point the Presbyterians called a halt. They would not lift a hand against the Lord's anointed.

Then the Independents and the Baptists, the element strongest in the army, purged the Presbyterians from Parliament and forged ahead to bring to book " that man of blood, Charles Stuart." The theory of course changed, and again Milton became the spokesman and now urged the covenant theory of government, that the king is bound in compact with the people and if he violate the covenant is no longer king. In that case Parliament, as the representative of the sovereign people, may constitute itself into a court of high judicature to sit in judgment on his person, even to the point of depriving him of life. Charles went to the block. Then Cromwell and the saints began their reign and Milton's disillusionment recommenced. Liberty, he perceived, cannot be conserved by giving power to the mass of Englishmen nor even to the saints. Cromwell's parliaments were less tolerant than he, and soon the protector found himself confronted with a choice between democracy or freedom. His Parliament desired to suppress *The Book of Common Prayer*. He did not approve. Either, then, he must flout Parliament and compromise democracy in the interests of liberty or else give democracy the rein to the detriment of tolerance. He chose democracy and the prayer book was suppressed. The protector then, lacking the divinity which " doth hedge a king," found himself even more than the monarch an object of scurrilous and seditious attacks. He had no mind to suffer England to be flooded with such subversive pamphlets. His secretary, John Milton, was called upon to exercise the office of licenser.

Milton became almost embittered against " the common

rout, that wandering loose about, grow up and perish, as the summer fly." He inquired:

" And what the people but a herd confus'd,
A miscellaneous rabble, who extol
Things vulgar, and well weigh'd, scarce worth the praise.
They praise, and they admire they know not what;
And know not whom, but as one leads the other;
And what delight to be by such extoll'd,
To live upon thir tongues and be thir talk,
Of whom to be disprais'd were no small praise?
His lot who dares be singularly good.
Th' intelligent among them and the wise
Are few."

The brutish, ignorant, and wayward are to be held in constant check; if once they are given the bit, their capricious stupidity will throw off the yoke of reason and order.

And even the leaders filled Milton with foreboding. To Cromwell he addressed a sonnet, reminding him that peace has its victories no less renowned than war, and General Monk was warned to surround himself with a perpetual council. The guarantee of liberty should be the rule of the wise, but the end actually was martial law.

And then came the Restoration. The regicides in their turn went to the block. As Harrison was led to execution, someone called out, " Where is now your good old cause? " With cheerful smile he clapped his hand to his breast and said, " Here it is and I am going to seal it with my blood." He was first hanged, then pulled down while still alive. He was emasculated, his entrails were burned before his eyes, then his head was severed and his body hacked into quarters. His head was then pilloried on a pike and his quarters exposed upon the city gates. When the turn of Hugh Peter came, the rabble made so much noise that he could not be heard. Another who was similarly hooted, remarked, " It is a very mean cause that will not hear the words of a dying man." Evelyn recorded in his diary: " I saw not their execution but met their quarters mangled, cut and reeking as they were brought from the gallows in baskets on a hurdle. O the marvelous providence of God! "

And all this, be it remembered, took place in merry England only three hundred years ago!

Milton, though he had justified tyrannicide, was spared by the clemency of Charles II, who was loath to make excessive martyrs, and Milton had not signed the death warrant. Besides, he was a poet of reputation and was blind. Then let him alone. In his retirement Milton voiced one more plea for liberty, brave and futile. It was all the more brave because of those to whom he would accord religious liberty. " We suffer," said he, " the idolatrous books of the papists to be sold and read as common as our own; why not much rather the Anabaptists, Arminians, and Socinians? There is no learned man but will confess he hath much profited by reading controversies."

The problem had come, however, to be much more serious than the way to truth. The deepest question was as to the ways of God with men. One could understand why He should suffer the rabble to perish, but how explain the fall of the saints?

> " Such as thou hast solemnly elected,
> With gifts and graces eminently adorn'd
> To some great work, thy glory,
> And peoples safety, which in part they effect:
> Yet toward these thus dignifi'd, thou oft
> Amidst thir highth of noon,
> Changest thy countenance, and thy hand with no regard
> Of highest favours past
> From thee on them, or them to thee of service.

" Nor only dost degrade them, or remit
To life obscur'd, which were a fair dismission,
But throw'st them lower then thou didst exalt them high,

   .   .   .   .   .

Oft leav'st them to the hostile sword
Of Heathen and prophane, thir carkasses
To dogs and fowls a prey, or else captiv'd:
Or to the unjust tribunals, under change of times,
And condemnation of the ingrateful multitude."

To find an answer Milton had to reach beyond the immediate to contemplate the design of God and the nature of man. He must unfold the drama of Creation, Fall, and redemption. Not Arthur and the Table Round enlisted his pen, but the sublimer task of justifying the ways of God to men. When *Paradise Lost* was finished, it had to be scrutinized by the licenser. He examined minutely to discover any veiled contemporary allusions, but could smell out nothing, and he was right. Milton was pillorying no persons under the guise of Satan, Belial, or Beelzebub. England and humanity were his concern.

The opening scene of *Paradise Lost* obscures the problem of why the saints should be brought low, for here it is the archrebels who have been cast into the lurid abyss. Milton, himself an outcast, felt the sympathy of common circumstance with those who had been ejected but yet were not broken in spirit. Many commentators have sensed in the poet an unavowed admiration for the magnificent rebel's courage " never to submit or yield " or for that yet more audacious outcast who counseled wearing out the patience of the Most High. But one must not confuse Milton's dramatic artistry with his final judgments. To be sure an uncowed spirit evokes a transient ejaculation of applause, but in the end, as the cause makes the martyr, so also the cause justifies or confounds the insurrection. Implacable resistance to tyranny is noble, but the most superb defiance of God is ultimately base. Courage cannot justify itself. There is some higher and absolute reference. Milton would not begin by relativizing God.

The opening scene of the poem is of course a conspiracy, a council of war among the fallen chiefs as to how best to recover their forfeited estate. Some propose direct attack, but Satan, who quivers from the shock of the encounter, dismisses such a fatuous suggestion. The plan that at length commends itself is that of seeking to undo God at the point of his creation, and Satan therefore insinuates himself into the Garden with intent to seduce God's glorious and frail creation, to beguile the primal pair by false ideas — one is tempted to add, as the Restoration pamphleteers were then doing in their legends of Charles the martyr.

The story then moves back to give an account of the Creation. Adam is made of the dust of the earth, a superb creature. Eve is wondrous fair. Was Milton reminiscent of Leonora Baroni? The mother of mankind " infused sweetness into the heart unfelt before."

> " Grace was in all her steps, Heav'n in her Eye,
>   In every gesture dignitie and love."

Created because God saw it was not good for man to be alone, she was the perfect mate, whose " sweet compliance declared unfeigned union of mind." She plied her husband with questions and listened adoringly to his responses. The perfect wife!

Now Satan is abroad in the Garden. He is espied from Paradise, and a warning is sent to Adam and Eve, who well know that the condition of their bliss is that they shall refrain from the fruit of the tree of the knowledge of good and evil, for in the day in which they eat of it they shall surely die.

The fall begins before the Fall. Adam and Eve are dressing

the vines of the Garden when Eve proposes that they should divide their labors in the interest of greater efficiency.

> " Let us divide our labours, thou where choice
>   Leads thee, or where most needs, whether to wind
>   The woodbine round this Arbour, or direct
>   The clasping Ivie where to climb, while I
>   In yonder Spring of Roses intermixt
>   With Myrtle, find what to redress till Noon."

Adam requires the reason for such increased production in a garden where all things needful are supplied. He would not be deprived of her company for the sake of a little more fruit. " For not to irksome toil but to delight God made us." Of course, if Eve craves a little solitude, he will not begrudge it, for " short retirement urges sweet return." So far Adam had carried himself well, and had he stopped here, Eve might have been deterred. But he went on to add that by herself she would be more open to the seductions of Satan now abroad in the Garden. Then her back is up and she pours out upon Adam all the arguments of the *Areopagitica*. His fear bespeaks a lack of confidence in her " firm faith and love."

> " And what is Faith, Love, Vertue unassaid
>   Alone, without exterior help sustain'd? "

Adam is Milton the licenser, who must remind her that free will can be abused and even reason may " fall into deception unaware." Yet for all his misgivings he will not repudiate his liberalism and interpose constraint.

> " Go; for thy stay, not free, absents thee more;
>   Go in thy native innocence, relie
>   On what thou hast of vertue, summon all,
>   For God towards thee hath done his part, do thine."

And Eve trips blithely into the bushes.

Then Satan as a serpent raises his head and speaks. Eve is

amazed. Not that in Paradise any wonder should amaze, save this, that a lower creature should speak, inasmuch as God had conferred speech on man alone. The serpent explained that he had chanced upon a goodly tree laden with fruit of fairest colors, mixed ruddy and gold. He had eaten, and a strange alteration had given him the power of speech. Eve desires of course to see the tree, and at once recognizes it as the one of which she may not taste. Satan remonstrates. Not eat of this " sacred, wise and wisdom giving plant, mother of science "? It is Galileo speaking. What harm can there be in reading the riddles of the universe, charting the stars, splitting the atoms? How ridiculous the threat that he who tastes of this fruit shall surely die!

> " Doe not believe
> Those rigid threats of Death; ye shall not Die:
> How should ye? by the Fruit? it gives you Life
> To Knowledge."

" Meanwhile the hour of noon drew on." Eve hungered. The fruit was savory and she ate.

Her eyes were opened. Should she tell Adam, or should she enjoy this newly won advantage which overcame the inferiority of her sex? But she resolves to tell him, so dear to her is his love.

Now Adam meanwhile had " wove of choicest flowers a garland to adorn her tresses." She comes to him with countenance blithe and tells her tale. Adam, " astonied stood and blank, while horror chill ran through his veins, and all his joints relaxed." Well he knew that Eve would die and he alone live on forever. Might he perhaps give up another rib and let God make another Eve? Not that: " Loss of thee would never from my heart." Fully aware then of what he was about, Adam tasted of the apple in order that he might share the doom of Eve. Through chivalry he fell.

There follows a moment of voluptuous delight. Then bitterness ensues, and Eve starts to upbraid Adam for granting the liberty she had craved, just as children demand to have their way and, when things go wrong, reproach their parents for having given in. Adam and Eve are quarreling as they are cast out of the Garden. Having sacrificed integrity for love, Adam has lost also the love for which the sacrifice was made.

All this may seem to have wandered far from the theme of liberty — yet not so far. Love cannot thrive without integrity; no more can freedom. At long last all comes back to truth. For all its varieties, it is yet truth. And all refers to God and his laws of virtue and soundness of mind.

The archangel Michael points the lesson when he assures Adam and Eve that their plight is not hopeless. They can yet make of earth a paradise if they will observe that love and liberty can thrive only when blessed with virtue and right reason.

> " Yet know withall,
> Since thy original lapse, true Libertie
> Is lost, which alwayes with right Reason dwells
> Twinn'd, and from her hath no dividual being:
> Reason in man obscur'd, or not obeyd,
> Immediately inordinate desires
> And upstart Passions catch the Government
> From Reason, and to servitude reduce
> Man till then free. Therefore since hee permits
> Within himself unworthie Powers to reign
> Over free Reason, God, in Judgement just
> Subjects him from without to violent Lords;
> Who oft as undeservedly enthrall
> His outward freedom: Tyrannie must be,
> Though to the Tyrant thereby no excuse.

Yet sometimes Nations will decline so low
From vertue, which is reason, that no wrong,
But Justice, and some fatal curse annext
Deprives them of thir outward libertie,
Thir inward lost."

This, then, appears to be the moral, that the fall of the saints is but the nemesis of their own excess, and the guarantee of liberty is not, after all, the sound sense of Englishmen as Englishmen, nor even of the saints, but only of those qualities rooted in God which alone can make a commonwealth holy and free. Milton ends by no means with despair. In "Paradise Regained," the Saviour declines to establish his Kingdom by constraint, holding it rather "more humane, more heavenly first by winning words to conquer willing hearts and make persuasion do the work of fear."

Chapter Eight

THE SEEKER:

Roger Williams

Roger Williams, the lonely seeker who flanks the monument of the Reformation, has been selected to exemplify the struggle for religious liberty in the New World. He is a particularly intriguing figure because although banished by a Calvinist theocracy he was at certain points even more Calvinist in his theology than his opponents. Williams was an Englishman, born in 1603 and thus a contemporary of Milton. His career was divided between the Old World and the New. Williams illustrates full well the intimate relation of the coincident battle for freedom in the colonies and in the mother land. The aims were similar; the circumstances were distinct.

Roger Williams

The peculiar circumstance of the New World was that here " God hath set before us an open door of liberty," which by no means meant the establishment of a community where each should be free to go to hell in his own way. Liberty consisted in the opportunity to erect a commonwealth that would concede very little liberty to the dissenter. The hope was to do in the New World that which had failed in the Old. In virgin territory, untrammeled by all the incubus of a per-

verted tradition, a new Canaan should be reared in the wilderness. The objective was well voiced by John Cotton when
he said: "And therefore it is for us to do all the good we can,
and to leave nothing to those that shall come after us, but to
walk in the righteous steps of their forefathers. And therefore let us not leave, nor give rest to our eyes, until in family,
church, and commonwealth we have set a pattern of holiness
to those that shall succeed us."

The Puritan dream for a new world was an extension of the
optimism already ingrained in Calvinism that God through
the elect would achieve his purpose in the course of the historical process through the erection of his Kingdom. It was a
phase of that optimism which in the 1640's inspired Milton
with his confidence that the English were a people highly
favored and chosen of the Lord to sound the tidings of the
Reformation. And when hopes for England waned, all the
more were looks averted from a blighted land to a shore that,
though bleak, barren, and rugged to the outward eye, yet
was burgeoning with possibilities for those who would plant
in the spirit a new Israel of God.

But then, of course, arose again the problem of knowing
who constituted the New Israel. What were the marks of the
elect? The answer was basically Calvinist, that the chosen
are for all practical purposes those who profess the true creed,
exhibit a righteous life, and come to the Lord's Table. But
New England Calvinism added a fourth requirement of even
greater import. In so doing it was reverting to the test originally posited by Thomas Müntzer of a definite experience of
inner regeneration. The saints are those who can testify, not
only to the intellectual and ethical signs of grace, but also to
the emotional. Candidates for church membership must give
evidence that "they have been wounded in their hearts for
their original sin, and actual transgressions, and can pitch
upon some promise of free grace in the Scripture, for the

ground of their faith, and that they find their hearts drawn to believe in Christ Jesus, for their justification and salvation." What a ring of personal experience there is in the " solemn and public promise before the Lord, whereby a company of Christians, called by the power and mercy of God and fellowship with Christ, and by his providence to live together in the unity of faith, and brotherly love, and desirous to partake together in all the holy Ordinances of God, do in confidence of his gracious acceptance in Christ, bind themselves to the Lord, and to one another, to walk together by the assistance of his Spirit in all such ways of holy worship in him and of edification one towards another, as the Gospel of Christ requireth of every Christian Church and the members thereof "!

Such a test is of all the most difficult to discern, and the most tormenting to achieve and perpetuate, precisely because it is so inward. The problem was immediate as to the exact way in which the colony should be constituted and perpetuated. The founders were Protestants and would emphatically not base their commonwealth on celibacy with survival contingent upon a steady stream of new recruits. They were organized on a family basis and relied in part for perpetuation upon propagation. Then the question was how to preserve the pattern among their own children. To make Abrahams out of Isaacs is no easy matter, particularly if they have been sacrificed on the altars of their parents' devotion. One way of preserving the pattern is to shield the children from contamination by placing some sort of hedge about the community. This is the device employed by the Hutterites, Mennonites in the more extreme branches, and the Dukhobors. The Amish, for example, exclude the outside world by prohibiting automobiles, telephones, movies, comics, and the like.

The Puritans, however, did not choose the way of segregation. They had no mind to separate themselves from the mother country, " dear *England,* left indeed by us in our persons, but never yet forsaken in our affections." Neither did they desire for the most part to separate from the Church of England. The preface to the Cambridge Platform in 1648 declared that " we, who are by nature Englishmen, do desire to hold forth the same doctrine of religion (especially in fundamentals) which we see and know·to be held by the Church of England according to the truth of the Gospel." Their hope was not to lose contact with England, but rather, by their " hazardous and voluntary banishment into this remote wilderness," to stir up the old land to an emulation of the new pattern. Nor, again, did the emigrants seek to segregate themselves from the Indians; for the purpose in coming had been " chiefly to display the efficacy and power of the Gospel, both in zealous preaching, professing, and wise walking under it before the faces of these poor blind infidels." Finally they would not separate themselves from the " unregenerated, that are aliens to the commonwealth of Israel, strangers to the covenant of promise."

This is the most amazing element in all their program that a body with intent to plant a holy commonwealth should not insist at the very outset upon a homogeneous complexion. Even at the very beginning there were saints and strangers, " profane men who, being but seeming Christians, have made Christ and Christianity stink in the nostrils of the poor infidels." How could the pattern be maintained? How could the community be perpetuated if it were not pure even in the beginning? The answer was by conversion. The same power that had been operative in Old England in calling forth a regenerate people would no less manifest itself in the New World in winning and holding saints. The Indians should be converted, the children should be converted, the strangers should be converted. Surely in all history never was there a more transcendent optimism!

There was, nevertheless, one very definite safeguard. The saints should rule. Church members alone could vote, and they alone could be church members who exhibited all the evidences including the emotional signs of grace. State and Church were one, but Church, State, and community did not coincide. Those who were not of the Church were not citizens, but only inhabitants, even though they might constitute, as at New Haven, but nine tenths of the population. That they should be willing to subject themselves to the rule of the saints must appear very surprising. The only answer can be that, if they were not saints, they nevertheless aspired to be. They respected the saints, and were willing that they should set the tone for the community. Also it must be remembered that most of these people had not lost anything by way of political privilege, since in the old country they were debarred from the franchise by the property qualification. Here, then, was a community that did indeed display a pattern of liberty to an astonishing degree, in that it set out to preserve its quality, not by the rope and the gallows, but by producing conviction. They would " by winning words win willing hearts and let persuasion do the work of fear."

In the course of time, however, the rule of a handful of saints produced restiveness. The masses were eager to qualify for the society of the elite. The problem was all the more acute because the Puritans, if unable to transmit to their children an experience of grace, yet succeeded in instilling into them a rugged honesty which disdained to make a pretense of grace in order to be admitted to the Lord's Table and to the town meeting. Then the temptation became urgent, if the demands could not be met, to lower the qualifications. The Cambridge Platform already in 1648 was on the road toward relaxation. " Severity of examination should be avoided . . . and such charity and tenderness should be used as the weakest Christian if sincere may not be excluded." The tests should be only vigorous enough to satisfy a " rational charity." In this spirit the saints were defined as, first: " Such as have not only attained the knowledge of the principles of religion, and are free from gross and open scandals, but also do together with the profession of their faith and repentance, walk in blameless obedience to the Word, so as that in charitable discretion they may be accounted saints by calling (though perhaps some or more of them be unsound, and hypocrites inwardly) "; and, second, " The children of such, who are also holy."

Some proposed to go even farther and to include the grand-children of the saints, but the framers of the Cambridge Platform were not willing to see the elect of New Canaan degenerate into the elite of New England. They dug in their toes. Yet before the end of the century the Halfway Covenant had included even the grandchildren. The alternative to this method was a revival which would generate the requisite experience. Thus the Puritan commonwealth oscillated between efforts to lower the standards to the level of the community and revivals to raise the community to the level of the standards.

But what, then, should be done with those who rejected the standards altogether, who repudiated the very ideals on which the commonwealth was established? They might be of upright life. If so, they were only the more insidious and seductive because their exemplary demeanor would make their attack the more plausible. Here again was the old question whether the moral or the doctrinal offender constitutes the greater menace, and New England like Geneva displayed more leniency to the one who failed to live up to the ideal that he professed than to the one who refused to make any profession. But in that case what should be done with the nonconformist? There was more than one possibility. When Obadiah Holmes refused to have his child baptized, he was fined. He denied the jurisdiction of the court and declined to pay the fine. Then he was whipped. The favorite method of punishment was expulsion from the community. This did not appear to be an illiberal solution. It was the European system of territorialism: "To each region its religion," with freedom to migrate for dissent. Nowhere was this method less illiberal than in the New World, where open land was abundant and the hardships of moving no greater than those experienced by every other breaker of the wilderness. The Bay colonists believed in their right to stake off a piece of ground and ask of settlers only this, that either they should subscribe to the principles of the foundation or go somewhere else. But the Quakers denied the right to stake off a corner of the earth in which to intern oneself against the spokesman of the spirit. "The earth is the Lord's, and the fulness thereof," and no one has any authority to pre-empt a section. The Quakers invaded Massachusetts. The Puritans put them out. They said to them, in effect, this: "If you do not like it here, go back to Pennsylvania. You have your own colony. You can conduct it there as you please. Be satisfied with yours and leave us ours." The Quakers refused to be banished. They came back. They were again expelled, and again they came back. At last four were hanged on Boston Common. No one in this land would today condone such barbarous treatment, but one must not forget that an issue was involved. Has any group the right to erect a no-trespass sign in order to carry out an experiment in idealistic living according to some given pattern? May there be zoning laws in the things of the spirit?

At the moment when such issues were acute Roger Williams arrived in Massachusetts. The year was 1631. He was then twenty-eight years of age. He was given a pastorate in

Boston from which because of scruples of conscience he re-
tired to Plymouth and from there received a call to Salem.
After but four years of ministry in Massachusetts, he was
banished in 1635 because of a rejection of the cardinal tenets
of the theocracy. The manner of his dismissal was harsh, in
that he was forced to leave in the inclement season of the
year. Leaving for the time being his wife and two children,
he took refuge with the Narragansett Indians. Thirty-five
years later he declared that he could still feel the bite of that
winter snow as he sought an asylum " in the howling wilderness." The spot that harbored him was called Providence.

The first reason for his banishment was that he denied the
validity of the patent from the English crown conferring a
title to Massachusetts, because the English king has no right
to expropriate the lands of the Indians and confer them upon
his subjects. Nor would Williams concede the contention of
John Cotton that the Indians were the Amalekites, rightfully
to be displaced by the new Israelites, on whom God had conferred this Canaan. The war with Amalek, said Williams, is to
be spiritualized, and the only proper way to acquire land from
the Indians is not by conquest, nor by purchase, but only by
good will and free gift. The lands that he later acquired
around Providence he did not pretend to have paid for. What
he had given was merely a token of gratitude and not an
equivalent for the gracious generosity of the Indians.

The denial, however, that the Indians were the Amalekites
was much less disconcerting to the Bay than the rejection of
the claim of the Puritans to be the Israelites. Ancient Israel
did constitute a national Church, said Williams, but properly
speaking it is the only valid example in all history, because
after Christ the Jewish nation ceased to be the chosen people.
From that day forward the elect have been gathered into the
Christian Church, but this can never be identified with any
nation. There is no such thing as Christendom unless the

term be applied to the Church itself and not to any geographical entity, since no nation is really Christian. The Church and the world are not Christian. Among them are lukewarm Protestants who are worse than ignorant papists. No whole populace ever was or ever will be wholly regenerate. The entire Puritan dream of establishing a provincial Church after the pattern of a national Church is utterly illusory. Ancient Canaan was called " Jehovah's Land " and " Immanuel's Land," " which names and titles I think Master Cotton will not say are competent and appliable to any other lands or countries under the Gospel, but only to the spiritual Canaan or Israel, the Church and people of God, the true and only Christendom . . . to the then only Church of God Master Cotton can produce no parallel to that, but the Christian Churches and people of God, not national but Congregational." Part of the reason is that a Christian community should not and cannot be maintained and perpetuated by the methods the Bay employed. One method was the way of comprehension which modified the standards in order that a larger number might be able to attain. Such a dilution was in Williams' eyes fatal to the purity of the Church. When the hedge is broken down, the garden becomes a wilderness. The standards must be pitched so high that only the regenerate can qualify. Williams took more seriously the concepts of election and reprobation than did the Puritan colony itself, in that he would endeavor to fashion the Church only out of the elect. In this respect he was, of course, reviving the Anabaptist attempt to purge the Church of the tares, an ideal that Calvin had always disclaimed. And yet Calvin himself closely approximated the Anabaptist ideal by positing certain presumptive tests whereby the elect could be recognized. Williams proposed to heighten rather than to diminish the requirements, and thus refused to make the Church coterminous with an unweeded society. He declared:

" From this perverse wresting of what is writ to the Church and the officers thereof, as if it were written to the civil State and officers thereof, all may see how the Church and civil State are now become one flock of Jesus Christ; Christ's sheep, and the pastors or shepherds of them, all one with the several unconverted, wild, or tame beasts and cattle of the world, and the civil and earthly governors of them; . . . Christ's lilies, garden, and love, all one with the thorns, the daughters, and wilderness of the world." Williams was indeed so extreme in his separatism that " for a season he withdrew communion in spiritual duties even from his wife, till at length he drew her to partake with him in the error of his way." So reports John Cotton.

The standards, then, should not be reduced. At the same time Mr. Cotton's dream of converting everyone in the entire community in order that all might be able to meet the requirements was entirely fatuous. One ought indeed to make the attempt, but Mr. Cotton himself conceded that no wholesale conversion was to be expected until after the coming of Antichrist. Williams at this point was placing his finger upon a practical paradox in Calvinism in the combination of predestination and revivalism. A revival is very difficult to explain or justify unless its object be to save souls, but if the number of the elect is predetermined, no amount of revivalism can effect a change. The New England Calvinists did not suffer themselves to be impeded by this logic from employing the only sound method open to them for perpetuating their community. Williams pressed their premises with greater consistency.

If, then, the standards should not be diminished and conversions could not be expected, only one further expedient was open for maintaining the mores of the holy commonwealth, and that was constraint. Cotton did not propose to apply it in every direction. He distinguished between things indifferent and the fundamentals, and would use coercion only on behalf of the latter. Williams pronounced him wrong on both counts. He ought not to be tolerant with regard to the things indifferent, since nothing is indifferent that God has enjoined. Within the Church no easygoing tolerance should obtain. At the same time no coercion should be employed either to put men out or to draw them in. The whole fallacy of the national Church is that it cannot dispense with constraint because a national Church must be a single Church. If there is a single Church, there will be dissenters, because uniformity is impossible. Williams did not defend diversity as an ideal, and he drew no analogies from competition in trade or variation in poetry, but simply assumed that diversity is the law of life, and men will be no more satisfied with a single religion than they will fit themselves into one style of coat. Since, then, variety is a fact, a national Church without coercion is unattainable.

And if force be once allowed, it will be used not only to insure the norms of the community but also to extend its confines. The maintenance and the extension alike will be fostered by the sword. However great may be the disclaimer of any intent to convert by force, soon the commonwealth will be overreaching its borders. Wars of religion will ensue.

But whichever be the purpose, whether to maintain or to extend, force in religion ought to be disowned. The first reason is the grave danger of making a mistake. Often enough the saints have been put to death as heretics, as in the case of Hus, and Christ himself was condemned as a deceiver. Here once more is the rational argument that no infallible tests and no infallible persons exist by which and by whom to administer coercion. The rational argument in Williams is, however, comparatively scant.

He found much more congenial the considerations to be deduced from the cleavage of flesh and spirit. There is, he claimed, an order of the spirit and there is an order of the flesh. The sword belongs to the one and the word to the other. The State properly uses the sword. This Williams never denied, nor was he an Anabaptist in declaring that the Christian man may not assume the office of the magistrate and employ the sword as a servant of the State, provided he restrict himself to the proper sphere of the State. The point is not that the sword as such is inadmissible, nor that the State corresponds entirely to the reprobate and the Church exactly to the saints. Even Williams conceded that the Church contains some tares. The line between Church and State, therefore, is not exactly the line between the elect and the reprobate, but rather the line between the spirit and the flesh. The distinction was one that Luther had drawn, but he was at the same time insistent that spirit and flesh exist together in the same individual and that their spheres cannot be so neatly segregated. Williams affirmed that they can and must be separated. If the sword exceed its own province, it will but work havoc.

" I hence observe, that there being in this Scripture held forth a twofold state, a civil state and a spiritual, civil officers and spiritual, civil weapons and spiritual weapons, civil vengeance and punishment and a spiritual vengeance and punishment: although the Spirit speaks not here expressly of civil magistrates and their civil weapons, yet, these states being of different natures and considerations, as far differing as spirit from flesh, I first observe, that civil weapons are most improper and unfitting in matters of the spiritual state and kingdom, though in the civil state most proper and suitable."

The arguments that Williams adduced in support of his position were those formulated earlier by Castellio and since grown to be the commonplaces of the advocates of liberty. The first was that constraint must engender hypocrisy. " Can the sword of steel or arm of flesh make men faithful or loyal

to God? Or careth God for the outward loyalty or faithfulness, when the inward man is false and treacherous? Or is
there not more danger from a hypocrite, a dissembler, a
turncoat in his religion (from the fear or favor of men) than
from a resolved Jew, Turk, or papist, who holds firm unto
his principles? "

A carnal weapon or sword of steel may produce a carnal
repentance. "Faith is that gift which proceeds alone from the
Father of lights, and till he please to make his light arise and
open the eyes of blind sinners, their souls shall lie fast asleep
— and the faster, in that a sword of steel compels them to a
worship in hypocrisy." Even more serious is the effect that
compulsion to religion " carries men to be of no religion all
their days, worse than the very Indians."

As for ridding the commonwealth of inconvenient persons,
toleration is more effective. With regard to the Quakers, Williams reported: " We moreover find in those places where
these people aforesaid in this colony are most of all suffered
to declare themselves freely and are only opposed by arguments in discourse, there least of all they desire to come. And
we are informed they begin to loathe this place for that they
are not opposed by civil authority and with all meekness and
patience are suffered to say over their pretended revelation
and admonitions, nor are they like or able to gain many here
to their way." Williams was unquestionably too sanguine at
this point. The Quakers were before long to avail themselves
of the liberties of Rhode Island and the colony was to have
Quaker governors.

The consideration most frequently and ardently invoked
by Williams in favor of liberty was the violation of conscience entailed in persecution. Here he showed himself to
be a son of the seventeenth century, because under conscience
he included the erroneous conscience. Those who like Castel-

lio employed this argument in the sixteenth century were
few. One hundred years later their opinion had come more
nearly to prevail, and John Cotton appeared as almost an
anachronism in adhering to the ground of the earlier Reformers that one who obstinately rejects the fundamentals
sins against his own conscience. Williams stoutly defended
the integrity of the mistaken. His supporting evidences were
relatively few. He did not, like Milton, urge that truth is a
quest in which error may represent a necessary stage. He
did not regard error as an indispensable foil to truth. Nor
did he define truth as many-sided, so that those embracing
different and apparently discrepant aspects could yet both be
right. Williams' argument was simply that those who by
common consent of the Puritans were actually in error were
nonetheless as devoted and as sacrificial as those deemed to
be correct. And if devoted and if sacrificial, then to be regarded as sincere.

Let Williams speak. Here are passages culled from several
of his works:

"I have before discussed this point of an heretic sinning against
light of conscience: And I shall add that howsoever they lay this
down as an infallible conclusion, that all heresy is against light of
conscience; yet . . . how do all idolators after light presented,
and exhortations powerfully pressed, either Turks or pagans, Jews
or anti-Christians, strongly even to the death hold fast (or rather
are held fast by) their delusions? . . .

"Yea, God's people themselves, being deluded and captivated,
are strongly confident even against some fundamentals, especially
of worship, and yet not against the light, but according to the
light or eye of a deceived conscience. . . .

"Now all these consciences walk on confidently and constantly,
even to the suffering of death and torments, and are more strongly
confirmed in their belief and conscience, because such bloody and
cruel courses of persecution are used toward them. . . .

"I speak of conscience, a persuasion fixed in the mind and heart of a man, which enforceth him to judge and to do so and so, with respect to God, his worship, etc. . . .

"This conscience is found in all mankind, more or less, in Jews, Turks, papists, Protestants, pagans, etc. And to this purpose let me freely without offense remember you . . . [of the story] . . . of William Hartly in Queen Elizabeth her days, who receiving the sentence of hanging, drawing, etc., spake confidently (as afterward he suffered): 'What tell you me of hanging, etc. If I had ten thousand millions of lives, I would spend them all for the faith of Rome,' etc. . . .

"I confess in this plea for freedom to all consciences in matters (merely) of worship, I have impartially pleaded for the freedom of the consciences of the papists themselves, the greatest enemies and persecutors (in Europe) of the saints and truths of Jesus: yet I have pleaded for no more than is their due and right. . . .

"However, I commend that man, whether Jew, or Turk, or papist, or whoever, that steers no otherwise than his conscience dares, till his conscience tells him that God gives him a greater latitude. For, neighbor, you shall find it rare to meet with men of conscience, men that for fear and love of God dare not lie, nor be drunk, nor be contentious, nor steal, nor be covetous, nor voluptuous, nor ambitious, nor lazybodies, nor busybodies, nor dare displease God by omitting either service or suffering, though of reproach, imprisonment, banishment, and death, because of the fear and love of God. . . .

"It is to me most improbable that the number of Protestants turning papists will be great in a Protestant nation. . . . Why should not rather the glorious beams of the Sun of Righteousness in the free conferrings, disputings, and preachings of the gospel of truth, be more hopefully like to expel those mists and fogs out of the minds of men, and that papists, Jews, Turks, pagans, be brought home, not only into the common road and way of Protestantism, but to the grace of true repentance and life in Christ? I say, why not this more likely, by far, than that the mists and fogs of popery should overcloud and conquer that most glorious Light? . . .

" [But] if any or many conscientiously turn papists: I allege the experience of a holy, wise, and learned man, experienced in our own and other states' affairs, who affirms that he knew but few papists increase, where much liberty to papists was granted, yea, fewer than where they were restrained: Yet further, that in his conscience and judgment he believed and observed that such persons as conscientiously turned papists (as believing popery the truer way to heaven and salvation) — I say, such persons were ordinarily more conscionable, loving, and peaceable in their dealings, and nearer to heaven than thousands that follow a bare common trade and road and name of Protestant religion, and yet live without all life of conscience and devotion to God, and consequently with as little love and faithfulness unto men."

Some of the passages already cited indicate that Williams called for a sharp separation of Church and State. The reason was not simply that the spheres of their operation are distinct, but that the basis of their respective memberships must be different. The State includes everybody in a given area. The Church comprises only the regenerate, and they are bound to be few and incompatible with the world which will certainly subject them to persecution.

" Precious pearls and jewels, and far more precious truth are found in muddy shells and places. The rich mines of golden truth lie hid under barren hills. . . . The most high and glorious God hath chosen the poor of the world: and the witnesses of truth are clothed in sackcloth, not in silk and satin, cloth of gold, or tissue. And therefore I acknowledge, if the number of princes professing persecution be considered, it is rare to find a king, prince or governor like Christ Jesus the King of Kings . . . who tread not in the steps of Herod the Fox or Nero the Lion, openly or secretly persecuting the name of the Lord Jesus."

For the sake of the Church itself, it must be separated from the ungodly, who may and will persecute but cannot be suffered to have any part in its internal life. The Bay colony prevented this by excluding the unregenerate from the franchise. They stoutly resisted any extension of the vote, for fear that strangers would then dominate the saints. The common assertion must therefore be qualified that New England Calvinism transmitted the democracy of Congregationalism to the political order. This could become true only when the principle of Roger Williams was adopted which completely separated the two. The pattern of the Church could not be transferred to the State unless the State were distinct from the Church, because if the entire populace were admitted to the electorate, the Church would be subjected to aliens. Not until after such a fear was allayed by separation could the democratic pattern carry over into political relations.

The result of the separation was the emancipation of the Church but at the same time the secularization of the State. Williams pushed to extremes the principle of Luther that the State is not to be regarded as a Christian institution. Luther's point was simply that the State is not specifically Christian because it is valid equally among non-Christians and the Turks are perfectly capable of a sound political administration. For Luther this was no reason why Christian magistrates should not function as nursing fathers to the Church.

Williams began with Luther by pointing out how many States had been successfully administered without the benefit of Christianity.

" The commonwealth of Rome flourished five hundred years together, before ever the name of Christ was heard in it; which so great a glory of so great a continuance, mightily evinceth the distinction of the civil peace of a State from that which is Christian religion. . . .

"And since also the Turkish monarchy hath flourished many generations in external and outward prosperity and glory, notwithstanding their religion is false. . . .

"If none but true Christians, members of Christ Jesus, might be civil magistrates, and publicly intrusted with civil affairs, . . . then none but members of churches, Christians should be husbands of wives, fathers of children, masters of servants: But against this doctrine the whole creation, the whole world, may justly rise up in arms, as not only contrary to true piety, but common humanity itself. For if a commonweal be lawful amongst men that have not heard of God nor Christ, certainly their officers, ministers, and governors must be lawful also."

All this Luther could have said, but Williams went on to make much more drastic deductions, in that he affirmed that since a non-Christian could be a magistrate, a Christian when acting in the capacity of a magistrate could do no more than a non-Christian and should not therefore undertake to meddle with religion.

"A pagan or anti-Christian pilot may be as skillful to carry the ship to its desired port as any Christian mariner or pilot in the world, and may perform that work with as much safety and speed: yet have they not command over the souls and consciences of their passengers, or mariners under them, although they may justly see to the labor of the one, and the civil behavior of all in the ship. A Christian pilot . . . performs the same work (as likewise doth the metaphorical pilot in the ship of the commonweal) from a principle of knowledge and experience; but more than this, he acts from a root of the fear of God and love to mankind in his whole course. Secondly, his aim is more to glorify God than to gain his pay, or make his voyage. Thirdly, he walks heavenly with men and God, in a constant observation of God's hand in storms, calms, etc. So that the thread of navigation, being equally spun by a believing or unbelieving pilot, yet is . . . drawn over with the gold of godliness and Christianity by a Christian pilot, while he is holy in all manner of Christianity. . . . But lastly, the Christian pilot's power over the souls and consciences of his sailors and passengers is not greater than that of the anti-Christian, otherwise than he can subdue the souls of any by the two-edged sword of the Spirit, the Word of God, and by his holy demeanor in his place. . . .

" There goes many a ship to sea, with many hundred souls in one ship, whose weal and woe is common, and is a true picture of a commonwealth, or a human combination or society. It hath fallen out sometimes, that both papists and Protestants, Jews and Turks, may be embarked in one ship; upon which supposal I affirm, that all the liberty of conscience that ever I pleaded for turns upon these two hinges — that none of the papists, Protestants, Jews, or Turks be forced to come to the ship's prayers or worship, nor compelled from their own particular prayers or worship, if they practice any. I further add, that I never denied that, notwithstanding this liberty, the commander of this ship ought to command the ship's course, yea, and also command that justice, peace, and sobriety, be kept and practiced, both among the seamen and all the passengers. If any of the seamen refuse to perform their services, or passengers to pay their freight; if any refuse to help, in person or purse, toward the common charges or defense; if any refuse to obey the common laws and orders of the ship, concerning their common peace or preservation; if any shall mutiny and rise up against their commanders and officers; if any should preach or write that there ought to be no commanders or officers, because all are equal in Christ, therefore no masters nor officers, no laws nor orders, nor corrections nor punishments; — I say, I never denied, but in such cases, whatever is pretended, the commander or commanders may judge, resist, compel, and punish such transgressors, according to their deserts and merits."

Thus Roger Williams achieved religious liberty by the high price of opening the door to the secularization of the State. Often in our day this achievement is vaunted as his greatest contribution to liberty, and the new problems thereby created are overlooked. One may justly wonder whether, rather, his greatest contribution is not to be found in his tolerant spirit. He was commonly a reconciler. As one who had lived among the Indians and knew their speech, he sought to keep the peace among them and between them and the white colonists. The Bay recognized his services at this point and considered recalling him from banishment, but their gratitude could not quite bring them to reduce the standards of the holy commonwealth. He should remain in exile, yet esteemed and thanked.

His personal relations with the men of all parties were marked by both frank controversy and friendliness. A person who could retain the friendship of Cromwell, Milton, Endicott, and Winthrop was certainly, even if he were not a genius, yet a man of amazing quality. Williams had learned the high art of carrying on a battle of ideas without loss of respect, esteem, and affection.

He remonstrated very openly with the Bay for their dealings with the Indians. " Have they not entered leagues of love, and to this day continued peaceable commerce with us? Are not our families grown up in peace amongst them? Upon which I humbly ask, how it can suit with Christian ingenuity to take hold of some seeming occasions for their destructions? "

He remonstrated with the Bay over religious persecution. Nothing could have been more direct than his apostrophe to Endicott: " It is a dismal battle for poor naked feet to kick against the pricks. It is a dreadful voice from the King of Kings, and Lord of Lords: Endicott, Endicott, why huntest thou me? Why imprisonest thou me? Why finest, why so bloodily whippest, why wouldest thou (did not I hold thy bloody hands) hang and burn me? Yes, Sir, I beseech you to remember that it is a dangerous thing to put this to the

maybe . . . that in fighting against several sorts of consciences . . . I have not fought against God, that I have not
persecuted Jesus in some of them?"

He was equally forthright with Winthrop, telling him that
he mourned his nakedness and poverty in spirituals, yet at
the same time wished him well in a civil way and hoped that
the way of the Lord Jesus might be more fully disclosed to
them both.

Winthrop reminded him that they thought differently.
"Yes," replied Williams, "and the fire will try your works
and mine. The Lord Jesus help us to make sure of our persons that we seek Jesus that was crucified. However it is and
ever shall be . . . my endeavor to pacify and allay, where I
meet with rigid and censorious spirits who not only blame
your actions but doom your persons; and indeed it was one
of the first grounds of my dislike of John Smith the miller,
and especially of his wife, viz., their judging of your persons
as devils."

To young Winthrop, then living in Connecticut, the son of
the man who had subscribed to his banishment from the Bay,
Williams wrote saying, "Your loving lines in this cold dead
season were as a cup of your Connecticut cider."

Controversies of spirit with spirit and even body with body
we seem scarcely able to surmount. To be able to struggle
even to the point of banishing and being banished in the
winter's cold and yet to preserve the unity of the spirit and
the bond of peace may well be the highest of Christian attain-
ments.

Chapter Nine

THE APOLOGIST FOR THE ACT OF TOLERATION:

John Locke

The record of particular episodes in the struggle for religious liberty often reads like chapters in the story of lost causes. Doubly so is this the case if the biographical approach is chosen, because so often those who fought against persecution died themselves as the victims of persecution. Roger Williams in exile in the colonies and Milton in enforced retirement in England are scarcely the symbols of tolerance triumphant. Nevertheless, just as one cannot write off the toleration controversy of the sixteenth century as barren of results, neither can one dismiss the strivings of the sectaries in England and America

John Locke

during the seventeenth century as fruitless for liberty. At the close of the Cromwellian period England was more disposed to tolerance, if for no other reason on account of fatigue and yearning for tranquillity. Charles II rightly thought to facilitate his return to England by promising a general amnesty and by declaring " a liberty to tender consciences and that no man shall be disquieted or called into question for differences of opinion in matter of religion which do not disturb the peace of the kingdom."

Yet the reigns of Charles II and James II were marked by the last important resurgence of persecution. The reason was curiously in large part a fear of persecution. Englishmen would not tolerate Catholics because they did not trust Catholics to be tolerant of Protestants. However much a Catholic might aver his tolerance, the suspicion could not be allayed that if he were given the power, he would revert to the Inquisition and the stake. Such fears in the seventeenth century could not be considered groundless if one watched the course of events in France where, despite a political loyalty vociferously expressed by the Huguenots, Louis XIV progressively curtailed their liberties, suppressed their churches, and in the end, by the revocation of the Edict of Nantes in 1685, sent thousands of them into exile.

For that reason every move on the part of Charles II to fulfill his promise of indulgence, if it included any relaxation for Catholics, was looked upon askance by Parliament lest the glove should prove to hold the whip. And again such misgiving was not without warrant, for Charles did entertain a vast plan whereby England should be made Catholic in religion and absolutist in government. French arms should effect the revolution. But the kind of Catholicism that Charles envisaged was that of his grandfather Henry IV rather than that of his cousin Louis XIV. The Church in England should be dependent only in spirituals on Rome. Subscription in dogma should not be exacted with rigidity and the sects should be tolerated. Charles may very well have been sincere in saying, " I am in my nature an enemy to all severity for religion and conscience, howsoever mistaken it be, when it extends to capital and sanguinary punishments." But England was too impressed by the transformation of the tolerant Catholicism of Henry IV into the intolerance of Louis XIV to believe that Catholicism in power could long concede liberty.

Charles II was too astute openly to avow his grand scheme. He early perceived that the achievement of political absolutism in England was possible only on the basis of an ostensible adherence to the Protestant religion. For that reason he concealed his real position until his death. But enough about him savored of Romanism to evoke suspicion without any direct profession. His mother had been a Catholic; his sister in whom he confided was in France and was a Catholic; one of his natural sons was a Jesuit. The alliance with France and all the subsidies from France bespoke friendliness for the Catholic power. The king's brother, James the Duke of York, openly declared himself to be a Catholic and he was the heir to the throne. Hence there were plots to prevent a Catholic succession, with all the suspicion and severity that plots engender. The upshot of it all was, as far as the Catholics were concerned, that by the Test Act of 1673 all were excluded from public office who did not disclaim the doctrine of transubstantiation. Yet the succession to the throne was not altered, and James the Catholic followed his brother.

But if the hostility against Rome was motivated by distrust and fear of Roman intolerance, one might suppose that the attitude toward the sectaries would have been indulgent. It was not so, however. The reason was very similar. The sectaries themselves had been intolerant. Cromwell's spirit had not prevailed and the prayer book had been proscribed, and Cromwell himself had not scrupled to behead the Lord's anointed. The best hope for tranquillity appeared to lie in the maintenance of the middle way of the solid, sober Church of England. The sectaries were even looked upon as the allies of Rome, because by their defection from the national Establishment they weakened the solid front against the papacy. Then, too, there were those, especially of the clergy, who had old scores to settle, though one would suppose that their grievances could have been sufficiently redressed by restora-

tion to their former sees through the eviction of those appointed during the interregnum. That further steps were
taken in the direction of the suppression of sectarianism can
only be explained in part as a fear of disorder and in part as
a refusal to acknowledge the dissolution of Christendom. On
a European scale, of course, it was gone, but on a national
scale Englishmen still clung to the ideal of one State and one
Church embracing one people, born and baptized into a
commonwealth both of earth and of heaven. For this they
would make one last effort by constraint. The paradox of
persecution on the part of men weary of persecution is after
all no greater than recourse to war on the part of those weary
of war when new perils loom and new goals appear unattainable save by arms.

The actual measures against the nonconformists were enacted under Charles II in the Clarendon Code, including the
Conventicle Act, forbidding unauthorized meetings of as
many as five persons at a time, and the Five-Mile Act which
forbade ministers of the sects to come within five miles of
cities. The most drastic stroke was the Uniformity Act of
1662, which required all the clergy to give unfeigned assent
to *The Book of Common Prayer* newly revised. They must
also renounce the Solemn League and Covenant and profess
the unlawfulness of taking up arms against the king. Those
who refused to comply by the feast of St. Bartholomew
should be deprived. Some 1,700 declined. They were called
Bartholomeans because the terminus had been set for St.
Bartholomew's Day. If to them be added those earlier evicted,
the number approximates 2,000. The hardships of those thus
cast out with families and denied the right either to preach
or to teach were undoubtedly severe, yet Calamy's *Sufferings
of the Clergy* is far different from Foxe's *Book of Martyrs* or
Van Braght's *Bloody Mirror*. Calamy discovered a merciful
providence in that " few of them either perished or were ex-

posed to sordid, unseemly beggary." Either by manual labor or by the generosity of congregations or by teaching with the connivance of the authorities, a way was found to support wives and families. Greater were the sufferings of clergy and laity alike who for disobedience to the Conventicle Act and the Five-Mile Act suffered distraint of goods and prolonged imprisonments. In the course of twenty years some eight ministers died in prison. The last persecution, which kept Bunyan in Bedford jail and so many Quakers in durance, is not by any means to be minimized. Neither is it to be exaggerated, for the treatment of dissent had been greatly modified since the days of Torquemada or Servetus.

James II, when in 1685 he succeeded his brother Charles II, felt that the time had come for toleration; he therefore issued, in 1687, a Declaration of Indulgence, in which he candidly avowed his own adherence to the Church of Rome and his wish that all his subjects might be members of this communion. " Yet we humbly thank Almighty God, it is and has of long time been our constant sense and opinion that conscience ought not to be constrained nor people forced in matters of mere religion. It has ever been contrary to our inclination, as we think it is to the interest of government, which it destroys by spoiling trade, depopulating countries, and discouraging strangers, and finally, that it never obtained the end for which it was employed."

There were two counts that made this declaration unacceptable. The first was that the king was a Catholic, and Englishmen suspected his indulgence as a device for removing the restraints upon the practice of his own faith without sincere concern for the consciences of others. The king's previous behavior warranted distrust, for on his accession he had demanded of the Scottish estates the most sanguinary law enacted on the island against Protestant nonconformists. Under its provisions the aged widow Margaret Maclachlan and a lass of eighteen, Margaret Wilson, for refusal to say, " God save the King," without adding, " if it be God's will," were chained in the Solway at low water and engulfed by the rising tide.

The second count against the declaration was that it had been promulgated solely on the royal prerogative without parliamentary authorization. Seven bishops refused to read it in their churches, and on that account were sent to the Tower and tried for disloyalty. They were acquitted.

England had had enough. The king must be a Protestant. An invitation was therefore issued to the king's son-in-law, William, Prince of Orange, to come over from Holland to England and assume the government. Thus came to pass the Glorious Revolution of 1688.

The religious question had now to be settled. William would have been glad to make the Church of England more comprehensive by reducing its demands and thus allaying the scruples of many who remained without. He would at the same time tolerate all who could not subscribe and would make no religious tests for public office. The attempt to enact this program into law was only partially successful. The Bill of Comprehension designed to facilitate conformity through a reduction in the requirements was a failure. The Anglican leaders were not willing to augment numbers at the price of such dilution. But toleration for dissenters succeeded and found its expression in the famous Act of Toleration of 1689.

This document is commonly regarded as one of the milestones in the struggle for religious liberty. In and of itself it was not much. The older legislation of the Conventicle Act and the Five-Mile Act was not repealed, but the number of people to whom it might be applied was reduced. The Presbyterians and Independents escaped if they would subscribe to all of the Thirty-nine Articles save those bearing on polity and liturgy. The Baptists need not adhere to the article on infant baptism. Quakers received a special exemption from the obligation to take an oath. But Catholics and Unitarians were left still entirely without the pale, and disabilities as to public office and university degrees continued to apply to all nonconformists.

The Act of Toleration was very meager compared with the liberties subsequently achieved in England and the United States. Its significance is less to be found in its actual enactments than in its position on the boundary between two

A Cartoon: " A Delicate Dainty Damnable Dialogue Between the Devill and a Jesuite"

eras. Behind lay the Inquisition, the wars of religion, the dragonnades, imprisonments, and exiles. The sixteenth century had been marked by extensive use of the death penalty for heresy and the seventeenth, in England, by incarceration or exile plus many social distraints. The eighteenth century

was the age of the Enlightenment, with its war upon superstition, fanaticism, and bigotry, even to the point of its ex-
tinguishing all enthusiasm. The Act of Toleration stands at
the threshold of this change. Its ambiguity lies in the effort
to combine religious liberty with a national Establishment, to
bring together a union of Church and State and freedom of
religion. The concept of a Christian society, if only on a national scale, was still not abandoned, yet tacitly was relinquished when the sects were conceded an existence alongside of the Church.

The man who best epitomizes this whole development is
John Locke. He was not an exciting figure. His life, despite
one exile, was comparatively uneventful. His ideas were not
profoundly original albeit extremely influential, and his style
was drab. Drama belongs to the days of intense persecution.
Toleration was achieved by matter-of-fact people who, without any fanfare, had learned something about the everyday
art of living together.

Yet all this is true only in a comparative sense as over
against the days of Torquemada and Servetus. The times of
John Locke were stirring enough. Born in 1632, he was ten
years old when the civil wars broke out in England. His father supported the Puritan side and was well-nigh ruined in
the early reverses, but sufficiently recouped by the subsequent
triumphs to be able to send his son to Oxford. John Locke
thus studied there during the Puritan ascendancy. The problem of a public career then confronted him. The cloth was
rather too narrow of cut. Diplomatic service appealed, and
he went on a mission to Cleve in 1665. The decision, however, was for medicine, in which he distinguished himself;
and medicine curiously led him into politics — for in 1667
he became the physician and secretary to Lord Shaftesbury,
the progenitor of the Whigs. Ill health sent Locke to France
for a sojourn of four years from 1675 to 1679. On his return

to England he came to be suspected of complicity in an un-
successful attempt on the part of Shaftesbury and others to
forestall a Catholic succession to the throne by the way of rebellion. Locke, though able to satisfy interrogators of his in-
nocence, nevertheless considered withdrawal the course of
prudence and went therefore into exile in Holland for the
years 1683-1689. On the very ship with William and Mary he
came back to England, there to reside until his death in 1704.

Shortly after returning he wrote his *Letter on Toleration,*
the *Treatise on Civil Government,* and *The Essay Concerning Human Understanding.* These works taken together,
and particularly the two former, are commonly considered
an apology for the Glorious Revolution. They were not this
in the sense that the revolution had matured Locke's ideas
which had been conceived much earlier, nor in the sense that
his influence brought to pass the revolution, for he became
vocal in print only after its establishment. The point is,
rather, that he was himself so much a part of these events
that he was qualified to declare the word that spoke to men's
condition.

His ideas on religious liberty were not original. No one
could blame him for that. The best to be said on the subject
had already long since been said. The time had come, not
for better theories, but for an implementation of the old. But
the case did need to be restated and in terms pertinent to the
immediate situation.

One might indeed suppose that Locke would have re-
enforced arguments from the past by a skepticism drawn
from the advance of the natural sciences, in which he was
himself both interested and adept. But that in science which
intrigued him was " the improvement of natural experiments
for the conveniences of this life "; in other words, technology,
and not metaphysical implications. He could speak of the
universe as a machine, but did not think of it as a mechanism

subject to immutable law and immune from divine intervention. He had no objection to miracles on the ground of possibility. The only question was whether the evidence for their
occurrence was sufficient to warrant belief in their actuality.
The problem was thus not so much theological as historical,
and although he would scrutinize even Biblical miracles, he
did not for that reason come out with negative conclusions.
Even in his treatise, *The Reasonableness of Christianity,* there
was no rationalist attempt to discover natural explanations
for supernatural events. Locke is often classed with the Enlightenment, but this ascription is sound not so much because of his conclusions as because he restated the old problems in new forms, with which the succeeding age was to
grapple.

He was himself another of those Protestants in whom the
rigors of Calvinism and the mildness of Erasmianism were at
odds. Quite possibly the reconciliation of this conflict within
was the condition for the achievement of toleration without.
Locke was the son of a Puritan, ready to " let goods and kin-
dred go, this mortal life also." He knew the mettle of men
who counted faith above estates and the command of God
above the mandate of a sovereign. In his own justification of
revolution he was the heir of those who had dethroned and
beheaded a king.

But Locke was acquainted also with another aspect of de-
veloping Calvinism which, finding itself subject to persecution, had in the interests of liberty extended Calvin's view of
the English prayer book as containing " tolerable ineptitudes." The whole controversy in England was about just
such matters. The great doctrines were neither questioned
nor enforced, for in the area of faith the Established Church
was mild. Uniformity was required only with regard to polity and liturgy, and the defense of this policy was a curious
reversal of the argument advanced formerly by the Eras-

mians in the interests of liberty. When they distinguished the essentials from the nonessentials, and made the latter numerous in order to remove them from the field of constraint on the assumption that none would care to persecute over a matter unessential to salvation, then the argument proved to be a boomerang, for the leaders of the Anglican establishment said, in effect, to the sectaries, " You agree that all this great body of teaching and practice is not essential for salvation ? "

" Yes."

" And you will not be damned whether you do or do not conform on these points ? "

" Correct."

" Very well, then. If your eternal salvation is not imperiled, why will you not in the interests of order subject yourselves to the judgment of the Christian magistrate in order that all Englishmen may worship with seemliness, decorum, and after the same manner ? "

A refusal to comply under such circumstances was made to appear the height of obstinacy.

The answer fell to John Owen, the Independent who had been the outstanding figure at Oxford in Locke's early days. Precisely because the great dogmas of the Church were not in question, he was able in the tradition of Calvin's " tolerable ineptitudes " to avail himself of Castellio's argument that the controverted must be uncertain. These points are controverted and therefore they cannot be sure. But persecution over the uncertain is inappropriate. Such was the answer, but it was not adequate, for the Establishment was claiming precisely that the uncertain may be regulated, not in the name of an absolute but for the sake of good order, and he who refused to comply was punished not for his faith but for his obstinacy.

Locke, in the spirit of Owen, had a better answer. He

agreed with the Church of England that the magistrate might regulate nonessentials with several provisos: First, he must himself be a member of the Church that he regulates, and, secondly, he can regulate only that which affects the public peace, and the question is very real whether too much regulation may not itself be provocative of disorder. And finally, and this is the most drastic consideration, the essential and the nonessential in religion are incapable of determination because they belong to the inner life. Nothing is trivial to him who deems it important, unless first of all he be convinced of its triviality. This is but another version of the Pauline dictum that each to his own conscience must stand or fall.

On other occasions Locke employed the liberal argument in its traditional form, that persecution over trifles simply does not make sense. " Suppose," said Locke, " that I be marching on with my utmost vigor in that way which, according to the sacred geography, leads straight to Jerusalem." (In other words, I hold to the fundamentals.) Shall I then be " ill used because I wear not buskins; because my hair is not of the right cut; because I eat flesh upon the road, because I avoid certain byways, because I follow a guide that either is or is not clothed in white and crowned with a miter? Certainly, if we consider right, we shall find that for the most part they are such trivial things as these, which without any prejudice to religion or salvation of souls might either be observed or omitted—I say . . . such things as these—which breed implacable enmities among Christian brethren, who are all agreed in the substantial and truly fundamental part of religion." And granted that there be but one right road, the magistrate is in no better position to determine what it is than each private man by his own search and study. And if the magistrate undertakes to require that which is in itself indifferent, he thereby makes it essential because he has encroached upon God's province, who will say to him, "Who has required these or such like things at your hands?"

In this discussion Locke was, however, far from coming entirely into the clear. He appeared to rest his case upon skepticism as to the nonessentials, but plainly he thought they could be easily determined. The analogies from the trivialities of a journey have clearly that implication, and indeed he went on to make the point that certain matters were alike indifferent for salvation and innocuous as to the public peace. "Kneeling or sitting at the sacrament is no more injurious to the neighbor than sitting or standing at my own table. Wearing a cope or a surplice in the church can no more threaten the peace than a cloak or a coat in the market place. Being rebaptized can no more make a tempest in the commonwealth than in a river. Observing Friday with a Mohammedan, Saturday with a Jew, or Sunday with a Christian can make me neither a better or a worse subject of the magistrate or a worse neighbor."

"If, then, these points are nonessential and harmless, why not let them alone?" asked Locke. And the other side retorted, "If they matter so little, why not consign them to the magistrate instead of holding out obstinately for a private opinion?"

The answer to this question compelled one to go back farther and inquire as to the very nature of the Church itself. Should it be composed of those who took their religion so lightly that they were ready to permit even its outward forms to be settled by the civil power? What should be the basis of church membership? The whole Calvinist tradition had emphatically insisted that the members of the Church must be those who each for himself subscribed to the doctrine, gave evidence by a good life, and participated in the sacraments. And no lukewarm adherence was tolerable. Calvinism had endeavored to combine this Church with an entire community through a process of exclusion with regard to the unworthy as at Geneva, or by converting the entire populace as in Scotland, or by ruling the land through a militant minority as in England. But this latter program had collapsed, and now if all England could not be regarded as genuinely Christian, and if a convinced minority could no longer impose its will upon the aliens, then the Church had no recourse left, if it would maintain its integrity, other than to dissociate itself from the populace at large. In other words, the very logic of Calvinism pointed to the conventicle, the sect.

Locke had great difficulty in coming into the clear on this subject, because he was and remained an adherent of the Established Church, and sometimes argued for toleration on the ground that it would attract the nonconformists. At the same time he would not invite them save on the basis of sincere conviction.

" Open dissenters are better than secret malcontents. If all the dissenters were forced into the Church we should then have only an exasperated enemy within." Can anyone, he asked, question the sincerity of King James II, who gave up three crowns for his religion, or was Mr. Chillingworth less sincere when he became a Roman Catholic than when he returned to the Church of England? " It becomes all men to maintain peace and the common offices of friendship in a diversity of opinions, since we cannot reasonably expect that anyone should readily and obsequiously quit his own opinion and embrace ours with a blind resignation to an authority which the understanding of man acknowledges not."

But if the Church includes only convinced believers and the State embraces the entire populace, of necessity the theories of Church and State must differ and the union of the two becomes well-nigh impossible.

Adherence to the State depends on residence, adherence to the Church on voluntary subscription. This way of putting the case may seem to do violence to Locke's political theory because there, too, he adduced the principle of consent and often enough the analogy has been pointed out between his covenant theory of the Church and compact theory of the State. But there was a difference, because in the case of those born into a society after the original compact, membership was held to depend upon *tacit* consent to be inferred from the mere failure to remove elsewhere, whereas membership in the Church rested upon commitment. In other words, despite the compact theory of government, Locke held still to the birth theory of the State, and, despite his Anglicanism, to the new birth theory of the Church.

"A Church then," said he, "I take to be a voluntary society of men, joining themselves together of their own accord, in order for the public worshiping of God, in such a manner as they judge acceptable to him, and effectual to the salvation of their souls. I say it is a free and voluntary society. Nobody is born a member of any Church; otherwise the religion of parents would descend unto children, by the same right of inheritance as their temporal estates, and everyone would hold his faith by the same tenure as he holds his lands; than which nothing can be imagined more absurd. No man by nature is bound under any particular Church or sect, but everyone joins himself voluntarily to that society in which he believes he has found that profession and worship which is truly acceptable to God." And "if afterwards he discover anything erroneous, . . . why should it not be as free for him to go out as it was to enter?" If separatism be a sin, why should not a nonconformist who secedes from his own group in order to join the Church of England be regarded as sinful? The question of course makes sense only if one assumes the parity of the established Church and the sects, and that is precisely where Locke came out. With Roger Williams he reached the conclusion that "there is absolutely no such

thing, under the gospel, as a Christian commonwealth." And
he was even more logical than Williams in his denial that
there ever had been a Christian commonwealth, because even
in ancient Israel strangers were tolerated within the gates
and not exterminated because of their practice of idolatry.
Locke was the very epitome of the English system, with a
love for the national Church and a complete acquiescence in
a multiplicity of sects.

Alongside the Calvinist strain in Locke was the Erasmian,
and it was mediated to him through two lines: the first was
English and the second Dutch. In England the ethical emphasis that insists that only the pure in heart can see God was
cultivated by the Cambridge Platonists. One of their leaders,
Cudworth, was a personal friend of Locke's, and Cudworth's
daughter, Lady Masham, extended the hospitality of her
home to Locke in his declining years. The Neoplatonist tradition held that because the eye of the soul is impaired by impurity, the vision of God is attainable only after a purgative
process. One of the school of Cambridge affirmed that since
love was enjoined by Christ as the chief among the virtues,
therefore without love one cannot attain to Christian truth.
And Cudworth, the friend of Locke, preached before the
House of Commons an exposition on Paul's " Hymn of
Love," recalling that the way to heaven lies, not through
speculative knowledge, but through divine obedience. He
trusted that " a sweet harmonious affection in these jarring
times should tune the world at last into better music." Certain passages in Locke read almost as if they might have
been taken from this very sermon, for Locke held that " obedience to what is already revealed is the surest way to more
knowledge " and that " the indispensable duty of all Christians " is " to maintain love and charity in the diversity of
contrary opinions, since Christianity is not a notional science
but a rule of righteousness. Therefore we should lay aside all

controversy and speculative questions and instruct and encourage one another in the duties of a good life and pray
God for the assistance of his spirit for the enlightenment of
our understanding and subduing our corruptions. . . . Agreement in things necessary to salvation, and the maintaining
of charity and brotherly kindness with diversity of opinions
in other things, is that which will very well consist with
Christian unity."

Still deeper in its impact on Locke was a movement directly in the succession not only of Erasmus but also of Castellio, that of the Remonstrants in Holland. Locke spent
six years of his life there as an exile. For a time he lived in
concealment and under the assumed name of Mynheer Van
der Linden. But when he was removed from the list of the
proscribed in England, he feared no longer to reveal his
identity, yet declined the pardon procured for him by William Penn on the ground that to accept would be an admis-
sion of complicity in a plot of which he had been innocent.

Holland at the time of Locke's arrival appeared to be the
last stronghold of Protestantism and liberty. Elsewhere in
Europe the prospect was grim. The year 1685 saw the accession of the Catholic king to the throne of England, the revocation of the Edict of Nantes in France, the passing of the
Calvinist Palatinate into Catholic hands, and the cessation of
toleration in Savoy for the Waldenses. But in Holland old
sects and new survived either by toleration or connivance.
Here Locke met the Mennonites and the Labadists. For
some years he stayed in the home of an English Quaker,
Benjamin Furley. Here were new refugees from France,
Calvinists reconstructed and unreconstructed, and rationalists
such as Pierre Bayle. No subject was more warmly discussed
in these circles than toleration, and more important than all
were the native Hollanders, who cherished the memory of
the great Hollander, Erasmus of Rotterdam. Locke became

intimate with Le Clerc, the editor of the works of Erasmus, and, indeed, had it not been for the encouragement of Le Clerc, one may doubt whether Locke would ever have published anything. And there was Limborch, the leader of the Remonstrants and the exposer by historical science of the cruelties of the Inquisition.

Exile gave Locke leisure to think and to write, and the new pressures incited thought. The problem of conscience was here receiving a more searching consideration than had hitherto been the case. The sixteenth century, save for a few exceptions in men like Castellio, had claimed toleration only for a right conscience. The seventeenth century came to recognize also the claims of the erroneous conscience. But then the question was whether conscience could claim to be an absolute in the eyes of the State, and whether any particular course of action could be exempted by the State from penalty simply because the perpetrator was sincere. Castellio hardly saw the problem. Ochino raised it in the case of a conscientious tyrannicide, but left the problem in mid-air.

Pierre Bayle brought it to earth, in his discussion of the text, " Compel them to come in." He went so far as to say that if one is conscientiously convinced of his duty to spread his religion by force, then he is bound to do so, and this applies quite as much if he be in error. Thus Bayle either justified persecution when exercised by the erroneous or made it ridiculous, and in any case he pointed up the difficulties entailed in treating conscience as an absolute from the subjective point of view and a relative from the objective. Then came the question left suspended by Ochino of the conscientious tyrannicide. Bayle concluded that zealots, like the assassins of Henry III and Henry IV, if they believed it their duty to kill, must kill. But the magistrate who is not a searcher of hearts must at the same time punish. Thus Bayle emerged with an irreconcilable clash between the conscience of the citizen and the conscience of the State.

Locke could discover no better way out; if the magistrate conceived himself in duty bound to enact laws for the public good that appeared to his subjects to be clean contrary, there was no judge between them but God. The magistrate was bound to act, the subject was bound to suffer. Only if the magistrate's behavior imperiled the common weal might the subjects have recourse to revolution. The reconciliation of the problem, then, could not lie in any comparison of consciences, but only in constraint and resistance whether passive or active.

In such cases Locke could find no practical way of determining who was right. But it was for no lack of consideration of the question of how man can know what is true and right. Locke's fame rests largely upon his *Essay Concerning Human Understanding*. Curiously only two men in the course of the struggle for religious liberty have written treatises alike on the problem of liberty and the problem of knowledge and have sought to bring the two into relation. Those two men were Sébastien Castellio and John Locke. For that reason it is very interesting to discover in the letters of Limborch and Locke for the year 1693 a correspondence on the question of the desirability of publishing a complete edition of the works of Sébastien Castellio. Locke's opinion was that they would be received with high favor in England.

One wonders whether he was thinking only of the published works or whether perhaps he may have known the manuscript *On Doubt and Belief*. There is a bare possibility, though it cannot be pressed. This at any rate is certain, that Locke in Holland was moving in a succession of Castellianist thought, and the similarity between the ideas of Locke and Castellio is striking. Locke, like Castellio, took as the source of knowledge sense experience and revelation. Both were to be corrected and amplified by reason. And although Locke

rejected innate ideas, he accepted intuitive modes of understanding, which meant very nearly the same thing. Much he
was prepared to accept on faith, and if he attempted by reason to demonstrate the existence of God, yet for the character
of God he relied upon Christian revelation.

His main point was that faith and reason are not anti-
thetical, and that religion can be understood. Further, if it
cannot be understood, it is of no practical consequence. This
is where Locke distinctly sets himself in the Castellianist and
Erasmian antidogmatic tradition. It may in a sense be called
even antirationalist, since despite all the praises of reason it
disclaims any capacity on the part of reason to scale the
heavenly heights and pry into the ultimate mysteries. All
that has been vouchsafed to men is enough light to get home
by, a few simple truths, and a code of behavior. There is a
vast area that man cannot know, but should he complain
" that we are not furnished with compass nor plummet, to
sail and fathom that restless unnavigable ocean of the universal matter, motion and space "? Because, however great the
ignorance of mankind, no one who sincerely sought to learn
his duty with a design to do it had miscarried for want of
knowledge. Locke's system is rational only in the sense of
reasonable, and significantly he entitled his theological work
The Reasonableness of Christianity. The object of the book
was to discover an intelligible reason for the reticence of
Jesus with regard to his Messianic role. The gist of the whole
matter was this: what is needed to be known for salvation
must be accessible to the uninstructed and therefore clear
and simple. Locke was another exponent of the theology of
the penitent thief.

Curiously, his treatise on knowledge was brought less directly into relation with the problem of liberty than was Castellio's, and the reason was that in Castellio's day persecution rested on a claim to truth, but in Locke's day only on

a claim to order. He had no need to argue with the Church of England about truth, but only as to how much constraint was necessary for the preservation of the public peace.

And on this score he conceded the necessity of some constraint, notably in the case of the Roman Catholics, whose worship was by no means to be allowed. Practical experience had taught Locke much on this score. He had learned that Catholics may be urbane and less insufferable than argumentative Calvinists. Nevertheless they are not to be trusted in Church-State relations. In his judgment they were bound by their presuppositions to persecute, and therefore should not be tolerated.

His journals give some intriguing accounts of personal contacts with Catholics on the Continent. The first eye opener was on the mission to Cleve when he saw a Christmas crèche. To him it was but an instance of popish superstition and the images of the holy family appeared to him but the second cousins of Punch and Judy or their progenitors. The little models of sheep were but symbols of the people who were as sheep without a shepherd. Locke sprinkled himself with holy water and recorded in his diary that Catholics slobber over their ceremonies. But in the next entry he declared that " the Catholic religion is a different thing from what we believe in England. I have not met with any so good-natured people or so civil as Catholic priests, and I have received many courtesies from them. But the Calvinists are as bad as the Presbyterians, and one young sucking divine assaulted me furiously." Locke visited a Franciscan friary and conversed with the brothers in bad Latin. " The friar had more belly than brains and methought was very fit to be reverenced and not much unlike some head of a college and I liked him well for entertainment. The truth is they were very civil and courteous."

But the subsequent years in France revealed instances

enough in which Huguenot churches were being suppressed. Amid notes on relics, vineyards, uniforms, and irrigated orchards of Chinese oranges, Locke recorded that the Protestants had had three hundred churches demolished and within these two months twenty more condemned. Louis XIV was moving toward the revocation of the Edict of Nantes. Locke was convinced that this was the inevitable logic of Catholicism and never receded from his position that if any sect teach that promises are not to be kept to heretics or that excommunicated kings forfeit their crowns, such a sect is not to be tolerated.

The works of Locke written in exile with little hope of their ever seeing the light of day became, in fact, the apology for the Whig revolution when he returned on the very same vessel with William and Mary. His first letter on toleration, published in the year 1689, began with a protest in the spirit of Castellio:

" If the gospel and the apostles may be credited, no man can be a Christian without charity, and without that faith which works, not by force, but by love. Now I appeal to the consciences of those that persecute, torment, destroy, and kill other men upon pretense of religion, whether they do it out of friendship and kindness toward them, or no; and I shall then indeed, and not till then, believe they do so, when I shall see those fiery zealots correcting, in the same manner, their friends and familiar acquaintances, for the manifest sins they commit against the precepts of the gospel; when I shall see them prosecute with fire and sword the members of their own communion that are tainted with enormous vices, and without amendment are in danger of eternal perdition; and when I shall see them thus express their love and desire of the salvation of their souls, by the infliction of torments, and exercise of all manner of cruelties. For if it be out of a principle of charity, as they pretend, and love to men's

souls, that they deprive them of their estates, maim them
with corporal punishments, starve and torment them in
noisome prisons, and in the end even take away their lives
— I say, if all this be done merely to make men Christians,
and procure their salvation — why, then, do they suffer
' whoredom, fraud, malice, and such like enormities,' which,
according to the apostle, Rom., ch. 1, manifestly relish of
heathenish corruption, to predominate so much and abound
amongst their flocks and people? These, and such like things,
are certainly more contrary to the glory of God, to the purity
of the Church, and to the salvation of souls, than any conscientious dissent from ecclesiastical decision, or separation
from public worship, whilst accompanied with innocency of
life. Why, then, does this burning zeal for God, for the
Church, and for the salvation of souls — burning, I say lit-
terally, with fire and faggot — pass by those moral vices and
wickednesses, without any chastisement, which are acknowl-
edged by all men to be diametrically opposite to the profession of Christianity; and bend all its nerves either to the introducing of ceremonies or to the establishment of opinions,
which for the most part are about nice and intricate matters
that exceed the capacity of ordinary understandings? Which
of the parties contending about these things is in the right,
which of them is guilty of schism or heresy, whether those
that domineer or those that suffer, will then at last be manifest, when the cause of their separation comes to be judged
of? He certainly that follows Christ, embraces his doctrine,
and bears his yoke, though he forsake both father and
mother, separate from public assemblies and ceremonies of
his country, or whomsoever, or whatsoever else he relin-
quishes, will not then be judged an heretic."

One is not surprised that Locke was not satisfied with the
Act of Toleration. To Limborch he wrote, " It is not what you
would wish, but it is something." And then he set himself

indefatigably to urge that what had already been done should in all logic call for more. The arguments adduced in favor of abolishing the penalties of confiscation, maiming, and incarceration were valid equally for the removal of civil disabilities. And likewise the arguments against removing civil disabilities would be of equal force in favor of restoring confiscation, maiming, and incarceration. Then, England should go either backward or forward, and Locke was sufficiently confident that England would not move backward to be certain that his plea would impel it forward. Such, indeed, at long last was the outcome. England thus demonstrated the possibility of retaining a union of Church and State and of combining it with religious liberty.

A Cartoon: Two Devils Helping Nonconformists Pull Down the Dome of St. Paul's Cathedral

REFLECTIONS

A survey of the events and the theories described or alluded to in these brief sketches prompts at least certain reflections. The most obvious is that something was accomplished and that the process was exceedingly slow. The best things on religious liberty were said in the sixteenth century but not practiced until the nineteenth. From this observation we may derive alike comfort and concern. By way of comfort we have reason to hope that as the religious controversies of bygone days have been allayed, so also in time will the political and economic clashes of our time be assuaged. The day may come when men will think it preposterous to die and kill over a system of land tenure or a political constitution. On the other hand, if all this is to take two hundred years, quite conceivably there will be nobody here to celebrate the victory. Our situation differs from that of former times in that the very technology to which Locke looked to enhance the comforts of life has introduced the possibility of man's extinction. The only conclusion can be that either we perish or else the pace of social change must be accelerated. We cannot afford to wait two centuries to solve our present dilemmas.

Another reflection is that when one problem is solved, another will undoubtedly replace it. If one lion is persuaded to lie down with a lamb, another lion rampant leaps from his lair. Life does not seem to have been constructed for tranquillity. When the religious problem in the Western world was relatively solved, political and social upheavals emerged, which in turn set back religious liberty. Conceivably, now that at last all problems are being grappled with on a world front, we may, if we succeed at all, manage to achieve solutions that will offer a greater stability. But certainly the past discloses a never-ceasing bubbling of the caldrons. Eternal vigilance and unremitting labor are our mortal lot.

This is in part true because every solution, however wise and necessary, carries within itself the possibility of some new abuse. If doubt be invoked as a check on dogma, the course of skepticism may run so far that in the end neither God, nor right, nor neighborliness, nor decency survive. If reason be invited to temper orthodoxy, reason may erect its own guillotines. If to curb the arrogance of the Church or to check the meddling of the State the two be separated, then the State is prompted to remove from our coins " In God we trust." All of which is not to say that dogma is not to be curbed and orthodoxy is not to be restrained and Church and State are not to be separated. But even that which is imperative in any given situation opens the way to abuses of another sort. The ideal is to strike some sort of golden mean.

If formerly all the slogans of persecution deserved to be challenged, today many of the catchwords of liberty call for a re-examination if genuine liberty is to be conserved. The most serious problem is as to the certitude of truth in the field of religion. So far has relativity gone that now one idea is commonly held to be as good as another and one religion to have quite as much claim as another, provided only that it satisfies its own adherents. If they find in it peace, the character of the religion is inconsequential. Surely the rise of all the frightful isms of our time ought to have been enough to make clear that the satisfaction of adherents is no criterion either of the worth or of the truth of any system. The ideologies of racial extermination have been satisfying enough to those who pro-

fessed and practiced them, and yet they are not for that reason either right or true. Satisfaction and peace of mind are
not after all the chief end of man. We must square up to
what is actually so, whether or not it bring peace and satisfaction. If we are to deal with the tough in behavior, we shall
have to be tough in belief.

And yet we cannot return to the appalling dogmatisms of
former days. The protests of Erasmus and Castellio and all
the rationalists against unqualified pretensions to religious
knowledge were perfectly valid. The distinction between reason and faith is sound. Perhaps here another distinction should
be introduced which was never distinctly formulated in the
course of the long struggle, namely, the distinction between
knowledge sufficient for private consolation and knowledge
adequate for public legislation. Belief in immortality, for example, is a very great comfort to the bereaved, but our certainty of the future life and its details is not so great that we
can blithely blot out whole cities with the bromidic reflection
that after all we have not destroyed life but only transferred
it to another sphere.

We need likewise to rethink the common assumption that
superior knowledge has no right whatsoever to interfere with
religious conviction. A very thought-provoking instance is
related by Dr. Heiser in his book *An American Doctor's
Odyssey*. He was the health officer for Manila when cholera
was reported in various parts of the city. Simultaneously came
the news of a miracle in the bay, for a fisherman had observed
upon the surface of the water a black streak in the form of a
cross and the water was sweet. He summoned the priest, who
confirmed the miracle. The people then paddled out with
bottles and drank of the holy liquid. Investigation discovered
a break in the sewer. The doctor then appealed to the militia
to suppress the miracle. He was told that a riot might be expected, since the natives were already incensed over the burn-

ing of some of their huts for sanitary reasons. The doctor replied that he preferred a riot to an epidemic and the populace was kept back while the damage was repaired.

Here we have an instance where force was used to restrain people for their own good and the justification was superior knowledge. The difference between the American doctor and John Calvin was that the American doctor did know and John Calvin did not. At least that was the first difference. And a very much more important difference was that the militia did not burn the natives but merely kept them back until the sewer was mended. This introduces a sound principle, that although constraint may be justified when grounded on knowledge and genuinely directed to the welfare of those constrained, it must nevertheless be chary of means and confine itself to the very minimum needful.

This brings us directly to the problem of conscience. In the matter of religion its claims have come to be generally recognized, but not in matters of conduct, and conscientious objection to military service in the Western world fares very differently from country to country. Great Britain has been the most liberal. The problem was faced in other form clearly enough by Bayle and Locke, who saw that conscience cannot be regarded by the State as an absolute. If the individual be conscientiously convinced of a particular course of action that is deemed inconsistent with the public welfare, some degree of restraint will have to be exercised. There is no reconciliation of the clash other than by penalty from the one side and endurance from the other. But all this is not said to deny the rights of conscience nor to justify ruthlessness. Nothing is more precious than conscience, and no quality is more integral to the sound life of the body politic. The State in exercising restraint should be guided by several principles of limitation. First, the object of constraint should never be to break down integrity but only to prevent overt acts being inimical.

And when the peril is past, there should be no continuing penalty, let alone deprivation of citizenship, because he who out of conscience refuses to serve the State in time of war may well be in peace a most scrupulous and devoted public servant. The State ought ever to be ready to take such men into its service the moment they can conscientiously comply. Furthermore the State should cultivate humility, since acts that in one generation are deemed subversive often come to be regarded as innocuous by the next. Moreover, the State should exhaust every other recourse before employing the prison or the concentration camp.

The distinction so persistent throughout the struggle for religious liberty between the essentials and the nonessentials of Christianity calls for reconsideration. It is still a potent concept, for the whole Church unity movement within Protestantism and the continuing attitude of aloofness toward the Roman Church are based on the assumption that Protestants are agreed in essentials with each other, but that with Rome they are not. This is true, but the distinction cannot be maintained without continual inquiry as to what is essential. There is no answer other than through theology, and the contemporary revival of theological interest is wholesome, however much theology in the past may have been the symbol, if not the cause, of persecution. There are a number of points involved in this matter of the essentials and the nonessentials. One view is that in case of a difference both sides cannot be right, but there is no infallible way of telling which is right and, since the point is not vital, each may leave the other to follow his own preference. The other view is that both views may be right because truth is varied, just as God is diversified. If this theory be adopted to cover the varieties of Protestantism, then the question arises whether it may not be extended to cover all the religions of the world, and in that case a complete relativism ensues. No simple answer is ready to hand. This is one of the areas requiring constantly to be explored.

As for the theory of the Church, one observes throughout the course of Christian history a perpetual tension between permeation and withdrawal in the attitude of the Church to the world and the corollary has been the view of the Church either as coterminous with society or as separated in the form of a sect. All the previous failures to Christianize the world have more and more disposed Christians in the West to abandon the attempt at holy commonwealths and to regard the Church as an independent voluntary society. But this leaves the question only the more crying of what then becomes of the State and of society. The ideal is that of a national religion envisaged by Cromwell rather than that of an established Church, and in the United States, despite all the secularism, that ideal has perhaps more nearly been realized than anywhere else. Church and State are separated and friendly and exert a mutual influence. The Churches in some measure do affect public policy. The problem at the moment is most acute in the field of education, where the separation of Church and State has led to secularization. Some Church bodies feel the necessity of reverting to the system of the parochial school. Others seek to introduce religion on released time. Whatever the method, the need is acute.

The most devastating reflection to be deduced from this study is that much of the previous controversy is simply irrelevant now because the whole context has changed. In the past in Western Christendom those who debated persecution and liberty were on both sides concerned to make men Christian. Today the greatest persecutors desire to eradicate all religion. Even the argument that constraint will not make sincere Fascists or Communists will not weigh too greatly with them because they do not need many genuine converts so long as they hold the machinery of power. What they require of the others is only that they should not impede. A recantation is useful only in a few instances to affect public opinion. For the most part silent submission suffices. And even the old techniques of resistance are gone. Martyrdom is seldom allowed and obstructionists merely disappear.

The noblest achievement of the Western world has been the conduct of controversy without acrimony, of strife without bitterness, of criticism without loss of respect. But when men do not operate within the same framework, this becomes impossible. Only those who believe in universal right, in integrity, law, and humanity, if not in the Christian God, are in a position to clash on higher levels and retain personal friendship as did Roger Williams with most of his opponents. But if one side makes the will of a party into an absolute, and for it will lie and assassinate, then for the other side to fight according to the rules is very difficult.

The more the contestants are locked, the greater becomes the danger that the rules will be scrapped on both sides, and in that case the liberalism of the West is already undone. The very effort to control the unscrupulous foe leads to unscrupulousness. What is still more disconcerting is the Communist technique of insinuating agents under false colors, which breaks down faith, awakens suspicion, sows the poison of distrust, and produces panic and fevered witch hunts which are vastly more inimical to the innocent than to the guilty. In the United States at the present moment the greatest danger is not from a Communist coup but from anti-Communist hysteria.

Which again is not to say that the fear of Reds is entirely hysterical. Balance and again balance is what we need. In so many quarters of the globe whole peoples are incapable of considered judgment. War, privation, disease, fear have warped all sobriety of judgment. One word may be extricated from the long travail of liberty in the past and made a watchword for the present, and that word is " reasonableness."

These concluding remarks have gone beyond the immediate question of religious liberty into a discussion of all liberty and all rights, and the extension is justified because all freedoms hang together. Milton properly associated freedom of religion, freedom of speech, and freedom of the press. Civil liberties scarcely thrive where religious liberties are disregarded, and the reverse is equally true. Beneath them all is a philosophy of liberty which assumes a measure of variety in human behavior, honors integrity, respects the dignity of man, and seeks to exemplify the compassion of God.

Sources

Since this work is directed to the general public, documentation has been used only sufficiently to enable the specialist to find his way to the sources. The first six chapters are in a different category from the last three, because the sources are in foreign languages and the treatment is largely a reworking of books and articles of a more technical nature and previously published. All that is needful is to refer to the previous studies save for additional bibliography and references for new citations. The last three chapters are almost wholly new and the sources are in English. For that reason the documentation is complete.

FOREWORD: The opening section is a reworking of an article, "The Struggle for Religious Liberty," *Church History*, X,2 (June, 1941), 3–32. This article has three pages of bibliography. The theory of the Church in relation to persecution is more amply treated in the article "The Parable of the Tares as the Proof-text for Religious Liberty to the End of the Sixteenth Century," *Church History*, I,2 (June, 1932), 67–89.

CHAPTER I: TORQUEMADA: The sketch of the earlier history of the theory and practice of persecution in Christian history is condensed from my book, *Sebastian Castellio Concerning Heretics* (New York, 1935).

On the Inquisition in general, the classic work is that of Henry C. Lea, *A History of the Inquisition in the Middle Ages* (reprint, New York, 1922). A briefer and more recent treatment is that of A. S. Tuberville, *Medieval Heresy and the Inquisition* (London, 1920).

For the Inquisition in Spain, consult Henry C. Lea, *The Inquisition in Spain*, 4 vols. (reprint, New York, 1922), and Cecil Roth, *The Spanish Inquisition* (London, 1927).

For Torquemada, the following:

Hope, Thomas, *Torquemada Scourge of the Jews* (London, 1939).

Lucka, Emil, *Torquemada und die Spanische Inquisition* (Vienna and Leipzig, 1926).

Sabatini, Rafael, *Torquemada and the Spanish Inquisition* (Boston and New York, 1924?). The documents on the Franco case are printed in the article of Fidel Fita, "La Inquisition y el Santo Niño de la Guardia," *Boletín de la Real Academia de la Historia*, XI (1887), 7–160.

262 SOURCES

Some documentary material is in Juan Antonio Llorente, *Historia Critica de la Inquisition de España*, II (Madrid, 1822).
CHAPTER II: CALVIN utilizes the following previous studies:
"The Development and Consistency of Luther's Attitude to Religious Liberty," *Harvard Theological Review*, XXII,2 (April, 1929), 107-149.
Sebastian Castellio Concerning Heretics (New York, 1935).
"The Struggle for Religious Liberty," *Church History*, X,2 (June, 1941), 3-32.
The citations from Calvin's commentary on Deuteronomy will be found in the *Calvini Opera*, XXVI, and in the following order: pp. 150 ff., 177, 21, 77, 56.
The citation on page 71, line 1, is from the *Calvini Opera*, XXIV, 363.
CHAPTER III: SERVETUS: A detailed study is in preparation. The following articles have appeared:
"The Present State of Servetus Studies," *Journal of Modern History*, IV,1 (March, 1932), 72-92.
"The Smaller Circulation: Servetus and Colombo," *Sudhoffs Archiv für Geschichte und Medizin*, XXIV, 3-4 (1931), 371-374.
"Servetus and the Genevan Libertines," *Church History*, V,2 (June, 1936), 141-149.
The documents on the trial at Geneva are in the *Calvini Opera*, VIII. The best biographical study of Servetus is that by E. Morse Wilbur, *A History of Unitarianism*, I (Cambridge, 1945). He has translated "Servetus 'On the Errors of the Trinity,'" *Harvard Theological Studies*, XVI (1932).
Citations from Servetus:
ending
page 78, line 17, *De Trinitatis Erroribus*, 116b;
page 78, line 26, *De Trinitatis Erroribus*, 78a;
page 79, line 11, *Dialogorum de Trinitate libri Duo*, B6a.
CHAPTER IV: CASTELLIO is for the most part a reworking of materials in my *Sebastian Castellio Concerning Heretics* (New York, 1935), and especially of the earlier article, "Sebastian Castellio and the Toleration Controversy of the Sixteenth Century," in *Persecution and Liberty, Essays in Honor of George Lincoln Burr* (New York, 1931), 183-209.
The standard work on Castellio is the life by Ferdinand Buisson, *Sebastien Castellion* (Paris, 1892), in two volumes. Castellio's "De Arte Dubitandi" has been published by Elizabeth (Mrs. Felix) Hirsch in "Per la Storia degli Eretici Italiani del Secolo XVI in Europe," *Reale Accademia d'Italia Studi e Documenti*, VII (Rome, 1937).
The newly discovered manuscript referred to in the text was found by Dr. Bruno Becker, of Amsterdam, and is described in *Church History*, IX,3 (1940), 272. I have discussed Castellio's theory of knowledge in the article "New Documents on Early Protestant Rationalism," *Church History*, VII,2 (June, 1938), 179-187. The references to Calvin on page 103

are from the *Calvini Opera*, XXIII, 482–487; XXIV, 16–24. The passage from Beza on page 113 is from his *De Haereticis*, pp. 48–53 condensed, and his statement on page 114 is from the *Epistolae* (1575), 20.

The counsel to let Castellio alone mentioned on page 110 is from an unpublished letter of Simon Sulzer to Theodore Beza from Basel, May 2, 1560, cited here by the courtesy of Dr. Fernand Aubert, of Geneva, who is editing Beza's correspondence.

CHAPTER V: DAVID JORIS rests on my book *David Joris Wiedertäufer und Kämpfer für Toleranz in 16. Jahrhundert*, translated by Hajo and Annemarie Holborn, *Archiv für Reformationsgeschichte*, Ergänzungsband VI (Leipzig, 1937). My work has been corrected by Paul Burckhardt, "David Joris und seine Gemeinde in Basel," *Basler Zeitschrift für Geschichte und Altertumskunde*, XLVIII (1949), 5–106. He discovers a number of errors in my readings, but dissents from my conclusions at only two important points. The first has to do with Joris' reputed bigamy. A letter, the significance of which I overlooked, written by someone to the subsequent husband of the allegedly bigamous wife says that the father would not have been satisfied with the provision made for the children. The father appears to be Joris, in which case the charge is substantiated, but Burckhardt is not positive. The other point is my contention that at the end of his life Joris abandoned his messianic pretensions in favor of mysticism and allegory. In a region necessarily so vague precision is impossible, but I still sense a great difference between the earlier and the later Joris, and between the later Joris and some of his materialistic followers.

There is an illuminating discussion of Joris on religious liberty in Johannes Kühn, *Toleranz und Offenbarung* (Leipzig, 1923).

CHAPTER VI: BERNARDINO OCHINO rests on my book *Bernardino Ochino Esule e Riformatore Senese del Cinquecento*, translated by Elio Gianturco, *Biblioteca Storica Sansoni*, N.S. IV (Florence, 1940). The following study appeared slightly earlier, but too late to be used: Benedetto Nicolini, *Il Pensiero di Bernardino Ochino* (Napoli, 1939).

CHAPTER VII: JOHN MILTON: For the background of religious toleration in Milton's age, consult W. K. Jordan, *The Development of Religious Toleration in England*, 4 vols. (Cambridge, 1932–1946), and Thomas Lyon, *The Theory of Religious Liberty in England 1603–39* (Cambridge, England, 1937). There is an illuminating discussion in Michael Freund, "Die Idee der Toleranz im England der grossen Revolution," *Deutsche Vierteljahrschrift für Literaturwissenschaft und Geistesgeschichte*, XII (Halle, 1927). A section is devoted to Milton by Johannes Kühn, *Toleranz und Offenbarung* (Leipzig, 1923).

Among the recent books on Milton, the following have proved useful: Buck, Philo M., "Milton on Liberty," *University of Nebraska Studies*, XXV,1 (1925).

Hanford, James Holy, *John Milton Englishman* (New York, 1949).

Hutchinson, F. E., *Milton and the English Mind* (London, 1946).

Raymond, Dora Neill, *Oliver's Secretary* (New York, 1932).

Wolfe, Don M., *Milton in the Puritan Revolution* (New York, 1941).

The following two instructive articles are in the *Journal of the History of Ideas:*

Ogden, H. V. S., "Variety and Contrast in 17th Century Aesthetics and Milton's Poetry," X,2 (April, 1949), 159–182.

Siegel, Paul N., "Milton and the Humanist Attitude Toward Women," XI,1 (1950), 42–53.

The citations are from the Columbia edition of *The Works of John Milton,* 18 vols. (New York, 1931–1938), and are as follows: page 188, line 8: III, 1, 356; page 189, line 28: III, 1, 147–148; page 190, line 13: III, 1, 214; page 192, line 20: III, 2, 390–391; page 192, line 23: III, 2, 423; page 192, line 27: III, 2, 478; page 192, line 29: IV, 83; page 193, line 5: IV, 85–86; page 193, line 13: III, 2, 395; page 193, line 15: III, 2, 397; page 193, line 17: IV, 77; page 193, line 21: III, 2, 503–504; page 193, line 27: IV, 116–117; page 194, line 24: IV, 297–298; page 194, line 30: IV, 339; page 195, line 16: IV, 326–330; page 195, line 23: IV, 328; page 195, line 25: IV, 327; page 195, line 33: IV, 339–340; page 196, line 8: IV, 347–348; page 196, line 19: IV, 311; page 196, line 26: IV, 333; page 197, line 11: IV, 348; page 200, line 13: *Paradise Regained* III, lines 49–59; page 202, line 8: *Samson Agonistes,* lines 678–696; page 203, line 21: *Paradise Lost* VIII, lines 488–489; page 204, line 8: *Paradise Lost* IX, lines 214–219; page 204, line 22: *Paradise Lost* IX, lines 335–336; page 204, line 30: *Paradise Lost* IX, lines 373–375; page 205, line 17: *Paradise Lost* IX, lines 684–687; page 207, line 5: *Paradise Lost* XII, lines 82–101; page 207, line 15: *Paradise Regained* I, lines 222–223.

CHAPTER VIII: ROGER WILLIAMS: The biographical material on Williams is scant, and any treatment in the compass of a volume has to be filled out with copious drawing from the works of contemporaries. On the whole that by Emily Easton, *Roger Williams* (Boston, 1930), strikes me as the most sound. James Ernst, *Roger Williams, New England Firebrand* (New York, 1932), is interesting. The heart of the matter is in the succinct and discriminating evaluation by Lawrence Wroth, "Roger Williams," *Brown University Papers* (1937). The works of Roger Williams are published in six volumes by the Narragansett Club (1867–1874).

The opening section of the chapter is drawn from my article, "The Puritan Theocracy and the Cambridge Platform," in the commemorative volume entitled *The Cambridge Platform* (Cambridge, 1949). The article appeared also in *The Minister's Quarterly,* V,1 (1949).

The following citations from Roger Williams' works are identified by these abbreviations: *The Bloudy Tenent* — BT; *The Bloudy Tenent Yet More Bloudy* — BTB; *Letters* — L.

Page 215, line 11: L, 335; page 216, line 16: BTB, 277; page 217, line 9:

BT, 174–175; page 218, line 28: BTB, 23–24; page 219, line 19: BT, 132; page 219, line 29: BT, 147; page 220, line 6: BTB, 208; page 220, line 12: BT, 138; page 220, line 14: BT, 290; page 220, line 25: Works, V, vii; page 221, line 34: BT, 272; page 222, line 11: BTB, 508–509; page 222, line 16: BTB, 47; page 222, line 26: L, 328–329; page 223, line 16: BTB, 315–317; page 223, line 34: BT, 180; page 224, line 33: BTB, 71; page 225, line 3: BTB, 189; page 225, line 12: BT, 332; page 226, line 7: BT, 399–400; page 226, line 32: L, 278; page 227, line 25: L, 271; page 228, line 3: L, 225; page 228, line 18: L, 90; page 228, line 22: L, 306.

CHAPTER IX: JOHN LOCKE: The background is taken from chapters in Vol. V of the *Cambridge Modern History:* C. H. Firth, " The Stuart Restoration"; John Pollock, " The Policy of Charles II and James II"; and H. M. Gwatkin, " Religious Toleration in England." Useful is the book by A. A. Seaton, *The Theory of Toleration Under the Later Stuarts* (Cambridge, Eng., 1911). The ecclesiastical documents are printed in Henry Gee and W. J. Hardy, *Documents Illustrative of English Church History* (London, 1914). On the evictions, consult A. G. Mathews, *Calamy Revised* (Oxford, 1934). For the Cambridge Platonists, the most illuminating work is that of Ernst Cassirer, " Die Platonische Renaissance in England und die Schule von Cambridge," *Studien der Bibliothek Warburg* (1932). For Huguenot thought and the Glorious Revolution, consult Guy Dodge, *The Political Theory of the Huguenots of the Dispersion* (New York, 1947).

For Locke's own thought, the following were especially helpful:

Driver, Cecil, " John Locke," in F. J. C. Hearnshaw, *The Social and Political Ideas of Some English Thinkers of the Augustan Age* (London, 1928).

Gibson, James, *Locke's Theory of Knowledge and Its Historical Relations* (Cambridge, England, 1917).

Gough, J. W., *John Locke's Political Philosophy* (Oxford, 1950).

Hertling, Georg Freiherr von, *John Locke und die Schule von Cambridge* (Freiburg im Breisgau, 1892).

Citations are from the edition of Locke's works in 1801 and from the documents given in the biographies by Lord King, *The Life of Locke,* new edition, 2 vols. (London, 1830), and by H. R. Fox Bourne, *The Life of John Locke,* 2 vols. (London, 1876). These are as follows: page 237, line 32: King, I, 197–198; page 240, line 11: King, II, 84–87; page 241, line 2: Works, VI, 24–31; page 241, line 18: Fox Bourne, I, 177; page 242, line 19: Fox Bourne, I, 191; page 242, line 23: Works, VI, 376–379; page 242, line 28: Works, II, 279; page 243, line 12: Works, V, 395–410; page 243, line 28: Works, VI, 13; page 243, line 31: King, II, 202; page 244, line 5: Works, VI, 38–39; page 245, line 4: King, II, 65; page 245, line 8: Works, VI, 237; page 248, line 22: King, I, 164–168; page 249, line 33: King, I, 28–44; page 251, line 31: Works, VI, 6–7.

ILLUSTRATIONS

Page 33 Thomas of Torquemada, drawn from the painting by Pedro Berruguete in a detail from a work commissioned by Torquemada for the monastery at Avila, reproduced in Thomas Hope, *Torquemada*, 1939.

Page 45 A Burning at the Stake in the Spanish Inquisition, reproduced from an illustration in Adriaan Van Haemstede, *De Historien der Vromen Martelaren*, 1604.

Page 54 Monument of the Reformation at Geneva, drawn from a photograph.

Page 72 Michael Servetus, drawn from the copperplate in Johann L. Mosheim, *Historia Michaelis Serveti*, 1727.

Page 81 Portrait of Erasmus Censored by the Inquisition, reproduced from the *Cosmographia* of Sebastian Münster, available in Marcel Bataillon, *Erasme en Espagne*, 1925.

Page 97 Sébastien Castellio, drawn from the plate in his Latin Bible of 1729.

Page 125 David Joris, drawn from the painting in the Basel Museum.

Page 133 David Joris' Lion and Lamb, reproduced from Joris' *Twonderboeck*, 1542.

Page 151 Bernardino Ochino, reproduced from his *Dialoghi Sette*, 1542.

Page 165 A Cartoon of the Pope Receiving His Commission from Satan, drawn from an illustration in a Spanish translation of a work of Ochino entitled *Imajen del Antechristo*, 1557.

Page 179 John Milton, drawn from the picture of a bust reproduced in Denis Saurat, *Milton, Man and Thinker*, 1925.

Page 182 A Cartoon: Puritans Demolishing Crosses on Canterbury Cathedral, reproduced from Bruno Ryves, *Mercurius Rusticus*, 1647.

Page 187 A Cartoon: Archbishop Laud Dining on the Ears of Prynne, Bastwick, and Barton, drawn from an illustration in "A new play called Canterburie his change of Diet" as reproduced in Edmund W. Ashbee, *Occasional Fac-similie Reprints*, 1868–1871.

Page 208 Roger Williams, drawn from a photograph of the Monument of the Reformation at Geneva.

Page 229 John Locke, drawn from illustrations in Lord King, *The Life of Locke*, volume one, London, 1830.

Page 235 A Cartoon from *A Delicate Dainty Damnable Dialogue Between the Devil and a Jesuite*, by John Taylor, 1642.

Page 252 A Cartoon: Two Devils Helping Nonconformists Pull Down the Dome of St. Paul's Cathedral, drawn from an illustration in *The Limehouse Dream* (1710) by Andrew Marvell the younger.

Index

Canon Law, 18, 20, 61, 90

Castellio, Sébastien, 16, 21, Chapter IV, 125, 134, 137, 138, 139, 143, 147, 148, 157, 159, 161, 164, 170, 171, 173, 179, 184, 194, 219, 239, 245, 246, 247, 248, 250, 255

Castile, 44

Charles I, 182, 187, 199, 203
  II, 201, 229, 230, 232, 233
  V, 16, 27, 72, 79, 150, 159, 162

Chiliasm, 128

Christendom, 29, 33, 34, 36, 90, 197, 215, 232, 258

Church (see *State*)
  authority, 19, 20, 59, 77
  no salvation outside, 17, 24, 37, 38
  types, 23, 60–61, 83, 122–123, 139

Clarendon Code, 232

Codex Justinianus, 18, 61, 74, 90, 92, 93

Communism, 14, 70, 175, 258, 259

Comprehension, 26, 27, 28
  Bill of, 234

Congregationalists, 26, 27, 183, 198, 244

Connecticut, 27, 28, 228

Conscience, 21, 120, 171, 172, 215, 220–222, 230, 246, 247, 256

Constantine, 38
  Donation of, 56

Contarini, Gaspar, 156

Conventicle Act, 232, 233, 234

Cotton, John, 209, 215, 216, 217, 221

Counter Reformation, 29, 55

Covenanters, 128, 129

Cranmer, Thomas, 162

Creeds, 19, 21, 37, 67, 69, 92, 118, 136, 137
  Apostles', 56, 64, 148, 171

Cromwell, Oliver, 25, 29, 198, 199, 200, 227, 231, 258

Crusades, 33, 34, 35, 36, 40, 115, 149

Cudworth, Ralph, 244

Death Penalty, 19, 37, 61, 63, 93, 98, 149, 166, 179, 180, 183, 235

Declaration of Indulgence, 233

Decree of 1781, 20

Democracy, 25, 94, 199

Deuteronomy, ch. 13, 36, 69

Devotio Moderna, 22

Diggers, 183

Dominicans, 43, 46, 135

Donatists, 18, 38, 61

Dostoevsky, Feodor, 52

Dukhobors, 128, 210

Edict of Nantes, 20, 179, 184, 230, 245, 259

Edward VI, 28, 107, 108, 121, 161, 163, 164, 174

Elect, 25, 62, 63, 67, 138, 209, 215, 216, 219

Elizabeth of England, 16, 27, 162, 168, 181

Endicott, John, 227

England, 16, 19, 23, 27, 28, 35, 69, 99, 121, 133, 152, 161, 163, 164, 173, Chapter VII, 211, Chapter IX, 256

Enlightenment, 29, 56, 116, 120, 238

Episcopalians, 27, 28, 183, 189, 198

Erasmianism, 72, 73, 79, 80, 97, 114, 120, 238, 244, 248

Erasmus of Rotterdam, 21, 22, 29, 57–59, 60, 72, 73, 74, 79, 80, 81, 97, 106, 125, 126, 146, 154, 164, 194, 245, 255

Erastianism, 28, 163

Error, 17, 21, 30, 60, 63, 94, 114, 120, 138, 190, 196

Ethical, 21, 24, 58, 73, 117, 134

Fall of Man, 75, 116, 163, 203

Family of Love, 183

Farel, William, 55, 68, 94

Fascism, 14, 258

Ferdinand, 41–51, 72